Cover Illustration

'Last Sleep of the Brave', Isandlwana, Zulu War, 1879. Oleograph after Alphonse de Neuville, 1881.

This work depicts a patrol from the 17th (Duke of Cambridge's Own) Lancers discovering the bodies of Lieutenant Teignmouth Melvill and Lieutenant Nevill Josiah Aylmer Coghill, 24th (2nd Warwickshire) Regiment of Foot, who were both killed attempting to save the Queen's Colour of the 1st Battalion at the Battle of Isandlwana on 22 January 1879.

The depiction of the 17th Lancers is however anachronistic as when the bodies were retrieved the lancers had yet to leave England for South Africa.

"THE DEATH OR GLORY BOYS."

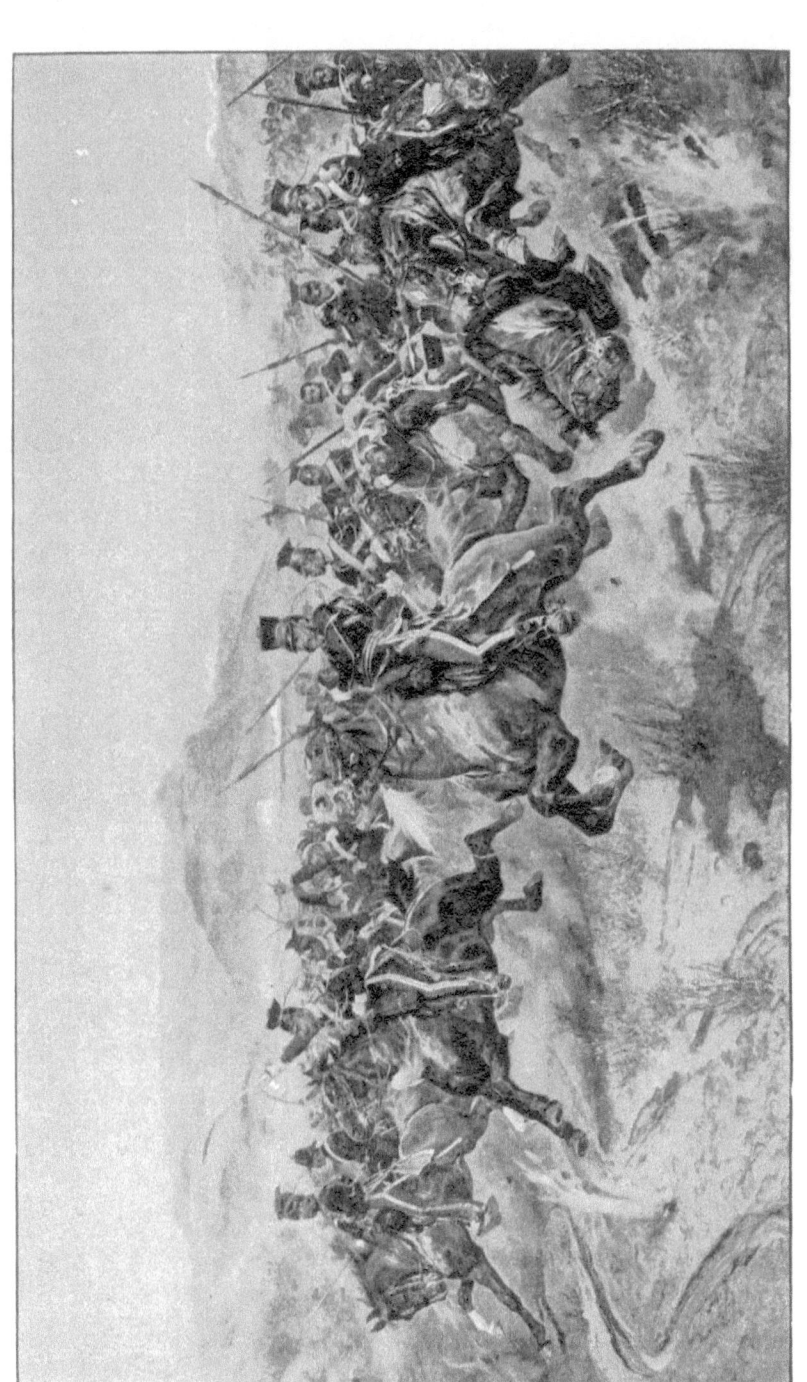

The Charge of the Light Brigade.
From the Painting by R. Caton Woodville.

By permission of Messrs. Henry Graves & Co., Ltd., Pall Mall, S.W.

"The Death or Glory Boys"

THE STORY OF THE 17TH LANCERS

1759—1903

BY

D. H. PARRY

AUTHOR OF "BRITAIN'S ROLL OF GLORY," ETC. ETC.

New Edition

WITH ADDITIONAL CHAPTERS AND
EIGHT FULL-PAGE ILLUSTRATIONS

The Naval & Military Press Ltd

Published by

The Naval & Military Press Ltd
Unit 5 Riverside, Brambleside
Bellbrook Industrial Estate
Uckfield, East Sussex
TN22 1QQ England

Tel: +44 (0)1825 749494

www.naval-military-press.com
www.nmarchive.com

In reprinting in facsimile from the original, any imperfections are inevitably reproduced and the quality may fall short of modern type and cartographic standards.

PREFACE TO THE PRESENT EDITION.

THE task of bringing this little record up to date, and giving an account of the 17th's South African trek, has been one of great difficulty, owing to the very complicated nature of the operations in which they took part.

Without the kindly help of various members of the Regiment it would have been an impossibility, and I desire to express my hearty thanks to Major V. S. Sandeman for allowing me to study his map, and for his valuable assistance so generously rendered; to Sergeants George Paul and Lawrence, V.C.; to Corporal C. J. Archer; and to many others.

To Corporal Archer's journal I have been particularly indebted, and only regret that considerations of space forbade my giving a greater number of extracts therefrom.

D. H. PARRY.

London, November, 1903.

CONTENTS.

CHAPTER I.
How they Raised the Regiment when George was King 1

CHAPTER II.
On March, and in Quarters 25

CHAPTER III.
How the Regiment Embarked for Active Service for the First Time 43

CHAPTER IV.
American War of Independence. The Campaigns from 1776 to 1779. 62

CHAPTER V.
The War in Carolina 75

CHAPTER VI.
An Eighteenth Century "V.C." 90

CHAPTER VII.
The Blue Dragoons—in Peace and War . . . 108

CHAPTER VIII.
Varied Service, 1795—1806 130

CHAPTER IX.
"Success to Grey Hairs, but Bad Luck to White-locks" 151

CHAPTER X.
Early Indian Service, 1808—1822 169

CHAPTER XI.
The Coming of the Lancers, and the Home Service of "Bingham's Dandies" 183

CONTENTS.

CHAPTER XII.
THE 17TH IN THE CRIMEA, AND THE REGIMENTAL STORY OF THE BALACLAVA CHARGE. 200

CHAPTER XIII.
THE 17TH IN THE MUTINY, AND THEIR SECOND TOUR OF INDIAN SERVICE, 1857—1865. 227

CHAPTER XIV.
GREAT BRITAIN AND ZULULAND. 252

CHAPTER XV.
THE LANCER BRIGADE IN SOUTH AFRICA. . . . 265

CHAPTER XVI.
"DEATH OR GLORY" ON THE VELDT. 297

CHAPTER XVII.
THE END OF THE WAR. 331

CHAPTER XVIII.
THE "OLD COMRADES" DINNER. 342

APPENDIX A.
THE SUCCESSION OF COLONELS 349

APPENDIX B.
THE WAR SERVICES OF THE 17TH 365

APPENDIX C.
THE TITLES OF THE REGIMENT; ITS FIRST UNIFORM, AND A RÉSUMÉ OF THE CHANGES IN ITS DRESS AND EQUIPMENT 367

APPENDIX D.
LIGHT DRAGOON KIT AND ACCOUTREMENTS, 1759 . . 372

APPENDIX E.
SOME OLD EXERCISES OF HALE'S LIGHT DRAGOONS ABOUT 1763 375

APPENDIX F.
THE TRUMPET DUTY OF THE LIGHT DRAGOONS. . . 378

INDEX 381

LIST OF ILLUSTRATIONS.

		PAGE
THE CHARGE OF THE LIGHT BRIGADE . .	*Frontis.*	
"SERGEANT MITCHELL WAS CUT DOWN, AND HIS COLOUR-POLE SMASHED"	*To face*	86
"SERGEANT STEPHENSON CHARGED THE FOE" .	,,	126
LINCOLN STANHOPE AND THE PINDARIS . .	,,	180
"ON REACHING THE BATTERY HE DROVE HIS LANCE INTO A GUNNER"	,,	214
"SEEING SOME RED-COATED REBELS FORMING INTO SQUARE, LIEUTENANT EVELYN WOOD SPURRED AT THE CORNER MAN ABSOLUTELY ALONE".	,,	236
"THE NEXT MOMENT THE 17TH WERE INTO THEM, DEALING DEATH RIGHT AND LEFT" . .	,,	244
"UP HILL AND DOWN DALE THE 17TH HARRIED THE FLYING NATIVES"	,,	260

"THE DEATH OR GLORY BOYS."

CHAPTER I.

HOW THEY RAISED THE REGIMENT WHEN GEORGE WAS KING.

General Wolfe's Dying Request—John Hale, the Father of the Regiment—Benjamin West's Picture—A Glance at the British Light Horse—Their Prowess at Culloden—The Light Troops of Dragoons, 1755—Elliot's and Burgoyne's—John Hale's Recruiting Appeal to the County of Hertford—Arming Warrant, 1759—The Skull and Crossbones—Old Time Recruiting—The Original Officers—The First Uniform—The Band—Horse Furniture—Pay—An 18th Century "Free Kit"—The Troop-Horse—Guard Mounting.

A DAPPER little red-haired man, clad in a bright, new uniform sadly sullied by the blood that poured from three wounds, lay dying on the field of his fame: in his nostrils the taint of the trampled grass and the powder smoke, the din of battle receding from his ear, and the shout of victory growing fainter and fainter.

Not far below him, reflecting the September gold of the Canadian woods, rolled the mighty river on whose bosom a few short hours before, the silence broken only by the plash of the muffled oars, he had whispered Gray's sublime elegy to his listening staff, under circumstances, and amid surroundings, perhaps the most dramatic in history.

B

And now, borne to the rear to die, while British bayonet and Highland claymore finished the gory work beneath the walls of Quebec, Wolfe had still sufficient strength left, even in his agony, to think of others.

"I am aware," he said to the sorrowing officers gathered round him, "that it is the aide-de-camp's privilege to carry the despatches home, but I beg, as a favour, to request that my old friend, Colonel Hale, may have that honour."

To that last wish of one of the most thorough and most accomplished leaders the British army has ever possessed, the 17th Lancers owe their origin, together with their significant badge and motto.

"Last night," we read in the *London Evening Post*, October 17th, 1759, "Colonel John Hale and Captain James Douglas, late commander of H.M.S. *Alcide*, arrived from Quebec."

Both officers, who had made the then long passage in the *Leasthop* frigate, received a gratuity of five hundred pounds, Douglas being knighted into the bargain; and the *Whitehall Evening Post*, November 6th–8th, announced that his Majesty had promoted Hale to be colonel of a regiment of Light Horse, to be forthwith raised, the announcement preceding the actual arming warrant by one day.

At that time, and, indeed, for long after the proprietary regiment had become happily a thing of the past, the rank of colonel carried with it emoluments hardly credible in our own day.

A colonel was then a demi-god, seated upon a regimental throne. The regulations for his control were few, and he was seldom interfered with from headquarters. Inspections were rare; a review by the king an honour never to be forgotten.

Each colonel received a lump sum, out of which he was to clothe his men; and, by arrangement with the contractor, he netted a considerable portion of it for his private purse, gentlemen of the highest standing holding it no disgrace thus to enrich themselves at the expense of the soldier.

The internal economy, drill, and often the equipment of a regiment followed the particular whim of its commanding officer—in some cases to its great advantage, in others the reverse.

Of John Hale, who was about to have this power vested in his hands, we must now speak, for he may be justly regarded as the father of the "Death or Glory Boys."

He was born in 1728, the fourth son of Sir Bernard Hale, Chief Baron of the Exchequer in Ireland, who died in Red Lion Square in 1729, and was buried at King's Walden, in Hertfordshire, the manor of which place had been bought by Richard Hale, citizen and grocer of London, in the reign of Elizabeth.

John Hale was originally intended for the Bar, and entered at Trinity Hall, Cambridge, but association with his brother Bernard, an officer in the Guards, turned his youthful aspirations towards a sword and sash, and obtaining a commission in the 47th Foot, then called "Lascelles'," he served with his regiment during the "'45."

"Lascelles'" lost their colours at Prestonpans, and this may account for Hale's subsequent bitterness against the Scots. Whether his friendship with Wolfe —who was aide-de-camp to Henry Hawley—dates from this period we cannot now tell, but the existence of that friendship is proof sufficient of John Hale's qualities, both personal and military.

He was promoted captain in 1752, and ordered to America the same year; obtaining his majority in 1755, and the lieut.-colonelcy of the regiment on the 19th March, 1758.

His career was distinguished by personal bravery, and he had the local rank of colonel at the storming of Quebec

He used to relate in after years how he had remonstrated with Wolfe before that action for wearing a new uniform, which rendered him doubly conspicuous to the Indian marksmen.

This is practically all that is known of the young man, up to that time, with the exception of one item, to be found in a letter from his daughter, written in 1839, which throws a curious light on the painting of historical pictures.

"General Hale's portrait is not inserted in that fine print of Wolfe's death," says Mrs. Anne Smelt, the lady referred to, "and why? Because he would not give the printer the monstrous sum of one hundred pounds, which he demanded as the price of placing on a piece of paper what his own country knew very well, viz., that he, General Hale, fought in the hottest of the battle of Quebec, whether the printer thought fit to record it or not!"

Is it possible, then, that West's celebrated canvas, which we have all admired as a bold departure from the classic custom of representing contemporary heroes in togas and laurel wreaths, was after all a speculation, and a particularly sordid one at that?

But now, leaving young John Hale to receive the congratulations of his friends, and, following the fashion of the time, no doubt to get most gloriously drunk in honour of his sovereign's distinguished mark of favour, we must hark back a few years and briefly glance at the origin of Light Horse in our service, for its adoption marks an epoch in military history.

When that picturesque individual whom we commonly call the Young Pretender made his romantic dash for a throne, and turned Great Britain upside down, Evelyn Pierrepoint, Duke of Kingston, "the exemplar of amiability," and later, the husband, by a bigamous marriage, of the notorious Elizabeth Chudleigh, raised a regiment of Light Cavalry to fight for the king.

His men were mounted on horses of various colours, "with swish, or nicked tails, their accoutrements as light as possible, of every sort and species; their arms, short bullet guns, or carbines, shorter than those of the Horse (*i.e.*, the existing cavalry proper), slung to their sides by a movable swivel to run up to their shoulder belt; their pistols upon the same plan, as they used both carbines and pistols on horseback indiscriminately; their swords very sharp, and rather inclined to a curve."

In all these details they departed from the accepted traditions of our cavalry; who were weighed down by mighty belts and pouches, heavily booted, and still more heavily mounted on mammoth steeds of one colour for a regiment, that being generally black or brown; and who carried huge basket-hilted swords of the claymore kind.

Divided into Horse, or cavalry proper, and Dragoons, who were trained to fight also on foot with musket and bayonet,* these cumbrous cavaliers went through stately evolutions, doing everything "decently and in order,"

---

* It is not generally remembered that bayonets in the Heavy Cavalry owed their final suppression to a submission drafted to George IV. as recently as 20th February, 1820.

and seldom charging until the enemy's infantry showed signs of breaking.

But Kingston's Light Horse, if only by reason of their more rational equipment, inaugurated a new era; and though nothing has come down to us of their drill—if, indeed, they ever had time for any—we know that they did terrible execution among Bonnie Prince Charlie's unfortunate adherents. At Culloden Moor they pursued the broken rebels for three miles, several of them killing their fifteen and sixteen apiece, three Nottingham butchers in the ranks each accounting for fourteen!

Whether or no these sanguinary circumstances were answerable for Cumberland's particular regard—it is not improbable—he took over the corps after the rebellion.

It was disbanded at Nottingham, 15th September, 1746, each private man receiving three guineas, and his saddle and bridle, and every officer a printed copy of a very laudatory letter from the Secretary at War to the Duke of Kingston.

With the exception of eight, who gave honourable reasons for not so doing, the entire corps rejoined for "The Duke of Cumberland's Light Dragoons," to be armed and equipped on a new and light plan; and mounted on horses from $14\frac{1}{2}$ to 15 hands; the men averaging from 5 feet 8 inches to 5 feet 9 inches, and wearing hats like the Heavy Dragoons', "and not helmets," which seems to point to the fact that Kingston's regiment had worn the latter.

Cumberland's Light Dragoons served with some distinction on the Continent; their colonel, Lord Robert Sutton, being captured with the gallant Ligonier at Laffeldt, the regiment also losing several officers and men at Val; but on the peace of 1748, they were finally disbanded, and for seven years Great Britain boasted no Light Horse. Then, towards the end of 1755, a light troop of three officers, a quartermaster, two sergeants, three corporals, a farrier, two drummers, and sixty-five men, disciplined in a different manner to the heavy troops, was added to the following eleven regiments of Dragoon Guards and Dragoons :—

1st King's Dragoon Guards .	(Lieut.-Gen. Bland's.)
2nd Queen's	(Major-Gen. Herbert's.)
3rd Prince of Wales'. . .	(Lieut.-Gen. Sir Charles Howard's.)
st Royal Dragoons . . .	(Lieut.-Gen. Hawley's.)
2nd Royal North British Dragoons	(Lieut.-Gen. Campbell's.)
3rd King's Own Dragoons .	(Major-Gen. Earl of Albemarle's) now 3rd Hussars.
4th Dragoons	(Gen. Sir Robert Rich's) now 4th Hussars.
6th Inniskilling Dragoons	(Lieut.-Gen. Cholmondeley's.)
7th Queen's Dragoons . .	(Lieut.-Gen. Sir John Cope's) now 7th Hussars.
10th Dragoons . .	(Lieut.-Gen. Sir John Mordaunt's) now 10th Hussars.
11th Dragoons . . .	(Major-Gen. Earl of Ancrum's) now 11th Hussars.

They were armed with carbines, having a bar and sliding ring, with a bayonet, but no sling. The carbines were carried in a bucket below the right holster, in which was a pistol, the left holster holding either an axe, hedging-bill, or spade. Their bridles and saddles were light, though the latter were made with burs and cantles like the heavies', and they were burdened with gay quarter-clothes and holster flaps elaborately broidered. Their belts were of brown tanned leather; they carried no side pouches, and the carbines were sprung to a swivel which played up and down the shoulder belt, a method afterwards universally adopted throughout the cavalry. The three-cornered hats bound with white tape gave place to helmets of strong black jacked leather, having bars down the sides, and a brass comb on the top, not altogether unlike the shape now so closely identified with the French Cuirassiers. The front of the helmet was red, ornamented with brass work with the cypher, crown, and regimental number; a tuft of horsehair adorning the back, in colour half red and the other half to correspond with the regimental facing.

These new troops won some renown in those ill-advised descents which we made about that time on the French coast, and when they were reduced, in 1763, their strength was one captain, two lieutenants, two cornets, a quartermaster, farrier, two drummers, four sergeants, four corporals, and 114 private men. Just previously to their reduction they had been put into a new helmet, with a rolled turban, and two tassels at the back tied in a knot, to fall down over their necks in bad weather, their former cap having had a rolled-up leather flap round it for the same purpose.

But, in the meantime, two regiments of Light Dragoons had been formed, which were not destined to undergo disbandment—the 15th, raised 10th March, 1759, by Lieut.-Colonel George Augustus Elliot, afterwards so well known as Lord Heathfield, "the Cock of the Rock," for his defence of Gibraltar; and the 16th, raised 4th August, in the same year, by Lieut.-Colonel Burgoyne, these corps figuring in our army list to-day as the 15th Hussars and 16th Lancers.

It is said that the 15th were partly recruited in

the first instance from a deputation of tailors, who, having come to London to present a petition to the king, were induced to enlist; and the poet Coleridge was one of our first Light Dragoons, serving for a short time in Elliot's under the *alias* of Silas Tompkin Comberbatch, until his friends rescued him from the depôt at Reading.

These two regiments had been in existence only a few months when Quebec was fought, and they would seem to have already given such satisfaction to George II. and his military advisers that it was decided to raise five additional corps on the same model, and John Hale, returning home on the flood-tide of victory, arrived at the right moment for his own fortunes, and, as this volume will endeavour to show, for the fortunes of the British Army.

In No. 2129 of the *Whitehall Evening Post*, Lieut.-Colonel Hale commenced operations by publishing the following notice:—

"To the Nobility, Gentry, and Freeholders of the County of Hertford.

"His Majesty having graciously permitted me to raise a Corps of Light Cavalry for his Service, a Son of your County, I humbly intreat your Interest and Assistance in raising such Men, and providing such Horses, as His Majesty's Service, and the Terms I offer, may with Reason expect.

'I dare to flatter myself that this Regiment, if 'chiefly composed (as I intend it) of Hertfordshire Men, may one Day reflect Honour on that County, which shall have generously offered them to the Cause of Liberty and the Service of their Country.

"Advertisements of the Conditions of Inlistment shall immediately be made public, and proper Persons appointed in the great Towns, to receive and entertain all Recruits, and purchase the Horses which shall be offered to Sale, if fit for the Purpose.

"Neither Time nor Circumstances permitting me to make a personal Application, it is hoped you will favourably accept this public Address, from

"Your most obedient Servant,
"JOHN HALE,
"Lieutenant-Colonel Commandant of a Regiment of Light
"Cavalry, forthwith to be raised."

The Royal Warrant for arming the corps, dated 9th November, ran as follows:—

"GEORGE R.
"Whereas we have thought fit to order a Regiment of Light Dragoons to be raised and to be commanded by our trusty and well-beloved Lieutenant-Colonel John Hale, which Regiment is to consist of Four Troops of 3 sergeants, 3 corporals, 2 drummers, and 67 private men in each troop, besides commission officers, Our will and pleasure is, that out of the stores remaining within the Office of our Ordnance under your charge, you cause 300 pair of pistols, 292 carbines, 292 cartouche boxes, and 8 drums, to be issued and delivered to the said Lieutenant-Colonel John Hale, or to such person as he shall appoint to receive the same, taking his indent as usual, and you are to insert the expense thereof in your next estimate to be laid before Parliament. And for so doing, this shall be, as well to you as to all other our officers and ministers herein concerned, a sufficient Warrant.

"Given at our Court at St. James' the 9th day of November, 1759, in the 33rd year of our reign.

"To our trusty and well-beloved Cousin and Councillor John Viscount Ligonier, Master General of our Ordnance."

A Board of General Officers sat the same night Hale's commission was signed, to wag their powdered heads over the knotty point of uniform, when scarlet was chosen for the coats, and white for the facings—the dress, by the way, of Hale's late regiment, the 47th—a mourning lace, and, according to the public prints a few days later, a death's head with two crossbones *above* it, and below, the motto, "Or Glory," on the front of their caps, and on their *left breasts.*

Whether the sepulchral emblem was ever actually displayed on the coat itself is uncertain; some writers say that it was, but we have found no warrant to confirm the statement.* Whether the badge was suggested by that worn by a distinguished regiment in the Prussian army, the "Death's Head Hussars," or whether the frequent use of it on the tombstones of the period gave John Hale the idea, matters little; but his sentiment is known to have been one of reverence for General Wolfe, and a desire that his men should hold him in mind as a pattern to follow in all their actions. Except that the skull now surmounts the crossbones, badge, motto, and facings have remained unchanged in the 17th for 140 years.

How Hale raised the four original troops can only be guessed at now, but guineas and beer undoubtedly played their part. Many an alehouse tap-room and many a red brick wall must have exhibited his recruiting placards in the quaint Hertfordshire villages; many a brilliant picture of the very dubious joys of soldiering under the Georges must have been drawn by glib-tongued agents and "Sergeant Kites."

Widowed mothers and pretty sweethearts must have wept unavailing tears in plenty when Giles and Lubin 'listed for the Light Horse and joined the throng of "brisk lads wanted to complete the Regiment now raising."

They did not do things by halves in those days, as witness the following authorised form of speech to be

* The 111th Foot, raised in 1760—scarlet with pompadour facings—had "Glory" embroidered on the left breast; and the 24th Light Dragoons, raised in Ireland in 1794, and disbanded in 1802, had "Death or Glory" on the front of their helmets.—D. H. P.

used in 1768 when beating up for recruits for the army:—

"To all aspiring heroes bold, who have spirits above slavery and trade, and inclinations to become gentlemen by bearing arms in his Majesty's ——— regiment, commanded by the magnanimous ———, let them repair to the drumhead (tow row dow), where each gentleman volunteer shall be kindly and honourably entertained, and enter into present pay and good quarters—besides which, gentlemen, for your further and better encouragement you shall receive one guinea advance; a crown to drink His Majesty King George's health; and when you come to join your respective regiment, shall have new hats, caps, arms, cloaths, and accoutrements, and everything that is necessary and fitting to compleat a gentleman soldier.

"God save their Majesties, and success to their arms.
"Huzza! Huzza! Huzza!"

A little light is thrown on the class of man wanted for the Light Dragoons by the instructions given in 1762 in the case of the Royal Foresters, for which corps no recruit was to be taken under 5 feet 5½ inches, nor above 5 feet 9 inches; "they must be light and straight, and by no means gummy," and while the bounty-money was not to exceed three guineas and a crown, the officers were to get them as much under as they could.

Recruiting officers drew on Mr. Calcraft, the agent, for forty pounds in the first instance, and when that sum was nearly expended, they could obtain more on application through headquarters, by submitting an account of their doings.

These rascals, as in the majority of cases they undoubtedly were, had orders to lay out the bounty-money as far as was possible on necessaries for the recruit; in other words, to make the poor beggar pay for the very things which he was led to suppose were to be given to him, and it is not too much to say that our army has very largely owed its paucity of numbers and its difficulty in recruiting, even to our own times, to the system adopted, which in private life would be justly stigmatised as misrepresentation and fraud.

The exact *modus operandi* of recruiting was this: the man having come forward, or having been talked over, and the bounty once placed in his hand, he was taken before the nearest Justice of the Peace (not being an officer in the army) within four days, but not sooner than twenty-four hours. He could then cry off his bargain if he were so minded by returning the enlistment-money and twenty shillings besides within the latter time; but, supposing him still willing to serve, either for the war or for life, the 2nd and 6th sections of the Articles of War were read over to him, and he took the prescribed oath to be true to the king, and to serve him honestly and faithfully, etc., etc., so help him God; after which he was in for it!

Curiosity led us to search the public prints for deserters during the first few years of the existence of Hale's Light Horse, without finding a single man "wanted," though other regiments advertised in plenty, the Guards in particular making anxious inquiries after five and six in a batch!

But whatever the method employed in Hale's particular case, it is said that his corps was complete in numbers in the short space of seventeen days, a record of which both colonel and county might well be proud.

The four troops were commanded and, according to Cannon, raised, by Captains Franklin Kirby, from lieutenant 5th Foot; Samuel Birch, from lieutenant 11th Dragoons; Martin Basil, from lieutenant Elliot's Light Horse; and Edward Lascelles, from cornet in the Royal

Horse Guards Blue; so that every arm of the service was practically represented among them with the sole exception of the Artillery.

Service in the Light Dragoons was evidently popular at that time, although in the same column that contains Colonel Hale's address there is an advertisement for one "James Slaughter, aged twenty-two . . . fair complexion and blue eyes. Deserted from Sir William Williams's troop of the 16th," a guinea to be given, over and above the usual reward, to whoever secures him in any gaol in Great Britain; and a few days afterwards, in the same paper, John Rowland is wanted, height 5 feet 5 inches, from Hon. Captain Gordon's troop of the 16th, who deserted in a "drab coat and his white shag regimental breeches, and regimental boots and spurs"; this misguided son of Mars being valued at two guineas above the usual reward, probably on account of the clothing of his nether limbs.

Hale's first rendezvous was at Watford and Rickmansworth, and early in December they bade adieu to the leafless woods and wintry uplands of Hertfordshire, and filed off two and two to the roll of their drums, the clatter of their nag-tailed horses muffled by the fallen leaves, and, no doubt, many a host of country folk at the lane ends to wish them God's speed.

There would be hand-shaking and leave-taking, ay, and heart-breaking too; with tender scenes in the cobble-stoned stable-yards, that still remain though the gallant lads who rode out to the parting muster, gay in scarlet and white, have long since gone to the last muster of all.*

---

* We may surely be allowed to assume that some of the uniforms were ready even at that early date, when we reflect what a potent factor in recruiting uniform has always proved.

Human nature was the same then as now, but the times were very different.

It was the year of Handel's death and Eugene Aram's execution; Johnson, Goldsmith, and Sir Joshua Reynolds—who afterwards painted a portrait of Colonel Hale — were meeting in London town, whither her ladyship repaired in her chariot to attend the play, preceded by linkboys.

Highwaymen haunted the heaths and lonely commons, malefactors hung dangling in chains along the roadside, the beadle and the stocks were part of the rustic economy; and in 1751 the good people of Tring had ducked two poor old women of seventy to death on suspicion of witchcraft—perhaps more than one of Hale's Dragoons had witnessed it as boys.

Bull-baiting, cock-fighting, hard-drinking times they were, and yet with a certain primitive charm about them when "read of in books and dreamt of in dreams."

There would not be much discipline in the scarlet column winding away towards Warwick and Stratford-on-Avon that December day; all that had to come, the first step being to remove them from home ties before the "gentleman soldiers, with souls above slavery and trade," were put through their facings, and made to feel the iron hand of subordination and restraint.

After a short stay of a fortnight at Warwick and Stratford the regiment went on to Coventry, where it lay until August, 1760; and while there it was increased to six troops, the two additional ones having been decided upon in December, 1759; while on the 28th January, 1760, another increase was ordered, viz. a sergeant, a corporal, and thirty-six men, to be added to each troop already in existence.

The following is the list of officers for 1759 and the beginning of 1760:—

LIEUT.-COLONEL COMMANDANT	John Hale.
MAJOR	John Blaquière (from captain 68th Foot).
CAPTAIN	Franklin Kirby.
,,	Samuel Birch.
,,	Martin Basil.
,,	Edward Lascelles.
,,	John Burton.
,,	Samuel Townshend.
LIEUTENANT	Thomas Lee.
,,	William Green.
,,	Joseph Hall.
,,	Henry Wallop.
,,	Henry Cope.
,,	Yelverton Peyton.
CORNET	Robert Archdall.
,,	Henry Bishop.
,,	Joseph Stopford.
,,	Henry Crofton.
,,	Joseph Moxham.
,,	Daniel Brown.
ADJUTANT	Richard Westbury.
SURGEON	John Francis.
AGENT	Mr. Calcraft, Channel Row, Westminster.

Nearly all the regimental papers were lost at sea in 1797, with the result that the meagre particulars of its birth and infancy have had to be gleaned from dry records and old newspapers.

Even the uniform is open to doubt for the first few years, though we may assume, with Fortescue, that the warrant of 1764 embodied the details adopted from the beginning.

In the Appendix, we give with some minuteness the first recorded costume, from the early clothing warrants and the very interesting "Discipline of the Light Horse," by Captain Hinde of the 21st, or Royal Foresters, a corps raised by the immortal "Markiss o' Granby"; here we will content ourselves with a brief glance at their outward appearance on the line of march.

To begin with, they were decidedly a red regiment; scarlet of coat, which was lapelled with white to the waist; red plumes of horsehair whisked about their powdered locks, and their drummers were resplendent in red vests and breeches. Their white saddle-cloths had red braiding about them, with silver tassels for the officers, and the commissioned ranks wore a crimson silk scarf over the left shoulder until 1764, when they tied it about their middles. The non-coms.' distinguishing rank-marks were, silver edging round the sergeants' collars, a silver fringe to their epaulettes, and a crimson sash with a white line round the waist; while the corporals had a silver sleeve edging and white silk epaulettes. The dark blue farriers, with their bearskin caps, would give a spot of relief to the scarlet and white of the rest; and the sun would find plenty of buttons and embroidery to glint upon, to say nothing of the white-metal skulls on the helmets, the carbine barrels, which were bright in those days, the long knee-boots with black tops, and the clumsy stirrup-irons of the period. Their helmets followed the fashion of the light troops, and had a brass comb from which the plume hung. The regimental badge was displayed in white-metal on the front, and round the body of the headpiece was a turban of white silk.

It was a handsome dress, with its white turned-down collars, then called "capes," and the morsel of lace ruffle at throat and wrist; and no doubt Hale's dashing fellows thought so too, and were prepared to uphold their opinion with their swords—perhaps some of them did, who knows?

Before the regiment was five years old a change of some importance was made by the substitution of trumpets in the place of drums. The use of the drum was a link with that past which had always viewed the Dragoon as more or less an infantry soldier, and it is not improbable that Lieut.-Colonel Dalrymple, of the King's Own Dragoons, assisted in its abolition by some very sensible comparisons in his essay (1761) on the merits of the two instruments. Be that as it may, in 1764 "his Majesty thought proper to forbid the use of brass side-drums in the Light Cavalry, and in their room to introduce brass trumpets—each troop has one trumpet, who when dismounted form a band of music, of two French horns, two clarinets, and two bassoons, and also one fife to a regiment; but when mounted the trumpets only sound."

A bugle horn was used instead of the old beating to arms, and for certain calls during exercise, one of the trumpeters slinging it over his shoulder, and the French horns also sounded some of the signals.

The uniform of these trumpeters in the 17th followed the almost universal plan of the time, namely, of reversing the colours of coat and facings; thus they had white coats elaborately braided with the mourning-lace, red collars, cuffs, lapels, waistcoats, breeches, and horse furniture, and wore cocked hats with white feathers, and a sword with a scymitar blade.

They were not to have the hanging sleeve which was used in some of the Heavy Cavalry regiments, and they were mounted on grey horses.

In those days a farrier was attached to each troop, dressed from head to foot in dark blue, with white collar and cuffs, and a white apron rolled to the left side, and an axe on the same side, slung in a white shoulder belt. These gentry wore a small bearskin cap with a silver plated horseshoe in front on a black ground, and on the front of their saddles they carried two budgets or churns, to hold their implements and spare shoes; their horse furniture of black bearskin with horseshoe badges in front, and crossed hammers and pincers on the housings.

Dalrymple speaks disparagingly of them as a class, and indeed the veterinary surgery of those days was little else than rule-of-thumb barbarity.

In 1764 fixed regulations for standards and guidons were laid down, which for the 17th were to be of silk, with tassels and cords of crimson silk and silver mixed, 1 foot in length, including the tassels. The lance was to be 8 feet long, spear and ferrule included, the colour itself 2 feet 8 inches to the end of the slit in the swallow-tail, and 1 foot 8 inches deep on the lance. There were three guidons, the first answering to the king's colour in an infantry battalion. This was of crimson silk, with rose and thistle conjoined in the centre, the crown above, and *Dieu et mon droit* underneath; in a compartment in the first and fourth corners, the White Horse of Hanover; in a compartment in the second and third corners, XVII. L. D., on a white ground. The second and third guidons were of white silk, painted with gold and silver; the "Death's Head" on a crimson ground in the centre, with "or Glory" below it, the whole encircled by a wreath of roses and thistles on the same stalk; the white horse on a red ground in the first and fourth corners, the rose and thistle conjoined on a red ground in the second and third, all three guidons being fringed with red and silver, and the third distinguished by a figure 3 on a red circle below the motto.

These guidons were carried by the cornets in a white belt edged with the regimental mourning-lace, and fluttered gaily until William IV. abolished standards in the cavalry of the Line.

It is perhaps worthy of note here that the 17th was one of the eight mounted regiments flying a motto in 1768.

Officers and men of the Light Dragoons were ordered to have black bridoons made in such a manner that the horses could be linked together when the regiment was dismounted, and all the swords, belts and knots, saddles, girths, surcingles, pistols, bits, gloves, boots and spurs were to be uniform in pattern for all ranks.

The officers affected a square stirrup in some regiments, and a round one in others, but which obtained in the 17th cannot now be told.

The arms and accoutrements of the privates were as follows:—A carbine with barrel about 2 feet 5 inches (bayonet a foot long), and a pair of 9-inch barrel pistols, pistols and carbine being of the same bore: a long sword, crooked or straight according to regimental regulation. The sword was carried in a white belt, $2\frac{1}{2}$ inches broad, passing over the right shoulder, and another belt crossed it, carrying the cartouche box that held twenty-four rounds, and having a swivel, chain, and T from which to spring the carbine. (The 16th had a cartouche box on the left hip, and their swords in a waist-belt.) The waist-belt in the 17th was $1\frac{3}{4}$ inches in width, or an inch less than in the horse, whose chest belts were $4\frac{1}{2}$ inches!

All ranks had a saddle very hollow in the middle, made without burs or cantle and rising high back and front, with a pad behind to carry the valise, or necessary-bags as they were then called. They used a snaffle bridoon with linking collar; a bit-bridle with nose, but no ear or throat band; the cheek-strap going through the ear-band of the bridoon and buckling on the left side, completing them both, and the bit having either a ring or chain for its curb. The collar was of brown leather without a bit, but having a leather or hemp rein fastened to a ring over the left holster. By the black leather carbine bucket was a loop which held the picket-post which they strapped up by their sides with the carbines, the whole of this kit, including weapons, weighing between 15 and 16 stone, and the men themselves, in watering-order, without accoutrements, from 9 stone to 11½.

A private's pay in the Light Dragoons at that time consisted of three items, viz. :—

Subsistence	. . . .	£9 2 0
Arrears	. . . .	3 1 0
Grass-money	. . . .	1 11 10
		£13 14 10

His helmet, coat, waistcoat, breeches, cloak, boots, and sword were supplied by the colonel by contract—coat, waistcoat, and breeches having to last two years, and the other items for four.

Out of a nominal eightpence a day, twopence was stopped for food, and the list of articles he was compelled to purchase out of his pittance would make the modern "grouser's" blood curdle.

A snaffle bridle.	Gaiters.	White jacket.
Goatskin.	Shoe brushes.	Black stock.
Surcingle.	A clothes brush.	Check sleeves.
Horse-cloth.	Curry-comb and brush.	Black ball.
Saddle-bags.		Powder bag and two puffs between two men.
Four shirts.	Mane-comb and sponge.	
Four pair of stockings.	Turnkey.	Scissors to each sergeant and corporal.
Two pair of shoes.	Awl.	
Leather breeches.	Horse-picker.	

Four pairs of boots and spurs were allowed to each troop every year to meet possible contingencies, and about thirty-six cloaks to the regiment every fourth year.

Horse furniture and standards were replaced every fifth clothing, or in about ten years.*

And now a word about the Light Dragoon's horse, which took up (his rider being in the saddle) 8 feet of ground by 3, and cost twenty guineas.

The animal was of the nag or hunter kind, with a docked tail, and the way they were purchased is described by Colonel Dalrymple, who is very severe on the system and the profits of the "middleman."

"A jockey goes to a market," says he, "buys a troop horse at twelve or thirteen guineas of the breeder, he meets a friend there, who, perhaps, wanting such a one, he lets him have him at a guinea profit.

"This horse, bought in Lincoln or Northamptonshire, is sold at Newport or Dunstable Fair for sixteen guineas, and brought to town, where he is sold for the Dragoon price, and sent down to quarters.

"During these several changes, the horse is stuffed in such a manner as to conceal his defects and ensure a surfeit to the purchaser; a cold stable, with difference of food and attendance at quarters, increase his complaints, which, however, with the assistance of the farrier, are at last removed; but carrying off with them his extraordinary flesh, the purchaser is often surprised to see a raw-boned ugly brute, instead of a fine sleek gelding, which he bought a month or two before.

"The summer's run, however, sets them up, and

---

* A list of all the necessary items for the complete furnishing of a regiment, with the prices of each, will be found in the Appendix.

habit reconciles them to the food which the scanty allowance for a dragoon horse can afford them."

According to Hinde, that allowance was three quarters of oats and twenty pounds of hay, the man drawing one day's feed in his corn bag, which he had to keep in his room and not in the stable, measuring out each feed in the regimental quartern measure in the presence of the quartermaster or one of the troop officers.

The horses were watered twice a day in summer and once in winter, and were to be "well dressed twice every day, and to have their tails and manes well combed, and their heels rubbed every time the dragoon goes into the stable." Weather permitting, they were exercised (aired is the quaint old term used) every day, one man to two horses, and twice a week the whole regiment was ridden out with saddles and bits.

A strange old-time custom was the turning of the horses out to grass from the 1st May to the 1st October, under a grass-guard of varying strength according to the distance from quarters, and the old formula of guard-mounting in the Light Dragoons may be of interest to the modern Lancer, who regards that important duty as purgatory.

A troop in quarters had to furnish a corporal and six men, or, in certain cases, a sergeant, corporal and twelve files, who turned out at troop-beating to receive the parole; on Sundays at eight, on other days at ten.

This guard formed up three deep on the left of the old guard, in the presence of all the officers and non-coms., and the whole having fixed bayonets, they went through the platoon firing to front and rear, standing and advancing, but the front rank not kneeling on this occasion. Then the old picket dismissed, and the new one mounted, furnishing a man in gaiters for the colonel's door, and, strangest of all, every man except the actual sentries had to attend stables, and return when they had done up their horses!

If they ever had to turn out the guard during that operation, there must have been a wild scramble.

CHAPTER II.

ON MARCH, AND IN QUARTERS.

Scottish Service—Aberdour's Corps—A Strange Incident!—Discipline of the Light Horse—On the March—Riding School—A Detachment to Germany, 1761—John Hale's Prize Money—His Marriage and Numerous Family—Reduction of the Army—The Light Troops "Broke"—Regiment goes to Ireland, 1763—Two Troops to the Isle of Man, 1766—Light Dragoons Renumbered—A Day's Pay to the Military Orphanage—Colonel Blaquière's Duel—John Hale leaves the Regiment, 1770—His Country Life and Death.

FROM Coventry the regiment proceeded in the autumn of 1760 to Berwick, and so into Scotland, where it arrived in the first days of October.

Their first headquarters were at Haddington, the rest of the troops going into quarters at Musselburgh. In August, 1761, they were at Perth (headquarters), Falkland, Aberdour, Cupar, Culross, and Leven; in June the following year headquarters were at Musselburgh, the remainder of the regiment at Dalkeith and Hamilton; while in September, headquarters had again been moved to Haddington, the rest to Dalkeith, Dunbar, Hamilton, Musselburgh, and Linlithgow, the same distribution, with the exception of Hamilton, applying to the early part of 1763.

In this latter year a little struggle in the matter of precedence between Hale's and a corps commanded by Captain Lord Aberdour, afterwards 15th Earl of Morton, was finally adjusted. Aberdour's called itself the 17th, or Light Corps of Dragoons, and Hale's had to content itself with the next numeral, although a difference of opinion existed, oddly enough in the regiment itself, Fortescue finding some of the muster rolls of troops styling themselves as of the 17th, and some as of the 18th Light Regiment of Dragoons. How the question ever came to be raised is strange, as Hale's commission was not signed until 7th November, while Lord Aberdour's bore date 10th October; but the difficulty was solved in 1763 by the disbanding of Aberdour's corps, which had never consisted of more than two troops.

And now we chronicle a long forgotten incident, very typical of the times, which took place within two or three days of the regiment's arrival in Scotland.

On Sunday evening, the 5th October, 1760, a party of five officers rode from Haddington to Musselburgh along the first turnpike road constructed in that country. They were Lieut.-Colonel Hale himself, Major Blaquière, Captain Sam Birch, Lieutenant Joseph Hall, and young George Birch, who had only been gazetted cornet in March. With their lace ruffles awry, and all of them flushed with wine, they reached the Ravenshaugh tollbar at the junction of the two counties, where, resenting some supposed insult, they attacked Peter Ker, the tollkeeper, and beat him so severely with riding whips and pistol butts that the red blood flowed. His "guid wife" Helen ran to his rescue, and they beat her until, her cries of "Murder!" bringing out the neighbours, the gallant Dragoons rode off in the dark towards Musselburgh.

But the salt breeze from the Forth brought no glimmer of reason to their fevered brows, and in less than a quarter of an hour they were back again, shouting "Revenge, revenge!" and some of them dismounting, they seized the unhappy Peter and haled him away westwards, crying, "G—— d—— him for a Scotch rebel —; knock him down!"

They then belaboured him brutally, dragged him about, and treated his wife in the same fashion; and after disabling her sister with a stroke from a pistol, they stormed the toll-house, whither the terrified neighbours had meanwhile taken refuge. "Bring out the men!" they yelled, warming to their work, but the women-folk interposing, these young bloods rushed the door, flogged the maid-servant, smashed a pistol which was afterwards produced against them, and did not desist until they had almost stripped Mrs. Ker, whose condition, let alone her sex, ought to have protected her.

Then, honour being satisfied, they hiccoughed away, with many a hearty curse, to their quarters at Musselburgh, leaving a storm behind them which well-nigh cost John Hale his regiment and the others their commissions.

Morning, with its attendant headache, gave them pause, and compensation was offered, only to be refused.

The local gentry, justly incensed, instituted a prosecution, with the result that all five officers appeared on their trial at Edinburgh on the 26th January following, when they very wisely pleaded guilty.

They made no attempt to justify the assault, or even to excuse it, save on the score of having drunk too freely that day; and, after expressing their regret and offering to make any reparation the Court should think fit, they were, after an adjournment, condemned to pay £206 to Ker and his wife, including doctors' fees, and fined £5 each into the bargain.

A strong reprimand was sent down from the king,

and on the 19th March it was administered by Lord George Beauclerc, commander-in-chief of the forces in Scotland, at the head of some troops drawn out for the purpose at Musselburgh, probably on the Links.

The whole story is a curious illustration of the conduct sometimes indulged in by officers and gentlemen at that period, and, indeed, for long enough after. But, this one discreditable *lapsus* excepted, John Hale seems to have been a remarkably good fellow, and worthy of the esteem in which he was held.

The regiment remained in Scotland till 1763, though it had been proposed to move it the year before, the *London Evening Post* announcing, May 31, 1762, that "This day the last division of Colonel Hale's Light Horse marched in grand order through this place (Edinburgh) for the East Country, where they are to halt for a few days until they are reviewed, [when] they are to proceed on their march to England."

Beyond the trial of an officer's servant for intimidation, which was "not proven," and the resignation of Adjutant Westbury, nothing further is recorded of its doings, and it is probable that the private men found Scottish quarters but dull; for the rising of "'45" was then a thing of yesterday, and the redcoat still viewed with disfavour, even in the Lowlands.

Certain rules had been laid down for the light troops when in quarters, and these, no doubt, formed the basis of the discipline used in Elliot's, Burgoyne's and Hale's regiments, at any rate up to 1763, if not later.

The sergeants and corporals were enjoined to use the men kindly, but avoiding too much familiarity;

the officers were to keep a sharp eye on the non-coms., and not trust too much to them.

The usual punishment in the Dragoons was called "picketting," a barbarous method of hanging a man to a post by one wrist for a quarter of an hour, the only relief possible being to rest his bare heel on a peg driven into the ground, the process inflicting great torture, and not unfrequently resulting in rupture and lameness for life. This was abolished for the Light Dragoons, and, in its stead, double duty, confinement, and bread and water diet, were substituted, or "some public rebuke."

Courts-martial were to be held only on extraordinary occasions, whipping resorted to as seldom as possible, and *esprit de corps* was to be fostered. In fact, with the raising of the Light Dragoon, the authorities seem to have first recognised the existence of intelligence in the rank and file, and to have taken some feeble steps accordingly.

Vicious men, however, were to be made examples of—to be punished with great severity, and turned out of the corps with infamy, to the strains of the "Rogue's March," that tune which afterwards became popular as "The Tight Little Island," and the nursery jingle of our childhood, "Poor Old Robinson Crusoe."

When on the march the regiment proceeded by divisions, at a minimum rate of four miles an hour, the divisions keeping as close together as possible, with a large front in open country, and a small one in the lanes "for the convenience of the troops and travellers."

Every five or six miles they halted, to dismount, tighten girths, fall out, etc., and then on once more, the quartermaster ahead to look for billets, the baggage rumbling in the rear under charge of a mounted corporal and two dismounted men. The first and last three miles were to be made at the walk, the rest of the march at a steady trot. When the Light Dragoon reached his billet, he had to take off his accoutrements, slacken his girth, pick his charger's feet, and rub his legs very dry; give him a little hay and tie him up to the rack, to prevent him lying down, after which he was at liberty to refresh himself and change his scarlet coat for the fatigue jacket, when he might loll about until the call for "stables."

When that all-important summons was heard, each man had to stand by until a troop officer, with the quartermaster and farrier, had examined the horse's back, before he was allowed to unsaddle and groom, which performance was gone through in one of those picturesque stables that George Morland has painted so often, full of sunlight and shadow, and, of a certainty, redolent of ammonia; with a knot of loafers in the doorway, and possibly among them some old veteran who had ridden with Honeywood's, or Portmore's, or Dormer's, Dragoons in the rising of 1715, criticising the new-fangled soldier with a dubious eye, and proffering scraps of archaic advice between the whiffs of his clay pipe.

There was something romantic in that system of a roving march from town to town, before barracks became a permanent institution, and if old walls could speak they would echo with strange oaths, and the laughter of girls, and whispered vows doomed to be quickly broken when the trumpets of Hale's Light Horse blared to "boot and saddle."

From Lady Day to Michaelmas the *revallie* went at half-past five; at eight, and again at four, to dress and water; at eight p.m. "rack up," and at nine "tattoo"; while for the rest of the year *revallie* was at half-past six, dress and water at nine and three, and tattoo at eight. Field days were to be very frequent but very short, and words of command were to be pronounced "strong and short."

The horses were never to be saddled until "boots and saddles" sounded, and just sufficient time was allowed between that call and "to horse" to render the men "expeditious and adroit in everything they do."

"The Light Dragoon," says Hinde, "is always to appear clean, and dressed in a soldier-like manner in the streets; his skirts tucked back, a black stock, and gaiters on, but no powder.

"On Sundays the men to have white stocks, and be well powdered, but not any grease in the hair. And to attend divine service."

The feeding regulations were curious at that time, the men having the option of either finding themselves, or being catered for by their host; if they chose the former, subsistence was paid to them twice a week, and an officer was supposed to see that they boiled the pot properly, but if the landlord fed them he was paid in person once a week.

A man who got drunk had nothing but bread and water, and his subsistence-money went, half to his horse, and the rest to the comrade who looked after it for him.

"But if any person shall chuse rather to furnish them with Candles, Vinegar, and Salt, and with either Small Beer or Cyder, not exceeding *Five Pints a Day, gratis* [the italics are in the original] and allow them the use of *Fire*, and the necessary utensils for dressing and eating their meat, and shall give notice thereof to the Commanding-officer . . . ; in such case they shall provide their own Victuals, and the Officer shall pay the sums out of the Subsistence money for diet and Small-Beer to such soldiers, and not to the persons on whom they are quartered, except on a March or Recruiting, that is, to every Trooper's, or Dragoon's, or Light Dragoon's, Diet, and Hay and Straw for his Horse, *One Shilling*, to be paid to the Innkeepers."

Picture the "Death or Glory Boy" of that day, if you can, prowling round in quest of prime cuts after a long ride, and the triumphant procession back to quarters with the spoil! and those five pints of small-beer at the end of it!

One of the chief points in the education of a Light Dragoon was perfect horsemanship, and some famous riders have been associated with that branch of the service.

Philip Astley served in the 15th, though it is only fair to state that he was an accomplished equestrian before he joined; and the Flying Highwayman had some practice in Burgoyne's regiment before he began to practise on a longsuffering public, which afterwards defrayed the expense of his last earthly ride!

The recruit had his work cut out for him when the riding-master took him in hand, for, although gentleness to man and beast was inculcated in the regulations, the "ride" must have been a rough and tumble affair, with plenty of the tumble.

The absence of proper barrack accommodation in those days led to much of the drill and training of all ranks being done in the open, and that fact, though embarrassing to a sensitive man, carried its compensation with it, as the presence of onlookers must have often curbed a violent instructor, who, in the dim seclusion of a riding-school, might have taken it out of a stupid recruit until further orders.

"If temper is recommended in the first part, it is

not less necessary here," wrote Colonel Dalrymple; "for nothing can be more awkward than a country fellow, or perhaps an artizan, mounted, still stiff with their former occupations; the riding-master must, therefore, speak mildly to the recruits, instruct them to sit upright, to turn in the flat of the thigh to the saddle, and to let the leg and foot hang down carelessly; they must be told to depend more on the poise of the body than their twists, and should therefore have an eye to the head of their horse, by which they may always foresee what he is going to do, if vicious, and be the better prepared to humour the motion."

From which we see that the animal was not always selected for his virtues, and many a poor lad must have returned to his quarters sad and sore, rueing the evil day when he took the king's shilling for Hale's Light Horse.

To mount, dismount, to passage, rein back, move forward, and halt, formed the groundwork of instruction; which was supplemented by a long course of foot drill, "to give attitude and supple the body."

It was also recommended that they should gallop gently in file, carrying the horses forward in a serpentine line, and turning to right or left at the word of command.

Their stirrups were to be short enough for the man when standing up in them to show 4 inches of daylight between seat and saddle, to give greater force to his blow.

All this, and much more upon which we need not dwell here, must have been the daily practice of Hale's men, to bring them to that state of efficiency which they seem to have mastered early and well.

D

All newly joined officers had to attend riding-school until dismissed by the commanding officer, and each had to have one horse regimentally trained and kept in proper condition for parade, a "first charger," in short, upon which he was never to appear at any time without a regimental bridle, pistols, furniture, or goatskin.

It is not generally remembered that, in addition to the docked tail (a barbarous innovation of Lord Cadogan's in the case of his Dragoon horses), the practice of cropping the ears was also in vogue rather later, though we are happy to note that, according to Hinde, it was not adopted in his time by the Light Dragoons.

Firing from the saddle was an important item in the training of the Light Horse, and he was enjoined to accustom his charger to pistol and carbine from the first, by putting them in the manger with his feed, showing them to him, and flashing and firing with a small charge. The proportion of ammunition in 1760 was sixty-four rounds per man for service, with three flints; and 405 rounds, with two flints, for exercise; the former being half ounce and the latter three drachm cartridges. A long feather was to be kept up the touch-hole, and a stopper in the muzzle to exclude dust when not in use; and no arms were to be mended by other than the regimental armourer, "unless in case of his illness." For the curious in such matters full details of the carbine drill of that period will be found with other technical information in the Appendix.

There were changes in the regiment even at its birth. Captain Kirby's name vanished with the year, and before six months had passed Captain Martin Basil exchanged again into his old corps, and, as captain-lieutenant, fell gallantly in that action which won for the 15th its motto, and the proud inscription long worn on the front of its helmets, " Five Battalions of French defeated and taken by this Regiment, with their Colours and nine pieces of cannon, at Emsdorf, 16th July, 1760."

Early in 1761, Hale's furnished a detachment of fifty men and horses to serve under Granby and Prince Ferdinand in Germany, but nothing is known of its doings beyond the fact that Lieutenant Wallop was taken prisoner by the enemy.

This same year Captain Edward Lascelles was returned to Parliament for Northallerton, and married Miss Anne Chaloner, of Guisborough, at the celebrated church of St. George, Hanover Square. He, too, severed his connection with the Light Dragoons the following year, ultimately became Earl of Harewood in 1812, and died in 1820 at the age of eighty, having had a grandson wounded at Waterloo in the 1st Guards.

In 1762, Lieut.-Colonel Hale, either yearning after active service or, perhaps, with an eye to the main chance, left his men in their northern quarters and went to Havannah as military secretary to Lord Albemarle, the fleet sailing on the 5th March.

With that expedition this history has no part, but the division of the prize-money is curious: the Earl of Albemarle taking £122,697 ; Lieut.-General Elliot, £24,539; William and Augustus Keppel (the earl's brothers), £6,816 apiece; John Hale, £10,000; and the *soldiers*, £4 1s. 8½d. per man !

During the war two of our ships captured the Spaniard *Hermione* off Cadiz, valued at £1,600,000, exclusive of the vessel herself, and the treasure, decorated with flags and escorted by marines with fixed bayonets, passed St. James's Palace a little while after the birth of the Prince of Wales, afterwards George IV.

At the head of the waggons rode "a company of Light Horse attended with kettledrums, French horns, trumpets, and hautboys," the kettledrum being very unusual for the Light Cavalry, and only coming into favour with the Heavy about that time.

In 1763, John Hale married Mary Chaloner, sister of Captain Lascelles' wife, by special licence; the ceremony in all probability also taking place at St. George's, as the lady, a minor, is described as living in Bond Street at the time. The chances are that it was a love match, for all the dowry he received with his blushing bride was a small farm called Tocketts, about a mile from Guisborough in Yorkshire, where he afterwards made his residence, adding largely to the old house, which from a print now before us was an ugly, barrack-like structure with several wings, set on a lawn, and only redeemed by a peep of wooded hill beyond it. Well might he indulge in building operations, as Mistress Mary Hale bore him twenty-one children in their forty years of wedded bliss, and if any are curious to know how they named such a batch of mixed blessings we can satisfy them.*

Hale's grant of land in Canada lapsed to the Crown, but his sons afterwards possessed a very extensive property in that country.

The eldest son, Hon. John Hale, while secretary to his uncle, Lord Amherst, Governor-General of India, realised a handsome fortune, and died as recently as 1838, aged seventy-four, leaving two sons officers in the army, besides other children; the Quebec *Gazette*

---

* Mary, Anne, Harriet, Emily, Fanny, Charlotte, Catherine, Octavia, Emma, Eliza, Jane, John, Henry, Bernard, William, Richard, 2nd Richard, George, Frank, Vicesimus, and Edward.

recording that, during fifty-two years' service, he satisfactorily accounted for more than fifteen millions of the public money that had passed through his hands.

We will now leave the Hales for a while, posting down to Guisborough, most probably, and return to the regiment.

On the peace of 1763, a considerable reduction was made in our army, and the Light Dragoons, despite their obvious usefulness and firm establishment in popular favour, were not exempt.

All the eleven light troops were "broke," together with Lord Aberdour's, Sir James Caldwell's, and the Royal Foresters. The disappearance of Aberdour's apology for a regiment gave to Hale's the undoubted right to its proper title at last, and the Light Dragoons to be retained in the service stood as follows: Elliot's 15th, Burgoyne's 16th, Hale's 17th, and Drogheda's 18th —the latter, a distinctively Irish corps, which in 1768 had full-green housings laced with red and white, and, as a dashing Hussar regiment gay in light-blue and silver, was disbanded in 1818, after a brilliant career in the Peninsula and at Waterloo.

John Hale was gazetted full colonel in 1763, the year the 17th was moved to Ireland, but though it remained on the Irish establishment until 1775, details of the regimental doings, and even stations, are more meagre at this period than during any other portion of its history.

Ireland was simmering at that time; the Whiteboys had only just been suppressed for a while, and the Oakboys were about to rise, and it is known that the new arrivals were frequently summoned to perform that most hateful of all duties to a British regiment, to assist the civil power.

The regiment had made a long march from the east coast of Scotland, to Port Patrick, in Wigtonshire, and crossing over to Donaghadee in Co. Down, entered Dublin on the 6th and 7th June, 1763.

On Sunday, the 10th, four troops set out for Munster, the remaining two following next day, and "the men and horses, notwithstanding their long march in Scotland, made a remarkable good appearance." The baggage, and some of the men, went round in a sloop to Cove, the regiment being reported on the 18th June as on its way to Mallow and the neighbouring cantonments. In July two troops of Hale's and two of Drogheda's were called north, and an extract from a private letter, dated Armagh, July 30th, gives some clue to their doings.

"I think it would be an act of great injustice," says the writer, "to pass over the conduct and gallant behaviour of John Bond, Esq., who so remarkably signalised himself on the landing of Thurot, and [who ?] was now at the head of a party of Hale's Light Dragoons, at three o'clock in the morning surprised a thousand Oakboys, took the two ringleaders, or captains, viz. Glass and Williamson, prisoners, and lodged them in Armagh Gaol; the engagement was very smart for some time, but happily ended with dispersing them all."

Whether they remained in that part of the country we know not, but on the 6th October, 1764, the regiment rode into Dublin again from *the north* "on their route to the counties of Kilkenny and Waterford, to join the Earl of Drogheda's Light Horse, in order to quell the rioters in those parts."

The muster rolls quoted by Fortescue only begin in 1772, when the headquarters were at Clonmel in Tipperary, but we have found several undeniable references to the regiment at an earlier date, and some which, while not mentioning it specifically, may be assumed to do so without much doubt. Five of the Light Horse escorted two men named Bourke and White from Carrickbeg into Waterford in February, 1766. In May a number of horses arrived in Dublin from England for the remounting of the cavalry, and in this year the price of a horse was increased to twenty-two guineas by royal command. In November, Francis Augustus, the only son of Lieut.-General Elliot of the 15th, was gazetted captain in Hale's, which reminds one that Hale himself sent no son into his old regiment.

Young Elliot's stay was short with them, as he was gazetted out again in January or February, 1768.

In 1766, the Light Dragoons were renumbered, and Hale's became the 3rd, but the experiment soon died out, and in 1768 or 1769 they resumed their old number, which they have retained ever since.

Fortescue finds that, in 1766, two troops were quartered in the Isle of Man; their mission being no doubt to help the excise officers, as attention had been directed a year or two before to the large trade in smuggling carried on in the island.

In February, 1767, the Governors of the Hibernian School for the Orphans and Children of Soldiers acknowledged the receipt of £17 19s. 5d., being one day's pay of the officers and privates of Hale's. In 1768 they were at Tullow in Co. Carlow, where Cromwell once played such havoc, and on the 17th June, two troops rode into Cork from that place, pushing on again the same evening to Bandon, where the barracks had been prepared for them.

There the surgeon, Mr. Christopher Johnston,

improved the shining hours, for it is recorded that in the April following he married Miss Herrick, of Bandon, with a handsome fortune, and in 1790 a cornet, Christopher Johnston, is borne on the list of officers.

In January, 1771, we find them beating up for volunteers in Cork, and in July, Lieut.-Colonel Blaquière kissed his Majesty's hand on his appointment as Secretary to the Embassy at Paris. In 1773, Blaquière was the hero of an extraordinary adventure which made him one of the best-known men in Ireland for the time being. The son of a Huguenot refugee, he had been born in London in 1732, and spent his early youth in the counting-house of a merchant. How he came to become the 17th's first major we know not, nor is there anything to tell us what kind of an officer he made; but from the date of his appointment to the Embassy he saw little of the regiment. When Lord Harcourt came to Dublin in 1772, Blaquière returned with him as his chief secretary, in which capacity he became involved in the adventure aforesaid.

A certain Mr. Beauchamp Bagenal, member for Carlow, and one of the most pestilent duellists of his day, wrote to the new secretary, asking for leave of absence for a relative serving in America; and, as the matter did not come within the scope of his department, Blaquière wrote politely to that effect, regretting his inability to oblige him, and getting an immediate challenge as the result. Realising that there was nothing for it but to "go out," Blaquière met him the following morning at the thorn trees in Phœnix Park, a popular rendezvous for those delicate little adjustments. At Bagenal's request they were posted nearer than was usual, and the colonel fired in the air, while Bagenal took deliberate aim, pressed the trigger, and the pistol failed to go off. A second and a third time Blaquière's life trembled in the balance, and still the weapon hung fire. The colonel suggested that Mr. Bagenal should adjust his flint, which he attempted to do by tapping the edge of it with a key, but it missed for the fourth time. The colonel then suggested that he should change his flint, which was done; and at this, the fifth shot, Bagenal sent a ball through his adversary's hat, grazing his temple. It was now the colonel's turn, but disdaining any advantage, he was about to fire in the air again, when, to quote Froude—

"De Blaquière said he had no quarrel with Mr. Bagenal, and could not think of it. Mr. Bagenal behaved with great politeness and intrepidity, entreating that the colonel would not refuse him the honour of, etc., etc. It was in vain. De Blaquière would not do him the honour at all. Bagenal would have made a new quarrel of it, but the seconds interfered. It was agreed that De Blaquière had behaved astonishingly well! The affair ended, and the colonel was the most popular secretary that had ever held office in Dublin."

This officer married a lady from Cork in 1775, was created a baronet in 1784, and raised to the Irish peerage as Baron de Blaquière in 1800.

Many improvements in Dublin were due to him, and after a long parliamentary career, both in Ireland and England, he died, a popular *bon vivant*, at Bray in Wicklow, 27th August, 1812.

But, meanwhile, other and greater changes had taken place, for in 1770 Colonel Hale, having been appointed Governor of Londonderry and Culmore Fort, severed his connection for good and all with the regiment he had so successfully raised. In 1772 he became major, and in 1777 lieut.-general, and finally reached the rank of general on the 12th October, 1793.

It is disappointing to find no record of his having kept in touch with the 17th after he left them, as one might reasonably have expected of a man who could provide so significant a badge and motto; we can, therefore, only suppose that the general had his hands, as he certainly had his quiver, full, and that had the lads in scarlet and white chanced to come trooping through the township of Tocketts during their old leader's lifetime, there would have been high revel.

In politics he was a Liberal. George Grote, the historian, who married one of his granddaughters, tells of a speech he made at York, about 1784, "a hearty radical speech on constitutional reform, and highly courageous in its tone."

Hale by nature as well as name, the old general farmed and planted, and pottered about his house, which he renamed "The Plantations," until the 20th March, 1806, when he died, his ashes being deposited in Guisborough church beside those of his wife (who had predeceased him by less than three years), leaving behind him many local traditions of generosity and disinterested benevolence, and, as Fortescue very aptly puts it, "seventeen children and the 17th Light Dragoons."

It only remains for us to add that, in 1809, Robert Chaloner bought the farm and again joined it to the Chaloner estates, and that the mansion, whose walls had often heard the stirring story of Wolfe and Quebec, was demolished about 1815.

CHAPTER III.

HOW THE REGIMENT EMBARKED FOR ACTIVE SERVICE FOR THE FIRST TIME.

The New Colonel — Excellent Condition of the 17th — Formation for Inspection and March Past—Under Orders for America—Embarkation Returns—America and the Coming Struggle—Strange Action by Colonel of 47th — Lexington — Bunker's Hill — A Yankee Marksman — The 17th turn a Church into a Riding School—All the Horses of the Regiment said to have been captured—Howe sails for Nova Scotia— Regiment increased—Starts with the Army against New York.

THE new colonel was a man who merits some description, being altogether above the average in those times in point of reputation and length of service, and being, moreover, what we call nowadays a "gentleman ranker."

Colonel George Preston began his military career, according to James Grant, by beating a drum in the Scots Greys as far back as the coronation of Queen Anne, and for more than half a century he fought with that distinguished regiment in all their campaigns, rising by slow degrees until he became their lieut.-colonel in 1757.

He it was who wore the last buff coat ever seen in our service, and whenever Geordie Preston rode to the head of his men in his old leathern jerkin they knew that hard knocks would soon be going!

To him it is possible the 17th may have owed the high reputation they acquired in the five years following on his appointment, but one cannot say positively that he ever even saw the regiment.

Fortescue quotes the following extracts from some of the inspection reports:—

1770.—"A *very good* regiment." 1771.—"A very fine regiment, and appears perfectly fit for service. Must have had great care taken of it." 1773.—"This regiment is an extreme pretty one, and in good order." 1774.—"This regiment is in great order, and fit for service."

In May, 1773, they foregathered at Kilkenny, from Carrick, Ross, and Leighlin-bridge; and on the 24th were reviewed by General Pierson on the racecourse, "when the officers and men went through their different manœuvres and firing, as well on horseback as on foot, with the greatest exactness, to the entire satisfaction of the general and the admiration of the greatest number of spectators ever known here on the like occasion."

The plan on the opposite page will give some idea of a regiment drawn up for such an inspection at that period.

THE ORDER OF REVIEW. 45

ORDER OF REVIEW IN THREE SQUADRONS, CIRCA 1760-1780.
* The King or reviewing general.

		. Chaplain.		
		. Surgeon.		
		. Farrier.		
		. ,,		
		. Trumpet-Major.		
		Trumpeter.		
		. Fifer.		
		. Sergt.-Major.	. Sergeant.	
		. Corporal.	. Corporal.	
	Captain .			
	Lieutenant .	Right		. Quartermaster.
Colonel .	Guidon .	Squadron of		
	Cornet .	Two Troops.		. Quartermaster.
	Capt.-Lieut. .			
		. Corporal.	. Corporal.	
		. Sergeant.	. Sergeant.	
		. Farrier.		
		. ,,		
		. Trumpeter.		
		. ,,		
		. Sergeant.	. Sergeant.	
		. Corporal.	. Corporal.	
	Captain .			
	Lieutenant .	Centre		. Quartermaster.
Major .	Guidon .	Squadron of		
	Cornet .	Two Troops.		. Quartermaster.
	Lieutenant .			
		. Corporal.	. Corporal.	
		. Sergeant.	. Sergeant.	
		. Sergeant.	. Sergeant.	
		. Corporal.	. Corporal.	
	Captain .			
	Lieutenant .	Left		. Quartermaster.
Lt.-Colonel .	Guidon .	Squadron of		
	Cornet .	Two Troops.		. Quartermaster.
	Lieutenant .			
		. Corporal.	. Corporal.	
		. Sergeant.	. Sergeant.	
		. Trumpeter.		
		. ,,		
		. Farrier.		
		. ,,		
		. Adjutant.		

On this page the regiment is represented marching past at review, but the post of the fifer is not given.

```
                        ☩

            Surgeon    .   . Chaplain.
            Farrier    .   . Farrier.
            Trumpeter  .   . Trumpet-Major.
                       . Colonel.
    Cpt.-Lt. Cornet. Guidon.   Lieut.   Capt.
       .       .       .         .       .
    ┌─────────────────────────────────────────┐
    │                                         │
    │           Right Squadron.               │
    │                                         │
    └─────────────────────────────────────────┘

              . Quartermasters .
    Farrier        .                  . Farrier.
    Trumpeter      .                  . Trumpeter.
                   . Major.
    Lieut.  Cornet. Guidon.  Lieut.   Capt.      * King, or re-
      .       .       .        .       .           viewing
                                                   General.
    ┌─────────────────────────────────────────┐
    │                                         │
    │           Centre Squadron.              │
    │                                         │
    └─────────────────────────────────────────┘

              . Quartermasters .
    Farrier        .                  . Farrier.
    Trumpeter      .                  . Trumpeter.
                   . Lt.-Col.
    Lieut.  Cornet. Guidon.  Lieut.   Capt.
      .       .       .        .       .
    ┌─────────────────────────────────────────┐
    │                                         │
    │            Left Squadron.               │
    │                                         │
    └─────────────────────────────────────────┘
              . Quartermasters .
                   . Adjutant.
```

The scene was a picturesque one; the general and his staff riding slowly down the line, the swords flashing from their scabbards, squadron by squadron; the officers—strange straining after uniformity this—

divided according to their horses among the various troops, "to match as near as possible to the colours of black, brown, bay, or chestnut," and the trumpets sounding a march, but the cornets holding the guidons immovably upright, the reviewing officer not being a prince.

As he came abreast of the regiment the general's keen eye would fall on Parson Griffith, not long appointed, in all the glory of well-powdered bagwig; and on Surgeon Johnston, perhaps conscious that the dark eyes of the heiress of Bandon were beaming upon him from the bevy of magnificent Irish beauties come to see the "Dhragoons."

Then the sombre farriers, axe on thigh, contrasting with the laced white coats of the trumpeters, until, behind the officers, appeared the scarlet and white mass of the right squadron, clean shaven and well groomed, sitting motionless with short stirrups, not a belt out of place, not a stock awry; the red horse tails pendant from the combs of their helmets, the metal skulls grinning as brightly as whiting and elbow-grease could make them.

And so on, down the line in solemn parade, and then for the manœuvres, destined to delight the spectators, to whom good horsemanship was everything.

Then came forming of squadrons and wheeling of the line, charges by the trumpet and retreats by the French horn, with skirmishers dashing gallantly through the intervals, until the whole plain was alive with galloping men; forming "half-wedge" on the right, or the line oblique, the retreat through the defile, the wheel up in line—all the thirty-six movements laid down for such occasions.

"THE DEATH OR GLORY BOYS."

"This regiment is an extreme pretty one and in good order," wrote the general when it was all over, and we are not going to gainsay him.

On the 21st May, 1774, the regiment had a preliminary field day at Carlow, and on the 1st June the Earl of Drogheda reviewed them at Kilkenny. A few days later they marched to new quarters, namely, three troops to Maryborough, and three to Mountmellick, where their sojourn was destined to be short, as the following January they were under orders for foreign service and all leaves cancelled. Early in March the transports were daily expected, and on the 17th of that month the regiment entered Cork, the drafts to bring it up to war strength encamping at Cove on the 30th. These drafts had been furnished by the 12th (made Light Dragoons in 1768) and the 18th, Lord Drogheda's. On the morning of the 10th April two troops of the 17th left Cork for Passage, to embark, the rest following on the two succeeding days.

Here is their embarkation return from Fortescue, dated Passage, 10th April, 1775.

LIEUT.-COLONEL	Samuel Birch.
MAJOR	Henry Bishop.
ADJUTANT	John St. Clair, cornet.
SURGEON	Christopher Johnston.
SURGEON'S MATE	Alexander Acheson.
DEPUTY-CHAPLAIN	W. Oliver.

MAJOR BISHOP'S TROOP.

Robert Archdale, captain.   Frederick Metzer, cornet.

1 quartermaster, 2 sergeants, 2 corporals, 1 trumpeter, 29 dragoons, 31 horses.

CAPTAIN STRAUBENZEE'S TROOP.

Henry Nettles, lieutenant.   Sam Baggot, cornet.

5 non-commissioned officers, 1 trumpeter, 26 dragoons, 31 horses.

Captain Moxham's Troop.

Ben Bunbury, lieutenant.   Thomas Cooke, cornet.
5 non-commissioned officers, 1 trumpeter, 26 dragoons, 31 horses.

Captain Delancey's Troop.

Hamlet Obins, lieutenant.   James Hussey, cornet.
5 non-commissioned officers, 1 trumpeter, 1 hautboy, 27 dragoons, 31 horses.

Captain Needham's Troop.

Mark Kerr, lieutenant.   Will Loftus, cornet.
5 non-commissioned officers, 1 trumpeter, 26 dragoons, 31 horses.

Captain Crewe's Troop.

Matthew Patteshall, lieutenant.   John St. Clair (adjutant), cornet.
5 non-commissioned officers, 1 trumpeter, 1 hautboy, 26 dragoons, 31 horses.

Once at the waterside, the horses were unsaddled and unbridled, and led by their collars into the flat-bottomed lighters, ten or a dozen in each, every man to his charger's head, and a railing round the lighter to prevent accidents.

It is doubtful whether a single animal of them all was destined to crop the lush green grass of old Ireland again, and possibly with that intuition of dumb brutes there may have been some frantic resistance, and not a few immersions in the Cove of Cork that day.

But eventually, as the lighters came alongside the transports, one after another, bays, browns, and trumpeters' greys, were hoisted in the sling of stout sacking, dangled a moment in mid-air, and lowered into the darkness of the hold, from which they were not to emerge until two weary months of head winds and Atlantic rollers brought them to Boston harbour and the front!

Think of it, ye who find a short week too long to cross the "herring pond," with all the modern luxury of electric light and "violet velvet lining,"—two months of noisome, rat-haunted, stifling transport, with all the discomfort so graphically described by Surgeon Smollett!

It was not a good send-off for the regiment, about to prove its worthiness for the first time before the enemy, and the agony of parting with friends on shore was unduly prolonged by mishap and weather; for two of the ships fouled and there was damage done, and when the convoy finally weighed anchor on the 19th the wind changed again and they had to put back.

At last, on the 28th, they got out to sea, eight regiments in twenty-four transports, the sun shining gloriously, though the head winds still retarded them.

Let us leave them tossing in mid ocean—they were sighted on the 12th May, little more than a fifth of the voyage done—and glance very briefly at events happening at their destination, and at that destination itself.

The American colonies consisted of thirteen states, each possessing a governor and council appointed by the Crown, and a house of assembly elected by the people.

The population was, roughly, two millions of whites and half a million of coloured people, and by industry and application they had become wealthy.

It had been a hard fight against great odds; the red man, the wild beast, the primeval forest, the impassable swamp, all had to be combated, and were combated, until, at the time of which we are writing, the cluster of log huts had grown into a town, the river had its ferry, the forest its beaten track; on Sunday the church bell called the faithful to worship, just as in the old country, and already the moss grew green on graves whose dates bore witness to a very respectable antiquity.

Save that strange foliage met the eye, that birds of different plumage and song flitted across the clearings; that the mountain was higher, the river swifter, and the seasons fiercer in their alternation of sunshine and storm, the 17th would find less change in their surroundings during the early portion of their stay than many of them imagined; afterwards, in the wilds beyond the settlements, and particularly when they were campaigning in Carolina, the difference would be more marked; but in the towns were the same red-brick mansions of the well-to-do merchant; ladies wearing the same *mode*, or nearly so, that they had seen in Cork, and the same universal language spoken everywhere, if it *had* a colonial burr in it.

But there was one section of this people distinctly marked by its environment,—the farmer, trapper, and backwoodsman,—a section which carried its life and its gun in the same hand; ever watchful and wary for the beast that prowled by night and the arrow that flew by day; a sturdy, self-contained, self-reliant class, admirable until it was stroked the wrong way, which was exactly what the 17th and its sister regiments had come to do.

And the cause of their coming was not far to seek. The increased prosperity of the colonies attracted the attention of our government at home, and several attempts were made to enforce taxation and duty upon the colonists without any adequate return by the mother country.

This policy being met by opposition, further attempts were made to cripple their trade and bring them to their knees by forbidding local manufacture, which the colonists defeated by a boycott of British wares, until our merchants suffered severely.

The Stamp Act of 1765 caused great excitement and had to be repealed, but Parliament still claimed absolute right to legislate.

Then Townshend, to make up a paltry deficit of £40,000, taxed tea, glass, paper, and colours, with the result that rioting took place, and when the British Government again conceded to the popular outcry in all those items but tea, it was done with so bad a grace as to have a still more injurious effect.

The colonists were beginning to feel their power, and the ministry at home, self-seeking, obstinate, and intolerant of anything but its own party, sent troops to settle matters which were beyond its comprehension, in the settling of which said matters the 17th played a gallant part, though the ultimate adjustment was of a nature very galling to our pride.

It must be borne in mind that up to the last moment the Americans had no thought of separation, and it was only when the step was deliberately forced upon them that they took up arms in their own defence.

Even then their troops were raw Militia, officered by inexperienced men, with local jealousies and party feeling in their ranks.

The Northern States were not in much sympathy with those of the South, and when George Washington was called to the chief command he had to combat a good deal of unjust suspicion in many quarters.

In Massachusetts, for example, the wealthy class were almost entirely for the king, and nearly every township had its faction. There was not at the outset that great universal banding together in a common cause which a cursory reading of history would seem to suggest, and the whole internal story of the war is one of strife and dissension.

Boston was the town where hostilities practically began, and Boston is to-day the most English city in tone and appearance of any in the United States.

In the winter of 1774-5 it was garrisoned by about 3,000 British troops, the inhabitants numbering some 17,000, and being the only place in the colony where the king had any real authority, it had had to submit to a variety of irritating restraints and interferences.

There, in 1770, occurred the riot between the people and the soldiery, known as the "Boston Massacre," followed two years later by the burning of the armed British schooner *Gaspee*, and in 1773 by the throwing of the tea into the harbour.

Then came the absurd Port Bill, by which no vessel was allowed in Boston harbour that had not previously unloaded its cargo at Marblehead, thirty miles off, entailing a long transit by road.

In 1774 the first Continental Congress met at Philadelphia, when all the colonies, for the first time unanimous, agreed to leave the settlement of their grievances, and they were many, in the hands of the delegates, Georgia alone being unrepresented.

An unfortunate contempt for the colonists was openly manifested by our officers, one of whom, writing home in 1774, says, "believe me, any two regiments here ought to be decimated if they did not beat in the field the whole force of the Massachusetts province."

Again, on the day ordained by Congress for an universal prayer and fasting for the entire colony, the "King's Own" played their drums and fifes within ten yards of the church during the whole of the service, under the eye of their colonel, and our officers interrupted the preacher with laughter and coughing at the solemn service in celebration of the "Massacre."

A strange story was current at the time, of the means taken by our military to stir up a quarrel. By way of provoking the people, Colonel Nesbit of the 47th ordered a soldier to offer an old rusty musket for sale to a countryman from Billerica, who gave him three dollars for it, and was immediately put in the guard-house. Next morning, on a trumped-up charge of tampering with the troops, the unfortunate man was stripped stark naked, covered with warm tar, rolled in feathers, and escorted in a cart to the tree of liberty by thirty grenadiers with fixed bayonets, twenty drums and fifes, playing the "Rogue's March," and headed by the colonel in person with a drawn sword. Representations to Gage met with no redress, but the story went through the length and breadth of the land.

In April, 1775, the colonists in Massachusetts could only muster twelve field pieces and about 17,000 pounds of gunpowder, but when the time came these were found more than sufficient for their purpose, though officered as they were by doctors and farmers, with few leaders that had any experience of actual warfare.

And that time was not long coming, for Governor Gage, afterwards colonel of the 17th, hearing that some brass guns were stored at Salem, sent a detachment, which found that the people had removed them before its arrival.

This was in February, and in April he made another attempt on the military stores collected at Concord, which resulted in the commencement of hostilities.

We all know Longfellow's stirring "Ride of Paul Revere"; and how, on the signal of two lights shown on Boston steeple, he galloped with a couple of comrades to warn the colonists that the troops were coming out!

Nine hundred Grenadiers and Light Infantry, under

Colonel Smith of the 10th Foot, with six light companies of Marines under Major Pitcairn, embarked silently on the Charles River, landed at Phipp's Farm, and marched swiftly in the moonlight towards Concord.

But the tocsin rang out from the village churches, and the roll of drums came on the night wind; the country was alarmed, and at five o'clock of the April morning they found thirty-eight Militia, under Captain Parker, drawn up on Lexington Green!

"Disperse, you rebels! throw down your arms and disperse!" cried Major Pitcairn. "Don't fire unless you are fired on," said Captain Parker to his little band; "but if they want a war, let it begin here!"

It began there! for the Marines fired a volley, killing 7 and wounding 9, and charged with a loud hurrah! The Militia fired, and retired, afterwards following us up and capturing seven stragglers; and at Concord we met 450 colonists under Isaac Davis.

"I haven't a man who is afraid to go," he had said as his company was placed at the head of the column; and he fell by the first shot!

We burned a few stores there, but had to fall back, and then we learned the deadly value of independent marksmen posted behind trees and walls, and in the homelike orchards of the scattered farms.

Earl Percy had been sent after the detachment with infantry and two guns, and, forming square near Lexington at two p.m., received the exhausted redcoats within his protecting ranks.

A terrible retreat followed, and it is recorded on good authority that in some cases the colonists used the scalping knife during the pursuit.

It was sunset before we reached Boston, having raised a whirlwind which "all the king's horses and all the king's men," directed by a *posse* of incompetent generals, were unable to allay.

The news spread rapidly, and the people rose in every colony.

They knew of these events in New York four days after the fighting, disarmed the garrison, and seized the magazines; in Charleston, South Carolina, they took the arsenal, and proclaimed themselves ready to "sacrifice their lives and fortunes."

On drums and colours were placed the significant motto, "God, who transplanted us hither, will support us"; and on 10th May Ethan Allen, with his "Green Mountain Boys," took possession of Ticonderoga, where the "Black Watch" had fought with such heroic valour in 1758.

Then an army was mustered to shut up our troops in Boston; an army, it is true, without discipline, but gradually growing in numbers until 20,000 men formed a chain of investure thirty miles in extent, with headquarters at Cambridge, a league westward of Boston.

While this siege was in progress the reinforcements arrived, among them the 17th Light Dragoons, which landed, according to Cannon, on the 24th May, but according to Fortescue, between the 10th and 15th June, which latter date is probably the more correct.

At any rate, they had not been long ashore before the battle of Bunker's Hill was fought (17th June), and a party of the regiment volunteered for dismounted duty during the attack.

The story of Bunker's Hill is short and sharp, and may be told in a few lines.

Across the River Charles to northward of Boston rose a bare, conical hill, with the busy town of Charlestown at its foot on the Boston side, the river about as wide as the Thames at London Bridge, the hill itself well within cannon shot of Boston, and consequently commanding it.

Gage neglected to secure the height, and when one morning the boom of firing from the sloop-of-war *Lively* roused the besieged from their beds, it was to see her guns playing upon the intrenchments which the colonists had been throwing up in the night on the hill opposite!

The apathy, or ignorance, of the British commander was to cost him the lives of nineteen commissioned officers and over a thousand killed and wounded, for after a brisk cannonade by the men of war the position was stormed with heavy loss.

Our troops passed over, in heavy marching order, laden with knapsacks, three days' rations, and all the cumbrous paraphernalia of the period, which amounted to 150 pounds per man; a brilliant scarlet company, gay with white braid, and facings of blue, yellow, green, and buff, the *élite* of five brave British regiments, under Howe and Pigott; to which were afterwards added Hale's old corps, the 47th, some Marines and flank companies, and the dismounted troopers of the 17th.

All Boston turned out to see, and the hills on the American side were also crowded with spectators, watching the thrilling spectacle of the storming.

Six thousand colonials manned the intrenchments and rail fences; the climb was steep, the hay grass knee high, and when the word to fire was given, a deadly volley strewed the hillside with redcoats, thick as poppies in a Suffolk cornfield!

One marksman was noted by a lieutenant of Marines to stand above the intrenchment and take deliberate aim, while his comrades handed him fresh muskets, and in ten or twelve minutes he is supposed to have killed or wounded about twenty of our officers, until the Grenadiers of the 23rd settled his account.

Our advance was slow, halting at times to allow the shipping to play on the enemy; and the air was filled with smoke and roaring flames from Charlestown, which we were burning, the wooden steeples in particular flaring like torches in the July afternoon.

Twice we were repulsed, Howe's twelve staff officers being all shot down at one time or another; at the second attempt the colonials reserving their fire until we were within forty yards, and then literally withering us out of existence!

We were obliged—the few indeed that remained—to retire again out of range; but the third attack was successful, and the colonists forced across Charlestown Neck, leaving five out of their six guns behind, and some thirty odd wounded. The slaughter of the British was almost incredible, only five men of the Grenadier company of the Welsh Fusiliers coming out of action, and the other regiments suffering in similar, if not quite so great, proportion. Like many another British victory, it was far too dearly bought, and, indeed, need never have been had General Gage taken the commonest precautions.

What part the 17th took in it is not known—nothing beyond the bare fact of that volunteering, which is all that has come down to us, owing to that unfortunate loss of the regimental papers.

The siege, or rather the blockade, of Boston was continued by General Washington, who, appointed Commander-in-Chief of the Continental Army on 19th June, joined it on 2nd July.

His description may be well quoted from the pen of a distinguished English cavalry officer :—

"He was a gentleman of independent fortune in Virginia, who had taken up arms in a sincere spirit of patriotism, and with some military reputation, but in accepting the command he had repudiated all idea of pay or emolument. He was forty-three years of age, in the prime and glory of manhood, and had acquired his experience in the command of different bodies of British provincials in the French war."

The following is to be found in the *Hibernian Journal* for August, 1775, and may or may not be true :—"Clonmell, August 17th.—A letter from a Captain of Foot, at Boston, to his father in this country, says that the Provincials have possessed themselves of the entire horses of the 17th Regiment of Light Dragoons but three, and they were shot. The horses had been out at grass, having neither corn nor hay for them in Boston."

The 17th had arrived in time to participate in several months of privation and discomfort, in common with the rest of the army; for, shut up in an already crowded town, the health of the troops began to suffer for want of fresh provisions, and, heavily bombarded during the winter, it was a relief to everyone when Howe took leave of the place in March, 1776.

Dr. Thacher, visiting the Old South Church on the 23rd March, tells us that the interior of the spacious brick building had been entirely destroyed, the place having been used as a riding-school for Burgoyne's regiment of Dragoons. "The pulpit and pews were removed, the floor covered with earth and used for the purpose of training and exercising their horses. A beautiful pew, ornamented with carved work and silk furniture, was demolished; and by order of an officer, the carved work, it is said, was used as a fence for a hogsty."

Now, as Burgoyne's Light Dragoons, the 16th, did not reach America until after the evacuation of Boston, it is very certain that the 17th, being the only cavalry in the town, were the real culprits in that very Cromwellian desecration.

Lieutenant Carter, of the 40th Foot, writing to a friend, 18th October, 1775, says of it, "a meeting-house, where sedition has often been preached, is clearing out, to be made a riding-house for the Light Dragoons."

There was some fighting towards the end of their stay, but Howe had the good sense to see that the position was untenable, and, informing Washington that unless the bombardment ceased he must burn the town to cover his retreat, the American artillery at once discontinued their firing, Howe on his side leaving the town intact, and sailing for Halifax with 150 ships.

In his interesting journal, Dr. Thacher tells us that on the 8th February, 1776, when Major Knowlton fired the houses in Charlestown, the British officers in Boston were attending a farce, supposed to be written by Burgoyne himself, called the "Blockade of Boston." At the moment that Washington came on the stage, a sergeant of the regulars also rushed on, crying, "The Yankees are attacking our works on Bunker's Hill!" the line being received as part of the play until Burgoyne called out, "Officers, to your alarm posts," and so brought the farce to a sudden conclusion.

The 17th were quartered at Windsor on account of the forage during the army's sojourn of two months in Nova Scotia, and while there the 16th Light Dragoons arrived from England, presumably with remounts, though in point of fact nearly half their horses were lost at sea.

Also an order came to increase the 17th by thirty men, a cornet, sergeant, and two corporals per troop, but, before the number could be made up, the regiment was again off to the front to take an active part in the campaign of 1776.

The capture of New York was the object of the new operations, and the army landed on Staten Island on 3rd July, where reinforcements of British and Hessians joined them.

The expedition against Charleston, in South Carolina, under Clinton and Cornwallis, having failed in its object, also joined the main army, and among the tardy arrivals from England were a thousand Foot Guards, Sir William Howe's force amounting to 30,000 men.

CHAPTER IV.

AMERICAN WAR OF INDEPENDENCE. THE CAMPAIGNS FROM 1776 TO 1779.

The 17th Attached to Highland Brigade—Americans driven back—Howe's Madeira.—The American Army—The 17th at Brunx River—They make Themselves dreaded by the Enemy—Irish Horses wanted for the Regiment—Camp Equipage of the Dragoons—Danbury—Saratoga and "The Derby"—The 17th at Philadelphia.—On Detachment—Barren Hill—Sergeant Tucker—The 17th's Pride in its Uniform—Dress of American Army.

SIR WILLIAM and his brother, Admiral Lord Howe (afterwards so famous for his victory of "the glorious First of June"), were appointed commissioners from the British Parliament, with powers to treat for peace and grant pardon to the offending colonists, who replied that "they who had committed no fault wanted no pardon," and all attempts at reconciliation having broken down, Howe took the field on 22nd August, landing on Long Island without opposition.

The 17th were attached to the Highland Brigade under Brigadier-General Sir William Erskine, which consisted of the "Black Watch" and the Frazer Highlanders, who were being specially trained for bush fighting, their broadswords and pistols being laid aside for ever and a day.

A range of steep, wooded hills traverses Long Island from east to west, and Putnam occupied the heights and passes, his main force being at Brooklyn on the north shore of the island, since connected with New York by the magnificent Brooklyn Bridge.

The 17th came in touch with the American pickets on the 25th, and at nine o'clock next evening formed the advance guard, as the army moved from Flatland towards a pass in the hills, where an American patrol was captured and the pass found to be unoccupied.

By this manœuvre Howe had turned Putnam's left flank, and in the engagement which took place next morning, the colonists, surprised and out-generalled, were driven back to their intrenchments, the 17th charging them with gallantry, Cornet William Loftus particularly distinguishing himself. The Light Dragoons chased them into the woods and the muddy marsh at Gowan's Cove, where many perished; and the orderly retreat being broken up, the rout was severe, three American generals and about 1,200 troops falling into our hands in spite of the exertions of Washington, who hurried over from the mainland.

But Howe ordered no pursuit, and calmly began to break ground for a regular siege next day; Washington holding council with his officers meanwhile, and carrying his army across the East River into New York in a thick fog on the morning of the 30th.

During the affair, which was known as the action at Brooklyn, though it was in reality spread over several miles of country, the 17th routed the American cavalry at the village of Jamaica, and were thanked by Lieut.-General Clinton and their own brigadier.

Washington decided to concentrate his forces and retire from New York, which was commanded by the English shipping; and Howe allowed him to proceed with the removal of his guns and stores without interruption until the 15th September, when the fleet came up, and, under cover of a heavy fire from five men-of-war, we crossed the river in flat-bottomed boats and landed unopposed.

It is said that Howe, though in hot pursuit of Putnam's rearguard and in a fair way to take it, suddenly halted at the residence of Mrs. Murray (mother of Lindley Murray, the grammarian), and spent nearly two hours in the consumption of her old Madeira, which gave rise to a popular saying at the period, that " Mrs. Murray saved the American army."

That army, at first brought together by a great outburst of enthusiasm, speedily became insubordinate and unreliable by reason of local jealousies and the even then existing distinctions of " North and South," but in 1776 Congress took the matter in hand and organised a permanent force " to consist of seventy-five thousand men, to serve for the term of three years, or during the war."

In addition to pay and rations, a bounty of twenty dollars and a hundred acres of land was offered to each man, and from two to five hundred acres to the officers, in proportion to their rank.

The monthly pay was: $75 for a colonel; $50 for a major; chaplain and surgeon, $33·33; captain, $40; ensign, $20; while a sergeant-major received $9; drum major, $8; fife major, $8·33; sergeant, $8; corporal, $7·33; drum and fife the same; and the privates, $6·67. Each commissioned officer could take a soldier servant from the ranks, who was exempt from duty except in time of action.

The officers also drew rations in proportion to their rank, a single ration consisting of—one pound of beef or pork, one pound of bread, or flour, one gill of rum or whisky per diem, and a small quantity of vegetables when procurable; and in addition, a small quantity of vinegar, salt, soap, and candles, drawn once a week.

All this looks very well on paper, but we read of officers holding bridle in one hand and trying to toast a bit of bacon on a stick with the other, and often having to mount and ride for it during the process, chewing the half-warmed rasher as they went; of generals muffled up in a cloak while their solitary shirt was being washed; and, when that army was disbanded and carried its rags and its traditions home, its arrears of pay were enormous and it had not a farthing in its pocket!

Washington established himself in a strong position farther up the Hudson River, to cover a possible retreat to the mainland in case of need, and we occupied the town of New York, which a few days after was fired, according to some authorities, by incendiaries, almost an entire third of the place being reduced to ashes.

On the 12th October Howe again embarked a part of his force in the lighters with the intention of dislodging the Americans, and, reinforced by the Hessians, attacked them at White Plains in a very strong position on the 28th.

The 17th were engaged at Pelham Manor on the 18th, during their march up country, and joining Howe's army on the 20th were in time for some warm work.

Under a heavy fire they forded the Brunx River, clearing the way for the 28th and 35th, who, supported by the 5th and 49th, rushed the enemy's works with the bayonet, the 17th pursuing the broken colonists towards White Plains, with a loss of one man and five horses killed, and Cornet Loftus, four men, and eight horses wounded.

A general attack ordered for the 30th was postponed by reason of a fearful rainstorm, and on the 1st November the Americans retired to a strong position, after burning their forage and the village of White Plains.

Howe now turned his attention to the American garrisons that still remained on Manhattan Island, and during the storming of Fort Washington the 17th had one man wounded while the regiment was supporting the Light Infantry.

The British army then went into winter quarters, the 17th in and about New York, with the exception of one troop, which accompanied Clinton's force in the capture of Rhode Island, where the troop remained for the next twelve months. "The dread which the enemy have of the Dragoons has been experienced on every occasion," wrote Howe in his despatches, and he also submitted a request for a remount of Irish horses, which, as he says, were "hardier and better accustomed to get over fences." It would have been as well if Howe himself had possessed the same excellent qualities, instead of allowing the colonists to recruit their numbers while he remained idle.

Fortescue gives the strength of the regiment then at 225 all told, or five more than are mentioned in the embarkation returns. During November, 100 horses and double that number of recruits came out from home, and Hinde puts down the establishment for the following year at 408 rank and file, mounted and dismounted.

The list of an officer's camp-equipage for the

campaign just finished, as quoted by the same authority, is not without interest, and shows the impedimenta with which they were burdened in those days.

"Each officer," he says, "had a small Markie and Tent. A Bedstead with Curtains and Bedding; most of them had Musketto Furniture for their Bedsteads. A Camp Stool, and Camp-Table, a Servant's Tent, 2 Blankets, 1 Coverlid, a Pailace, and Bolster-Case, a Water-Deck, Sunks, 2 Trunks, and a Pair of Canteens."

Among the items for the men of the Light Dragoons for the campaign of 1777 he notes: Tin flasks with corks, brass rings, and tape straps; nosebags with leather bottoms and straps; hair picketing ropes; scythes; and both round and square tents.

In April, 1777, a detachment of twelve men accompanied Tryon, who sailed with drafts from various regiments, to destroy the American magazines at Danbury, in Connecticut, and though the aim was accomplished, they were harried by the enemy on their return, and had to fight their way back to the ships, getting no rest for three days and three nights.

A little tradition of that raid, of some interest to the 17th, is preserved in the village of Bethel. An old man, named Hamilton, had lodged a roll of cloth with the tailor at the other end of the street, and, hearing of our approach, determined to save it if he could. He had just mounted, and was fastening one end of the roll to the front of his saddle, when the British advance guard came up, and three men of the 17th started after him. His horse was slow, and as they gained upon him one of the Dragoons cried, "Stop, old daddy, stop! We'll have you!" "Not yet!" replied the fugitive, and as he spoke the cloth unrolled, fluttering out like a banner in the wind, and so startling the troopers' horses that Hamilton gained several rods' start. They chased him, however, to the bridge at the upper end of the town, but as often as they tried to cut him down the cloth got in the way, and the old fellow finally escaped with his prize.

A dismounted troop of the 17th was also engaged in the attempt to clear the Hudson River in October, when Clinton made a diversion in the hope of aiding Burgoyne, who was coming down from Canada, and hotly pressed.

Fort Montgomery was evacuated, but we had to storm Fort Clinton in the teeth of ten guns and an abatis four hundred yards long, manned by Provincials, who fought with great bravery. The 17th took part in the storming, but do not seem to have suffered any loss, returning once more to their old winter quarters at New York, where, however, they were not destined to remain long.

If anything, the campaign of 1777 had proved more unsuccessful and ridiculous than that of the previous year.

Burgoyne had surrendered with his entire division, and though Washington's army was suffering acutely from want and desertion, we were gradually teaching it its trade by our repeated absurdities.

An American writer has said, with some justice, that unless Gates had beaten Burgoyne at Saratoga the "Derby" would in all probability never have been run.

"Without that defeat General Burgoyne would not have sold his hunting-box at Epsom to Lord Derby, and without the possession of that hunting-box by that nobleman there would have been no Derby race."

Still, one may doubt whether Great Britain could not have better dispensed with the "Derby" than with the 7,280 men and the thirty-five guns the Americans claim to have taken on that occasion!

Howe had won the battle of Brandywine in September, and occupied Philadelphia, where the 17th joined him during the winter.

Several foreigners of note had come over not long before to take service with the colonists, among them the afterwards well-known Kosciusko, who attained the rank of general; and young Lafayette, the future commander of the National Guard in the early days of the French Revolution.

Lafayette was wounded in the leg at Brandywine, but he was in the saddle again in the spring, when he had reason to remember the 17th.

At Valley Forge, twenty-six miles from the British cantonments, Washington was allowed to remain for five months, drilling his ragged regiments, while Howe did nothing.

They were in a land teeming with traditions of the old-time settlers, whose homesteads still dotted the fertile plains among the clumps of birch and willow; the very form and colour of the farms must have recalled the Quaker villages which lay so close to the birthplace of the regiment at home.

From contemporary accounts we fancy Howe's army made somewhat merry during its stay at Philadelphia, at the expense of discipline; and one entertainment has become historic, the *Mischianza* fête, in which the unfortunate Major André broke a lance in the mimic tournament in honour of Miss Margaret Chew, who afterwards married Colonel Howard, one of the bravest officers of Washington's army.

In the spring of 1778, the 17th was busy on detachment duty, escorting provisions, and occasionally getting in touch with the enemy.

Twenty-five men under Captain Lord Cathcart went out to reconnoitre one day towards Whitemarsh, and learning that ten American soldiers were in possession of a house on the road, surrounded it and summoned the party to surrender. But the little garrison barricaded themselves and refused, and the captain giving the order to dismount, several of the troopers swung out of their saddles and fired a carbine volley at the door, riddling it with balls, and then marched up to attack with the sabre. The Americans then surrendered and were marched in, prisoners, to Philadelphia, the whole reconnaissance representing twenty-eight miles, which were performed without a halt.

A detachment of the regiment marched on the evening of 3rd May to Crooked Billet, north of Philadelphia, forming part of a force of a thousand men destined to beat up the quarters of the enemy there. The affair was entirely successful, the Continentals losing 150 men and all their baggage, which was cut off by the Dragoons.

At Barren Hill, not far from Crooked Billet, they again smelt powder under command of General Grant, and this time there was plenty of glory to be gained had the British general known his business.

The young Marquis de Lafayette was in command of the Provincials, 3,000 in number, and occupied an isolated post with a river in his rear, dividing him from Washington's camp. Grant got between him and the camp, while General Grey marched along the Schuylkill, and yet another party advanced to Chestnut Hill to intercept every passage of the river, except Matson's

Ford. A troop of Provincial Horse, however, discovered our approach, and giving the alarm, Lafayette and his troops retired precipitately, leaving six field-pieces at the ford. Grant was so tardy in his pursuit, that they afterwards came splashing through the river and carried off the abandoned cannon, and, but for a swoop of the 17th, who captured forty prisoners, the whole force would have escaped.

"Barren Hill" was one of the names engraved on the magnificent sword of honour afterwards presented to Lafayette by the American Congress.

Fruitless negotiations having been again opened, to meet with no better result, Sir Henry Clinton, who had succeeded Howe in command, broke up from Philadelphia and crossed the Delaware.

The 17th were summoned from the baggage column to the rearguard during the sharp action known as Freehold, or Monmouth Court House, where the Americans descended from the heights on a blazing June day.

The 16th charged the enemy, but the 17th had no opportunity, though their formidable aspect and the glitter of their sabres produced a moral effect specially alluded to by Clinton himself. After driving the foe back from two positions, under the sweltering sun whose intense heat alone killed fifty-nine of our infantry during the attack, Clinton resumed his march in the middle of the night to Sandy Hook, whence he sailed for New York on 5th July.

The remainder of the campaign—heaven save the mark!—was spent in the usual muddle and mismanagement; the army was divided at its close, and the 17th eventually found winter quarters at Hampstead, on the east end of Long Island, where they took over some men and all the horses of the 16th, then going home.

Only eighty of them were English mounts, but every horse was a godsend at that time, and the regiment was soon to need all the animals it could lay hands on.

In the year 1779, one Sergeant Thomas Tucker of the 17th is specially mentioned for gallantry during the almost daily skirmishes around New York, where the regiment occupied a position in front of the lines, to assist in keeping the roads clear and facilitate the approach of the badly needed supplies. The sergeant, who had come out from England as a volunteer with the regiment, was out with a party of twelve men when they came on a small fort unexpectedly. The account is meagre in its detail, simply stating that the sergeant leaped into the fort and made the garrison prisoners, and we must fill in the details for ourselves, with a background of woodland, a fortification of logs most probably, and the rush of the troopers in their patched and weather-stained red coats.

It is unfortunate that the early years of the regiment's history leave so much to the imagination; the story of those marches and long-forgotten actions must have yielded many a dramatic incident, many a fine scene for brush and canvas amid the romantic setting of the wild American landscape.

Tucker, so says the record, was rewarded with a cornetcy on the 10th April, 1779, and his name appears in the list of the officers of the 17th until 1788, when he ranked third among the lieutenants, the name of Evan Lloyd following.

While the regiment was in New York, presumably

in 1779, Prince William Henry, afterwards William IV., reviewed them (he was a young naval officer at the time), and more than fifty years later, at the close of another review of the 17th in Windsor Park, he recalled the fact to the officers at dinner, Evan Lloyd being still among them as senior lieut.-colonel.

One of the king's reminiscences was of the pride taken by the men in their uniforms during the American War, they preferring to wear their shreds and tatters, rather than don the green jackets of Tarleton's Legion, to which some of them were attached.

The uniforms of the American army of that period are little known to-day on this side of the Atlantic, but some plates now before us, prepared by the American War Department, show them to have been decidedly picturesque.

Washington recommended the hunting-costume, as most serviceable and easiest procured, and many corps adopted it in consequence. It was a handsome garb, consisting of a "shirt" gathered at the waist by a leathern belt, often white, and fringed with worsted, or trimmed with fur at the whim of its wearer. Sometimes moccasins, at others breeches and gaiters, were worn with it, and a looped-up hat.

Rawlings' and Allan's men wore green; Morgan's were entirely in white; a Virginia rifleman is shown in ordinary everyday costume, with cocked hat and flapped waistcoat.

The City Troop of Philadelphia were not unlike the 17th, save that the coat was brown, but it had white lapels and turned-over collar, slung carbine, and black top boots, and a round leather helmet with a buck's tail for a crest.

The Governor of Connecticut's Foot Guard might

have passed for our own at a distance, wearing scarlet, with elaborate yellow wings and lace, and bearskin caps with a brass plate in front, while General Washington's Body Guard—a corps of picked infantry—had the familiar blue and buff of their leader, with scarlet waistcoats, and white cross belts.

The Pennsylvania regiments adopted the Quaker brown, with buff or white facings; the New Yorkers, blue, brown, or grey coats, with a variety of facings, buff, white, crimson, blue, and green.

At first the clothes were cut, and the accoutrements worn, in the British manner, but before the end of the century everything was upon the French model, and one might be looking at a picture of the Republican army, so closely was their military costume copied.

CHAPTER V.

THE WAR IN CAROLINA.

A Troop for Carolina—Banastre Tarleton—The New Campaigning Ground —Raiding the Thoroughbreds—Goose Creek—A Night March—Brutality engendered by the War—The Ubiquitous Tarleton and his Dragoons— Scarlet Cloth—Hot Work—Pursuit of Buford—Charge on the Enemy's Position—Struggle for the Colour—Tremendous Sabring—Our Men lose their Heads and cut the Americans to Bits—Detachment returns to New York, leaving few Men in Carolina.

A CHANGE came over the fortunes of the 17th with the winter of 1779 and the spring of 1780.

France, after a long negotiation, sent troops to help the Patriot Army, and though one squadron was shut up in the harbour of Brest by our fleet, another crossed the Atlantic, and ultimately landed 6,000 men on Rhode Island in July, 1780.

Clinton had long had designs on the Carolinas, where a large section of the people were believed to be loyal to the king, and with the coming of the French, the need for carrying the war into other fields was increased.

A system of flying columns was to be organised, and a troop of sixty men of the 17th prepared to embark.

On the 26th December, Clinton sailed for Charleston in South Carolina, but a furious storm scattered the fleet; nearly all the horses were lost, and it was not until they had been tempest-tossed for close upon five weeks, that the troop of the 17th, and Tarleton's Legion, were landed at Port Royal, while Clinton and the rest of the force got ashore to the southward of Charleston, which place they intended to take and afterwards make the base of future operations.

Colonel Banastre Tarleton was one of the most capable officers outside any purely regimental command that the annals of the war bear record of.

Born at Liverpool, 1754, he was Lancashire on both the paternal and maternal side; intended for the Bar, like John Hale, and entered at the Temple, but took a commission in the King's Dragoon Guards instead. Volunteering for service in America, he saw a good deal of fighting, and gave proof of great physical courage and personal energy. He was appointed captain in the 79th Royal Liverpool Volunteers in 1778, and afterwards held the command of the cavalry of the Legion, to which a portion of the 17th was attached. Terrible tales are told of his cruelty in Carolina, and he was the popular bugbear of the American mothers for generations; but it must be remembered that party feeling ran at fever heat, and excesses were not confined to one side.

After the war, he contested Liverpool against his own brother, and carried the seat; became a friend of the Prince of Wales, and took the fair Perdita off his hands. She is believed to have helped him in the compilation of his history of the campaigns, a work which must be read with considerable reservation, from the "intolerable quantity" of Tarleton in its pages. He was made colonel of various Light Cavalry regiments, and finally, in January, 1818, obtained command of the 8th King's Royal Irish Light Dragoons, dying a general, G.C.B., in 1833. There is a fine mezzotint of him, in the dress of the Legion, published from the portrait painted in 1782 for his mother, by Sir Joshua Reynolds. Of marvellous activity, and with a positive genius for guerilla warfare, he made himself respected by his opponents, and his name remembered to this day in the Southern States.

His green-coated Legion—with whom the detached troop of the 17th was so closely associated that it is difficult to distinguish between the doings of the one and the other—went into quarters at Beaufort, after procuring some weedy mounts in place of those lost at sea, and while there they received orders to march up country without delay and join Brigadier-General Patterson's infantry, which was going up from Savannah to Clinton's assistance.

It must be remembered that the detachment of the 17th was now in a portion of America which had preserved perhaps more of the social characteristics of the old country than the Northern States, as regards the habits of its landed gentry.

The Carolinas and Virginia were the home of planters who lived pretty much as the old *seigneurs*, holding the lives and liberties of their people in their own hands, indulging in the gorgeous hospitality of an older period, and with it all the little details of horse-racing, cock-fighting, gambling, and "fine gentlemanism."

The country itself presented features of great natural beauty, semi-tropical birds, magnificent scenery, wild swamps where the muffled roar of the alligator was heard in the first flush of sunrise, and the screech of the crane in the short twilight that closed the sultry day. Cedar and cypress, pine and poplar, water-oak and palmetto, alternated with dreary stretches of sand barren and cane brake—a romantic country for campaigning, with a strong "Tory" or loyal element among its population, from whom great things were expected.

Tarleton's first duty was to rehorse his cavalry, and, the neighbouring islands being duly raided, a supply of indifferent mounts was obtained by the time General Patterson ordered him to join him on the march to Charleston.

Although there was a growing dislike to the war on the part of the inhabitants of Carolina, the cavalry met with active opposition at the very start, for the people, calculating on the unhorsed condition of the troops, collected together and attempted to oppose the march.

The 17th and the Dragoons of the Legion charged them, and captured several prisoners and a goodly number of mounts.

There were many thoroughbreds of considerable renown in the country at that period, and great shifts were made to prevent their falling into our hands; though not always attended with success when we learn that a Mr. Peter Sinkler, near Eutaw, lost no less than sixteen blood horses, and twenty-eight mares and fillies.

Two celebrated animals, Flimnah and Abdallah, were conveyed out of reach for a time by a volunteer party under Captain Thomas Shubrick, who, rowing with muffled oars to John's Island, where they were stabled under a guard, found the sentry asleep, secured him just before sunrise, and sent the horses off to a neighbouring ferry.

The shrill neighing of the stallions, however, warned our Dragoons, and a resident, opening his window, told the captain that he was in great danger, as a troop of cavalry under a smart officer was quartered near at hand; and the party had scarcely re-embarked before the bugle horns blew the alarm.

The Arabian Abdallah was ultimately recaptured, and is said to have died from hard usage during the campaign.

After a toilsome march of nearly a fortnight, Patterson joined Clinton, and on 1st April Major André, then deputy adjutant-general, directed Tarleton by letter to cross the Ashley River and join also, giving him strict injunctions only to forage, but not to invite hostilities.

Snapping up some more horses and a quantity of provender the 17th and the green-coated Legion reached their destination, passing close to the American force which lay at Middleton's Plantation near Goose Creek.

With the actual siege of Charleston we have nothing to do, for the energies of the red Dragoons were soon turned in another direction.

A force of Militia, and three regiments of Continental Horse under General Huger, held the forks and passes on the Cooper River, and kept open communication with Charleston itself. This force it was necessary to dislodge, and Lieut.-Colonel Webster with 1,400 men was ordered to attack it; the moment chosen being, when news reached Clinton that a large train of waggons and stores had arrived from the northward.

On the 12th April, Tarleton moved his cavalry and a picked corps of marksmen under Colonel Patrick Ferguson to Goose Creek, where Webster joined him next day with the 33rd and 64th Foot. The same evening, when the shadows were lengthening, and mysterious noises began to be heard from the cotton patch and the dense brake, the cavalry filed off along the dusty road, the ragged plumes of the 17th glowing a deeper red in the rays of the sinking sun.

Not a word was spoken, not a pipe alight; they were the eyes and ears of a little army on its way to a night attack, and keen glances were cast among the rustling palmettos as they rode past the deserted plantations into the country north.

Here and there where a by-path trailed away from the track two or three troopers would be told off to guide the rest of the column, as laid down in the directions for night marching, and when the main body came up these men would hasten forward to join the advance guard stealing noiselessly on, carbine on thigh.

Some distance beyond Goose Creek a nigger was spied, trying to hide himself, and when pounced upon he was found to be carrying a message from the Americans at Biggins' Bridge.

Tarleton says a few dollars procured some valuable information from the man. From a knowledge of Tarleton's methods it is more probable that a little stirrup-leather, or a carbine butt on his bare toes, was the means employed; but be that as it may, the leader learned that the enemy's cavalry was posted on our side of the river, and the Militia on the other bank.

Pushing on with renewed caution through the black night they came on the main guard of the American Light Horse at three o'clock in the morning, and charged with vigour.

A few shots probably, a loud yell of a certainty, and the Dragoons went pounding down the road between two swamps, driving the enemy before them.

It was short and sharp, sabre and spur; the picquets no sooner dashing back into their camp to give the alarm than the British were upon them, and everything in confusion.

A mad helter-skelter among the waggons, a scattering

of the embers of the bivouac fires, and then a *sauve qui peut* into the swamps, leaving everything in our hands and the bridge open!

Tarleton instantly sent his infantry over at the double, and they routed out the Militia posted there and in the meeting-house at the point of the bayonet.

Our loss was 1 officer and 2 men wounded, and 5 horses; that of the Americans, 15 killed, 18 wounded, and 63 prisoners; 42 of their waggons being captured, about 200 horses, and a quantity of stores of all descriptions.

Unhappily our victory was sullied by a brutality that became proverbial; our Dragoons gave no quarter, and the dead and wounded were slashed in an unnecessary manner; indeed, nearly all Tarleton's actions exhibited the same characteristic, arising from the strong party feeling that entered into the southern struggle.

It is to be regretted that the deeds of Tarleton's men are generally recorded under the ambiguous heading of the "British Legion," so that it is as impossible to exonerate the 17th as it is to saddle them definitely with participation in the far too numerous excesses perpetrated during the campaign.

The temper of the British army is well described in the following extract, from a contemporary hand:—

"Their (the British) troops were of the choicest kind, excellently equipped, and commanded by active, ambitious young fellows, who looked on themselves as on the high road to fortune among the conquered rebels. They all carried with them pocket-maps of South Carolina, on which they were constantly poring like young spendthrifts on their fathers' *last testaments*.

"They would also ask a world of questions . . .

and when answered to their humour they would break out into hearty laughs, and flourish their swords, and *whoop* and *hoic* it away like young fox-hunters just striking on a fresh trail.

"'Huzza, my brave fellows!' they would say to each other; 'one more campaign and the *hash* will be settled with the d——d rebels, and then stand by the girls!

"'Prepare the baths, the perfumes, and spices! bring forth the violins and the rose buds! and tap the old Madeira, that our souls may be all joy!'"

In the darkness, realising that resistance was useless, General Huger, Colonels Washington—a nephew of the celebrated George—Jamieson, and half a dozen others, escaped into a swamp on foot, but Charleston was practically isolated by the energy of Tarleton and Webster's excellent dispositions; the latter officer ordering the seizure of Bonneau's Ferry, which commanded another fork of the Cooper River.

Then ensued a brief period of watch and ward, when every man was busy, and patrols moved along the roads day and night; for the Americans were soon mustering again, and might be expected at any moment.

The croak of the frogs in the marsh, the note of the whippoorwill, and the screech-owl, were familiar sounds by that time to the troopers of the detachment; and as the novelty of the country wore off, and no foe came trailing down the tussock, our fellows would seem to have grown lax.

Meanwhile, protected by the Carolina Militia and two Virginian infantry regiments, the American cavalry collected for a swoop. Colonel W. White brought some Dragoons from the north, and gathered up the fugitives from Monk's Corner; a detachment joined him from Georgetown, and Colonel Hugh Horry came in with his Light Horse, and crossing the Santee at Dupin's Ferry on 5th May, they fell upon an officer and seventeen troopers next morning, foraging at Ball's Plantation.

The little party surrendered without resistance, and White, feeling he had done a good morning's work, marched his prisoners towards Lenew's Ferry, where he intended to recross the Santee under cover of 200 infantry sent thither by Colonel Buford.

But as chance would have it, Tarleton was out patrolling that day with 150 men of the 17th and Legion cavalry, and, receiving news of the affair from a Tory who had escaped, instantly pushed on for the ferry in the hope of rescue.

The day was blazing hot, the leagues were many, but at three in the afternoon he came in touch with the enemy's videttes, formed up at once, and charged on the grand guard without hesitation, utterly routing them their leaders having to take to the river for their lives.

Five of their officers and 36 men were killed, 7 officers and 60 Dragoons made prisoners; poor Colonels White, Washington, and Jamieson* again had to swim for it, and we were just in time to stop the passage of the ferry boat, which in another moment would have pushed out into the stream with the captured foraging party!

Our loss was 2 men and 4 horses killed, but on the twenty-six-mile march back to Cornwallis's camp at Huger's Bridge, 20 more horses gave out and died on the road.

Charlestown capitulated on the 12th May, and one

* Jamieson was the officer to whom Major André was handed after his capture.

of the results of its capture was that the partizans and troops in the interior could get nothing but *scarlet* cloth for a long time.

Many curious mistakes occurred in consequence, and two Militia men on furlough, who had dyed their jackets with roots, the dye of which had washed partially out, were saved with difficulty from death at the hands of their own side, who insisted that they were King George's men!

Even Marion had to wear a crimson red jacket instead of the blue of his own regiment.

Sir Henry Clinton—a Guards' officer, who had seen some service during the Seven Years' War and acquitted himself well—sent three expeditions into the interior to finally subjugate the state and consolidate the loyal element, and with one of these expeditions went the detachment of the 17th.

"If you chuse to keep the 17th Dragoons you are heartily welcome to them during this move," wrote Clinton to the earl.

On the 18th May the column started; 2,500 men in all, with five field pieces, under command of Lord Cornwallis.

They took the same route that the cavalry had followed as far as Lenew's Ferry, and their object was to cross the Santee, march up the north-east bank, and, if possible, fall on Colonel Buford (it is spelt variously, Beaufort, Buford, and Burfort), who was retreating to North Carolina *via* Camden, where Huger had ordered him to pick up his waggon train.

There was a difficulty in passing the river, the Whigs having burned or hidden all the boats, but the negroes from the neighbouring plantations helped in the search and the light troops were ferried over.

When the 17th and the Legion had passed, Tarleton was ordered away with them to Georgetown, a seaport on the estuary of a congeries of streams which find their way into the Atlantic there.

The country was populous and Tory in its feeling, so that he was soon back with the main column again, after a sweltering ride which must have lathered the horses, and added a few more stains to the 17th's dingy scarlet.

The heat was fearful, and it is doubtful whether the luxury of an unfastened stock would be permitted in those days. How the infantry got on, buttoned up in tight coats, white-breeched and black-gaitered, the Grenadier companies wearing bearskin caps, and the whole weighed down by packs and heavy muskets, can be better imagined than described.

They had plenty of beef, however, as a corps of mounted negroes was employed to drive in cattle, which were slaughtered as required by the regimental butchers.

When the column had reached Nelson's ferry, Cornwallis again sent Tarleton off on an independent command, with 40 of the 17th, 130 of the Legion Dragoons, and 100 mounted infantry of the same corps, carrying with them a 3-pounder gun.

Their object was to overtake Buford at all costs, Cornwallis despairing of coming up with him with the infantry.

On the 27th May accordingly, the 17th and their comrades were in the saddle and away in hot haste, killing their horses by sheer hard going, and pressing others into the service where they could; arriving at Camden next day, after a march of over sixty miles, only to find Buford still ahead.

The American leader had left Rugeley's Mills twenty

miles off, on the 26th, and when, after another night march, Tarleton reached that place, it was to learn that his flying foe had put yet another twenty miles between them. Men and horses were done up, but Tarleton, having come thus far, was determined to go farther. To gain time, he despatched Captain Kinloch, of the Legion, to Buford with a flag of truce, and proposals to surrender, assuring the American that a force of 700 men were close at hand, and Cornwallis coming up with nine battalions! Buford disbelieved the statement—in spite of Kinloch's assurance upon his honour that it was true—and held a council of officers, all of whom, with one exception, were in favour of rejecting the demand and continuing the retreat. He accordingly wrote in reply: "Sir, I reject your proposals, and shall defend myself to the last extremity."

All this time, Buford's men seem to have continued on the move, but Tarleton was soon upon them, and at three o'clock on the afternoon of the 29th May, his advance-guard slipped round the American infantry and carried off a Light Dragoon sergeant and four men.

Buford then prepared for combat at a place known as Wacsaw, in an open wood to the right of the road, forming up his infantry in one line with a small reserve, Sergeant Mitchell carrying the colours in the centre, and the baggage and cannon continuing their march.

His numbers are uncertain. Tarleton says they were nearly 400 Virginian infantry (11th regiment), a detachment of Washington's Horse, and two 6-pounders; but if Tarleton had Murat's genius for cavalry combat, he had also a most Napoleonic method of narrating his exploits. Still, from the return of killed and wounded, he is probably nearer the mark

"SERGEANT MITCHELL WAS CUT DOWN, AND HIS COLOUR-POLE SMASHED"
(*p.* 87).

than Colonel Bowyer, then adjutant to Buford, who puts their strength down at 200.

Tarleton formed up his troopers without delay, weary and wayworn though they were; sixty of the Legion Dragoons on his right wing, with nearly as many mounted infantry under Major Cochrane, with orders for the latter to dismount and gall the flank of the enemy before the charge. The 17th and part of the Legion, under Captains Corbet and Kinloch, were to take the centre of the enemy, and Tarleton himself, at the head of thirty picked Horse and some infantry, intended falling upon Buford's right and reserve; the 3-pounder and such of the troops as had not yet come up being ordered to form on a little hill in the rear as they arrived.

The two forces were 300 yards from each other, and for about a quarter of an hour the dismounted men advanced on our right, peppered the Virginians and killed most of their officers on that flank.

Suddenly the trumpets rang out the charge; the dusty, perspiring line of British cavalry undulated, and young Tarleton, in his bearskin crested helmet and round green jacket of the Legion, led them, sword in hand, at the wood.

When the cavalry were at fifty paces, the Continentals presented; a vicious row of long barrels flashed in the sunlight, but the American officers shouted to them to reserve their fire until the distance was lessened.

At ten paces the volley rang out, men and horses pitched forward in the dust and rolled in their death agony, but our fellows got well home and the enemy were quickly routed.

Sergeant Mitchell was cut down by some of the

17th and his colour-pole smashed, but, clinging to it, he was dragged along for nearly twenty yards.

The troopers then gathered round him, and he would have been slashed to pieces had not Captain Kinloch sprung to the ground and saved him.

Buford, seeing his left in confusion, and all the officers down, ordered his men to ground their arms; but Captain Adam Wallace, a better soldier than his leader, ordered them to sell their lives dearly, and made a most determined attempt to kill Tarleton.

He reached him and made several thrusts, but a sabre cut on the back of his neck nearly severed his head from his body, and he was found dead beside the corpse of one of our officers whom he had slain.

Tarleton declared that his bravery entitled him to immortal honour.

Buford at length sent Adjutant Bowyer with a handkerchief on the point of his sword to say that he was willing to accept the terms offered before the action began.

As he reached the British leader, a ball struck Tarleton's horse on the forehead, and down they went, the colonel underneath.

He was so exasperated, that he is said to have told his men to cut the American down; and Bowyer was certainly badly wounded by the Dragoons before a lucky volley frightened their horses, and he managed to get off.

But the report had spread that Tarleton was killed, and a ghastly massacre followed, the Dragoons losing all control over themselves, and sabring without mercy.

They killed 14 officers and 99 men, and wounded 8 officers and 142 rank and file—"unable to travel and

THE MASSACRE.

left on parole," says the despatch, which, however, omits the fact that these unfortunates had an average of *sixteen* wounds apiece, and were many of them stripped absolutely naked!

With a fury happily rare in our annals, our men also turned on the peasantry who had come to peep at the fighting, and spared no one!

It says something for the regard in which Banastre Tarleton was held by his followers; it would have said more for the man had he bidden the white-coated trumpeters of the 17th sound the "rally" on their bugle horns!

The regiment had Lieutenant Matthew Patteshall wounded, our other losses being 2 subalterns of the Legion, and 3 privates killed, 12 wounded, and 31 horses.

For the time being, South Carolina was cleared of the enemy's troops, and Tarleton rejoined Cornwallis at Camden a few days after this affair.

Clinton returned to New York, Cornwallis went down to Charleston, and Lord Rawdon was left in command at Camden with various outlying posts.

The detachment of the regiment was ordered back to New York also, but a few men were left behind, including some sick, and by the presence of these men the 17th's thread of participation in coming events remained unbroken.

CHAPTER VI.

AN EIGHTEENTH CENTURY "V.C."

Resumption of Hostilities in the South—Battle of Camden—Brave Stand of the Marylanders—Tremendous Pursuit—Marion—The Swamp Fox—"Liberty or Death"—Strict Discipline—A Stammering Commander—Fresh Detachment of the Regiment—Fiasco at Cowpens—Gallant Charge of the 17th—Guilford Court House—The 17th and the French Lancers—Dennis O'Lavery: a Forgotten Hero—Private McMullins—York Town and Gloucester—"The World turned upside down"—British Mismanagement—The Closing Scene—The Greased Flagstaff.

In consequence of the intense heat, operations were to be suspended until the latter end of August, and the bulk of the infantry was quartered about Camden in huts specially constructed to resist the sun.

A strong force of Americans, under Baron de Kalb, a gallant Prussian Protestant officer, who had served in the French army and then offered his sword to America, was assembled on the borders of North Carolina, ready for an attack on the British.

De Kalb, an experienced soldier, and an accomplished man speaking five or six languages, English among them, was unfortunately for the American cause superseded by Gates, the general whose defeat of Burgoyne at Saratoga had given him a reputation he was far from deserving.

He advanced against our numerous posts, and various skirmishes took place, until Cornwallis, knowing his position at Camden to be a bad one, resolved to march on Gates at Rugeley's Mills, and by a strange

THE BATTLE OF CAMDEN. 91

coincidence Gates started out to attack Cornwallis almost at the same moment and by the same road.

At ten the opposing armies started in search of each other, and at two in the morning their advance guards met in the woods and there was some firing, until, as if by mutual arrangement, they both fell back to wait for day.

De Kalb, wiser of the two, was for retiring to a good position at the Mills again, but Gates, rather elevated with peach brandy—so says tradition—insulted him, and stayed where he was.

Dawn came; Cornwallis reconnoitred and found he had the best of the ground, his flanks secured by swamps, and seeing Gates attempting to change the position of two Militia corps on his left, ordered Colonel Webster to charge with the 71st, 23rd, and 33rd regiments and four guns.

Out of the woods they poured, with rolling drums and booming cannon,—the "Fraser Highlanders," the Welsh Fusiliers, and the "Haver-cake Lads," bayonets glistening, and the red flash of Macleod's Artillery among their ranks.

Out, too, came the Volunteers of Ireland, Hamilton's corps and Bryan's, with the infantry of the British Legion; and behind, their time to come, the green cavalry, with a sprinkle of the scarlet 17th, waiting in reserve, with Tarleton at their head.

The grey moss hung in festoons from the trees; the dark green water oak loomed sombre among the light acacias; the squirrels fled, alarmed at the red tumult beneath them; and the American line broke, and fled also.

Virginian and North Carolina Militia flung down their arms and helter-skeltered away through the tree trunks!

In vain Brigadier-General Stevens led his brigade forward, crying, "My brave fellows, you have bayonets as well as they. We'll charge them!" They were not brave fellows, and they incontinently bolted.

Gates—and I quote from contemporary writers of his own side—galloped off to the rear to bring them back, but somehow he never returned himself, and the next one heard of him was that he had reached Charlotte, eighty miles away, killing three horses on the road!

On the American right, however, the Colonials stood to it boldly.

They were the 2nd Maryland Brigade under Brigadier-General Gift, with Smallwood's 1st Marylanders about 300 yards behind, the whole commanded by De Kalb.

De Kalb received eleven wounds, and in spite of the most particular assistance from the British surgeons, died a few days after the battle.

The final rout of the American right wing is said to have been due to our right, who, instead of pursuing the fugitives, wheeled against the Marylanders and broke them.

Then Tarleton was let loose, and there was another carnage.

For twenty-two miles the ruthless troopers harried the flying Yankees with fire and sword, and the aspect of the battle ground and the line of retreat is said to have been ghastly in the extreme. Between 800 and 900 of the enemy perished during the action and the pursuit, 1,000 being taken prisoners.

General Gift, with 100 men, managed to escape through a swamp, but seven cannon and the entire waggon train were captured, our loss being 69 killed, 245 wounded, and 11 missing.

Young Rawdon, afterwards Earl Moira and Marquis of Hastings—he was then only twenty-five—acquitted himself well. Webster was, as usual, beyond praise, and the entire British strength was a little over 2,000, only 1,500 of whom were regulars.

Tarleton pursued as far as Hanging Rock, but was soon afterwards down with fever.

Captain George Hanger then commanded the corps, and under his guidance the Legion deliberately funked it at Charlottestown, and, in spite of a spirited address by Cornwallis himself, would not charge until Webster's men had cleared the way for them. This was the afterwards well-known George Hanger, bosom friend of the Prince Regent, ex-Guardsman, coal merchant, eccentric, and writer on sport; a figure familiar to all students of that bacchanalian period through the medium of Gillray and Cruickshank.

It was about the period when Tarleton returned to duty that he came into close contact with one of the most remarkable leaders of irregulars that it was our fortune to meet—Colonel Francis Marion, of the 2nd South Carolina Regiment.

Marion was no ordinary man, and many well-authenticated traditions of his talents, kindliness, and high sense of honour are preserved. Tarleton nicknamed him the "Swamp Fox," and the sobriquet was deserved, for he led us a terrible dance; by bridle-paths that a horse could hardly follow, taking advantage of every natural obstacle, doubling back along his trail; here to-day, forty miles off before the sun rose again; forming ambush, and then disappearing, to the dismay of his baffled pursuers, who never knew in which quarter to expect him next. He was obliged to retire from active service for a time, and the cause was indicative of the man. Severely temperate in his habits, an attempt was made to inveigle him into one of those orgies so common to the period; glasses were filled, and the health of the defenders of Fort Moultrie proposed—Marion was one of them—but when he put his glass down after a mere sip there was an outcry. Their host, locking the door, said, "Gentlemen, by the laws of good fellowship no man leaves this room till all the liquor is drank!" and with that he flung the key into the street. Marion followed the key, and, the room being on the second storey, he broke his ankle!

The brigade of which he took command soon after his recovery consisted of six companies, of mounted infantry for the most part, and with a strong Irish element, but soon after the battle of Camden it was reduced to sixty men.

It was something of a coincidence that the leathern cap he wore (part of the 2nd Carolina equipment) was very similar in shape to that of the 17th, and bore the motto, "Liberty or Death," on a silver crescent in front.

Always in the thick of the fight, he only tried to draw his sword on one occasion, and then failed because it was rusted in the sheath!

Hearing that Tarleton and his men were to cross Nelson's Ferry one November day, on their way to Camden, Marion planted himself in the swamp, cut a rampart of bushes and waited for two days, only to learn that Tarleton had passed along the road before he laid the ambush!

Nothing daunted, he set off in pursuit, and a ten-mile ride brought him into the Richardson country, where the light of a huge fire put him on his guard

Word was sent him that Tarleton was there, with two field-pieces, and double his numbers, and at the same moment he heard that one of his own people had just deserted to the British.

Silently they left the road, and put six miles of trackless swamp between themselves and the enemy, only halting to sleep on the bank of Jack's Creek, which they abandoned for a securer post on the Black River at sunrise.

Meanwhile, Tarleton found his trail and made a circuit round the first morass, but drew up at Ox Swamp, where the wild vines spread like a net.

"Come, boys," said he, "let us go back, and we'll soon find the Game Cock (Sumpter), but as for this —— old Fox, the devil himself could not catch him."

This was the kind of work that formed the almost daily duty of the men of the 17th, early and late, in all weathers; often varied by the crack of muskets from an invisible foe, when some ford had to be fiercely fought for, or the bugle horn sounded "spurs home!"

Some of Marion's orders when with the 2nd Carolina Regiment throw a light on the American soldier of that day.

"Every officer to provide himself with a blue cloath Coatie, faced and cuffed with scarlet cloath, and lined with scarlet; white buttons, and white Waistcoat and Breeches."

"Any soldier who comes on the parade with Beards or hair uncomb'd, shall be dry shaved immediately and have his head dressed on the parade."

Again, four men "for absence from duty on the Day of Engagement received 200^d Lashes dress'd in Petticoats and Caps," and, on the occasion of a dinner given to the regiment by some ladies, the Colonel "hoped that the men would behave themselves with sobriety and decency in honour to those Ladies who had been so kind as to give them so genteel a treat."

Of Colonel Peter Horry, an active partisan officer under Marion, they tell a good story. Horry suffered from an impediment in his speech, which was apt to come upon him at a critical moment or when unduly excited. Once when in ambush against Tarleton the moment arrived for him to give the word "Fire," but his old enemy took possession of his tongue, and he could only get out the first half. "Fi-fi-fi!" gasped the unhappy Horry, and then, by a superhuman effort— "*Shoot!* d——n you; *shoot!*" he yelled. "You know very well what I would say!"

On October 1st, 1780, Major André, as gallant and accomplished an officer as any in the service, was hanged in full regimentals at Tappan, having been found guilty of being a spy.

Many wild statements have been made, and much nonsense written, about the injustice of this act, and Washington has been held up to obloquy by successive generations of British writers, but the hard, unyielding facts remain, viz., that André was taken within the American lines, in uniform, it is true, but that uniform concealed under a civilian great-coat; that his mission was to tamper with the loyalty of the infamous Benedict Arnold, and arrange for his escape to our side; and, while one could have wished that André had been shot instead of hanged, there is something to be said in favour of the American Generals' decision.

Fifteen good men and true signed the decree that sent him to the gallows, including such names as Nathaniel Greene, Lafayette, and Steuben, and if the law of reprisal has any justification, that justification is to be found in the treatment of Captain Hale by Sir William Howe during our occupation of Long Island.

Hale volunteered to discover our movements, was taken, and acknowledged his rank and motive.

Howe ordered the provost-marshal to execute him next morning, and circumstances of peculiar barbarity attended his last moments.

He wished to see a clergyman; the request was denied him. He asked for a Bible; one was not forthcoming!

Even the letters which, in the grey of his last earthly morning, he wrote to his *mother* and friends, were destroyed on the ground that "the rebels should not know that they had a man in their army who could die with such firmness."

After this, surely the fate of John André, sad as it was, might be allowed to sink into oblivion.

The remainder of the year 1780 was spent by Tarleton in chasing Sumpter and Morgan; and we learn from a letter of Cornwallis's, that the 17th must have been in want of many things, their accoutrements being spoken of as "coming up by the slow process of Gen. Leslie's corps."

Fifty Dragoons of the 17th are mentioned as having escorted a convoy of waggons from Brierley's into camp, and on the 6th January, 1781, another detachment arrived from New York, in time to participate in the campaign against General Morgan, who threatened Fort Ninety-Six.

Like Marion's, Morgan's men, sturdy trappers and farmers, wore the legend, "Liberty or Death," on the breasts of their white shirts, and their leader, a man of powerful frame and magnificent courage, is one of the popular heroes of the war.

On the 16th January, Tarleton was within six miles of Morgan's encampment, and next day the American made a stand near Cowpens, in a bad position, a river in his rear, and the country excellent for cavalry.

His Militia were so unreliable that he gave them orders to fire two shots apiece and then retire behind the rest.

Up came Tarleton in hot haste, and attacked before his troops were properly in position. our men yefling loudly.

There were about 1,000 men on each side, but the advantage in numbers, if any, was with the British leader. Morgan's first line, all Militia, was soon disposed of, but the Continentals in the second line stood firm. Tarleton led on the Light Infantry and that of the Legion, with the 7th Fusiliers, in line, fifty Light Horsemen at each flank, and seeing that we were making no impression, ordered his right squadron under Ogilvie to charge. They did so, and threw the Americans into some confusion, in the midst of which, Colonel John Eager Howard gave the command to his 1st Marylanders to change front. By mistake the company fell back, and the whole of the American second line retired on the cavalry. At the same moment Ogilvie was driven off by Washington's Dragoons, and Tarleton's reserve coming up (1st Battalion, 71st Foot), we advanced hurriedly, thinking the foe was in retreat. Howard instantly faced his Marylanders about, and they poured such a withering volley into the scarlet line, and charged so boldly with the bayonet, that our men, exhausted by long marching, and surprised at the resistance, were seized by a sudden panic and broke!

In vain Tarleton shouted to his cavalry reserve, in vain the horns blared out the charge—the green Legion would not face it, and in desperation Tarleton gathered a few men about him and charged himself.

This little band consisted of fourteen mounted officers and about forty men of the 17th, and right gallantly they spurred into the open wood that formed the American position.

A fine picture this: Tarleton in his green jacket with black velvet facings, the knot of officers in various dresses, for they were not all of the 17th, and the gallant troop of the regiment, dashing madly on the Marylanders in the thin wood, in a desperate attempt to retrieve the fortunes of the day.

Washington's cavalry—also in green, which caused more than one unfortunate *contretemps* during that war—spurred down upon them, Washington shouting, "Where is now the boasting Tarleton?"

But Tarleton's horsemen, urged onward we may surely suppose by the horns of the 17th, broke through them and recaptured the British baggage.

Cornet Patterson, of the 17th, hearing Washington's cry, rode straight for him, and maybe would have slain him had not the American's orderly trumpeter shot him dead!

Lieutenant Nettles, of the regiment, was also wounded, and no doubt some of the scarlet lads that rode behind him, but the heroic dash was useless; Tarleton's ill-advised haste in the beginning lost us the day, and the 17th were the only troops practically remaining with the Lancashire Lad when he drew rein out of the press.

His narrative seems to have been grossly unfair—at any rate, it drew forth some sledge-hammer strictures from McKenzie of the 71st Regiment, and it would almost prove that in pitched battle Tarleton was not the man to sustain his reputation as a daring irregular leader.

At the close of the fight Colonel Howard held the swords of seven British officers in his hand. He afterwards married Miss Margaret Chew, in whose honour poor André had broken a lance at the *Mischianza* fête, and their youngest son married the daughter of the author of the "Star-Spangled Banner."

Morgan wisely continued his retreat, but Cornwallis was hard put to it during the pursuit by the loss of his best Light Infantry.

At McCowan's Ford on the Catawba River he fought a brilliant action, where the Foot Guards upheld their ancient name and fame, and Tarleton's mixed Horse, Legion and 17th, made a fine swoop on the foe, but the two divisions of the American army joined forces at Guildford Court House.

A blow to our cause was dealt soon after this by a detachment of Loyalists, 300 strong, under Colonel Pyle, mistaking Lee's Legion for Tarleton's, and when surrounded, being sabred to a man!

I cannot find any statement of the services of the 17th at Guildford Court House, though the chances are strongly in favour of their being represented with the Legion, but a little later they are definitely named in a skirmish which has some interest, as being the first occasion that the regiment came in contact with the lance!

A force of French had landed in America, and among them was the Duc de Lauzan, with a mixed regiment of Lancers and Hussars.

They were gay fellows enough as regards their dress, being clad in blue jackets, black braid, and breeches of yellow ochre, and their leader was that unprincipled rascal whose vanity afterwards caused his name to be coupled with that of Marie Antoinette in a certain matter of an aigrette, which caused Lauzan, afterwards guillotined as the Duc de Biron, to be dismissed from Court.

On the 3rd October, 1781, the Legion, the 17th, and some of Simcoe's Dragoons reconnoitred the Hussars in front of Gloucester, and a lance penetrating a horse of the Legion, the animal plunged, and upset Tarleton's charger.

The rest came up helter-skelter, Legion and 17th, and if we are to believe the French story they were overthrown. At any rate, Tarleton from his own showing was unable to make an impression, and, obtaining another horse, ordered a retreat.

Lauzan's corps on its return to France became the 6th Hussars of the Monarchy; by the desertion of the regiment of Saxe, in revolutionary times they took the number five, and fought under that numeral through the Napoleonic wars; but, reverting to the original number at the Restoration, it is possible to trace in the present *Sixième* the lineal representatives of those troopers who gave the 17th their first rough lesson in the lance exercise.

And now we come to a story so heroic that it is strange to find it so little known.

Cornwallis, unable to help Rawdon (afterwards the Marquis of Hastings, of Indian fame), sent messengers to warn him that he must not rely on his support.

All the messengers were cut off, but one—Corporal Dennis O'Lavery, of the 17th Light Dragoons—got his despatch through in a manner that would have earned for him the Victoria Cross had he lived in our day.

Chosen for his known courage and experience, he accompanied the despatch-rider, and before they had gone far they were attacked and dangerously wounded.

The messenger died on the road, but O'Lavery took the despatch, all bleeding as he was, and continued to gallop on, growing weaker and weaker as he went, until at last he reeled in his saddle and fell.

The country was full of the enemy's troops, the paper he carried was of great importance, and crawling—heaven only knows how far—he crept into a deserted house to sink exhausted, with one hand on his sabre hilt.

They soon found him, ransacked his clothes in vain for the document, and then left him to his fate.

All through that night he lay in agony and alone, expecting every moment to be tracked to his hiding-place and further maltreated, seeing the light fade slowly out of the west, and telling off the long, dark hours only by the ever weakening throb of his own gallant heart.

At last dawn came, and with it some women belonging to our army.

He was too far gone to speak then, but he had just strength enough left to point to the gash in his groin that had drained his life blood, and with that gesture Dennis O'Lavery went to meet his God.

And then they saw that something more than a dead corporal of Light Dragoons lay on the floor at their feet, in his frayed and faded scarlet, with the silver rank-mark on his tattered cuff—for in his anxiety to save his despatch he had rammed it deep into the wound, lacerating the quivering flesh and rendering his hurt mortal!

Such was the verdict of the surgeons, and Rawdon

is said to have erected a monument in the hero's native county, Down—but, according to Lindsay, in a Dublin church.

In "The King's Own Borderers" James Grant utilises the story, none too accurately; Lindsay, of the 46th, embalms it in his volume; and Fortescue copies it from Cannon; but outside the works of these writers O'Lavery is unknown—I cannot even trace the monument. Yet here was a man of whom the nation should be proud; and if Great Britain ever rears a column of fame, the name of Dennis O'Lavery, of the 17th, should be carved in good bold characters upon its face.

Another gallant fellow of the regiment, Private McMullins, performed a brilliant feat of arms when carrying a despatch to the commander-in-chief.

Four Militia men set upon him, and in so doing caught a tartar; for one he shot, another he sabred, and the two last he brought in prisoners to headquarters.

If, as it is stated, the bulk of the 17th remained with Lord Rawdon, while the detachment only accompanied Tarleton, then the regiment must have shared in the victory at Hobkirk Hill and the defence of Fort Ninety-Six; but the operations in the South at that period are very difficult to follow, and nothing can be stated with absolute certainty.

After many ups and downs Cornwallis at last retired on York Town, through the orders of Clinton, and there he fortified himself.

In the letter in which Clinton suggests a defensive policy (11th July, 1781), he asks for the return of certain regiments to New York, among them being "remains of the detachment of 17th Light Dragoons."

Whether the demand was entirely complied with is uncertain, but some of the detachment remained, as twenty-five are mentioned at the capitulation of York Town.

They were under Tarleton at Gloucester, across the river, and there were many sharp skirmishes with the French and American troops before Washington finally invested the place.

The combined effect of the French fleet and forces, the masterly dispositions of Washington, and the wretched, war-worn condition of our men, produced the inevitable result, unconditional surrender.

The trenches were opened on the night of the 6th October; red-hot shot, sallies, and vigorous attack and defence made up the story, which approached its termination on the 17th, when Cornwallis beat a parley.

Washington, with that Roman sternness which characterised him, gave us two hours only in which to digest his terms, and the Marquis was in no position to decline them.

When Colonel Laurens, of the American army, met Colonel Ross, Lord Cornwallis's aide-de-camp, to discuss terms, a curious point was raised by the British officer, who exclaimed—

"'*This is a harsh article.*'—'Which article?' said Colonel Laurens—

"'The Troops shall march out with colours cased, and drums beating a British or a German march.'"

"'Yes, sir,' replied Colonel L., with some *sang froid*, 'it is a harsh article.'

"'Then, Col. Laurens, if that is your opinion, why is it here?'

"'Your question, Col. Ross, compels an observation which I would have suppressed. You seem to forget, sir, that I was a capitulant at Charleston—where Gen. Lincoln, after a brave defence of six weeks' open trenches, by a very inconsiderable garrison, against the British army and fleet, under Sir Henry Clinton and Admiral Arbuthnot, and when your lines of approach were within pistol-shot of our field-works, was refused any other terms for his gallant garrison than marching out with colours cased, and drums *not* beating a British or a German march.'—'But,' rejoined Col. Ross, 'my Lord Cornwallis did not command at Charleston.'—'There, sir,' said Col. Laurens, 'you extort another declaration. It is not the individual that is here considered—it is the Nation. This remains an article or I cease to be a Commissioner.'"

In the end, on the 19th October, 1781, the garrisons of York Town and Gloucester marched out with the honours of war, their colours cased, "the swords of the cavalry naked," and trumpets and drums playing the appropriate air, "The world turned upside down!"

The 17th certainly had bad luck during the early years of their existence, and, represented by the remnant of the detachment at the capitulation of York Town, the regiment also shared in the closing scene of all, the surrender and evacuation of New York.

Whether we ought to have given up the struggle is not for us to decide here. National pride whispers "No!" Strict justice tells us that the struggle was criminal, and should never have been provoked by us.

One thing is certain, we were out-generalled.

The whole war is a living commentary on the folly of favouritism and influence, and it is irritating to see how each British commander in succession entangled the skein still further, and then retired when he had had enough of it—a series of Pontius Pilates, in red coats and hair powder, washing their hands of a matter they were incompetent to set right.

The official intimation that there would be peace came to America in the March of 1783, Captain Stapleton, of the 17th, handing it to Washington on the 16th of the following month, and on the 19th General Washington proclaimed to his army the final cessation of hostilities.

We held, at that time, two places on the coast—the mouth of the Penobscot River and New York, which latter had been in our hands, and had constituted the base of our operations, since 15th September, 1776.

Our garrison in New York, according to the documents in the Record Office, consisted of Artillery, the 17th Light Dragoons, the Light Infantry and Grenadiers, the 7th, 22nd, 23rd, 38th, 40th, 43rd, 76th, and 80th regiments—a total strength of 3,795—and of Germans, the Chasseurs, a few Artillery, and the regiments of Lengercke, Donop, and Losberg Junior—3,762 strong.

Great difficulty was experienced by Sir Guy Carleton in finding transport for the numbers of Tory loyalists who, dreading reprisals when their countrymen should come in, insisted on embarking with the army; and it was November before the British leader could name a date for his departure.

Meanwhile, Washington disbanded his forces, reserving only a handful with which to take possession of the place.

The 22nd was at length agreed upon, but heavy rains began on that day, and there was a further postponement until the 25th. On the morning of that day, however, the blue-coated American Light Infantry, and the 2nd Massachusetts regiment, two companies of New York Artillery, and a troop of mounted militia, drew up in readiness, parading at eight o'clock on a sharp November morning, and marching down the old post road into the Bowery. At one o'clock, an officer informed them that the last British guard had been withdrawn, and they filed in along streets gaily decked with garlands, greeted by the cheers of the multitude.

Out on the broad river the stately fleet lay about Governor's Island, and the last boatloads of British soldiery were being pulled slowly from the shore.

The flagstaff on Fort George was watched with keen interest by our fellows as it grew smaller and smaller, for some wag had removed the halyards and greased the pole from top to bottom! Three times did a sailor lad try to swarm it, and as often did he come down with a run, until, filling his pockets with cleats, he nailed them one by one to the mast, and in the end the American flag floated out and the boom of thirteen guns thundered the Republican salute.

Apropos of the shifts to which the troops were put; when the flag was first adopted by Congress, the garrison at Fort Stanwix, or Schuyler, made theirs from alternate stripes of a soldier's white shirt and a campwoman's red petticoat, the field being cut out of an old blue overcoat. Later on, in a recent campaign, we shall tell how the 17th patched their tunics with brown paper!

CHAPTER VII.

THE BLUE DRAGOONS—IN PEACE AND WAR.

Return of the Regiment from America—New Colonels—Prices of Commissions Regulated—The New Dress of the Light Dragoons, 1784—Later Alterations—British Disregard for Old Uniform—The 17th take an Active Part in Irish Troubles—Soldiering in Ireland—Clouds in the West Indies—Detachment ordered there—A Light Dragoon's Letter—Mutiny of British Regiments in Ireland—Jamaica—Dragoons *v.* Maroons—Sad Death of Colonel Fitch—Smart Action by 17th—Campaigning in the "Cockpits"—Bloodhounds Imported from Cuba—Major-General Walpole inspects them under Difficulties—Sergeant Stephenson—Gallantry of Mr. Werge of the 17th—The General's High Opinion of the Regiment.

DURING the November of 1783, the regiment left America and returned once more to Ireland, where they were stationed for the next eleven years.

In April, 1782, Lieut.-General Preston had gone back to his old corps, the Scots Greys, and was succeeded by General the Hon. Thomas Gage, who came to the 17th from the 22nd Foot. His stay was short, for in February, 1785, he was transferred to the 11th Dragoons, and Thomas, Earl of Lincoln, got the colonelcy, from half-pay, 75th Regiment, disbanded in 1783. Early in 1794 he became Duke of Newcastle, and died the following year.

In 1783, the prices of commissions had been regulated, and stood, in the Dragoons, for a lieut.-colonelcy, £5,350; a captaincy, £3,150; a lieutenancy,

£1,365; and a cornetcy, £1,102 10s.; but the figure varied considerably in different regiments, notwithstanding the regulation.

On its arrival the regiment was fixed at a peace strength of 204 non-commissioned officers and men, and was stationed in King's and Queen's Counties.

Nothing of any note seems to have occurred during the next few years, except one very drastic alteration in the outward appearance of the 17th, which happened three months after its arrival in the Emerald Isle.

In April, 1784, the British Light Dragoon uniform underwent a complete change. The coats were no longer to be scarlet, but a dark blue, laced with white, and short in the skirts, which were turned back with the colour of the facings, white for the 17th, as were also their collars and cuffs. The lacing on the front of the jacket was not in parallel bars as the Horse Artillery jacket of to-day—that was adopted later—but arranged in a curious geometrical pattern in the place occupied by the old lapels, looking at a little distance like four white squares on each side of the jacket, each square divided by two cords passing from angle to angle, and crossing in the centre. The officers' lace was silver, as were their epaulettes, the men wearing wings of the same cloth as the jackets.

The swords were carried from a belt over the right shoulder, the belt having a ring under the left arm from which the weapon dangled, and a new helmet was adopted, perhaps the handsomest ever seen in our service. In shape it was practically a "bowler hat," made of leather, a black bearskin crest crossing it from front to back, a turban encircling it, and a scarlet and white plume standing in a socket on the left side. On the right side was displayed the badge in metal, and behind were two little tassels, still having for their object the protection of the neck in bad weather. Breeches and knee boots with black tops formed the clothing of the nether limbs, as before, and this new uniform continued in use for nearly twenty years.

There is hanging in that desolate shrine of long departed glory, the Brighton Pavilion, an interesting coloured print of George, Prince of Wales, in the dress of the 10th Light Dragoons, which shows the braiding of jacket and collar with great minuteness.

Somewhere about 1800, the skirts were done away with, a jacket very similar to the modern Horse Artillery being given to the Light Dragoons, with Hussar boots only coming to mid-calf, and I am inclined to think that they then reached their most picturesque period of uniform, subsequent changes evincing an almost total lack of taste, to say nothing of utility, on the part of our military reformers.

It must have cost some of Gage's "Lights" a pang to put away for ever the red rags in which they had seen such rough work, and it is very doubtful if a shred of one of them remains in existence to this day.

It is unfortunate that so little regard is paid to the changes of uniform in our country.

There should be a national museum of military costume, where the artist and the antiquary might find, not merely the unsatisfactory coloured plate, showing one side of an officer or private, but the actual uniforms themselves.

Hidden away in various parts of Great Britain, there are mouldering at the present moment, jackets, caps, helmets, and portions of equipment, which if gathered together would form a most interesting collection.

In 1793, the 17th were called upon to uphold the civil power in the North of Ireland. The spirit of the French Republic permeated the Irish people, and their newspapers for the previous ten years are full of a great volunteer movement, which, when the Revolution finally broke out, threw off all restraint and became openly disloyal.

At Belfast, in particular, things were fast coming to such a pass that a strong body of troops was drafted thither, among them four troops of the 17th.

The regiment arrived in Belfast on the 7th or 8th March, and on the 9th (Sunday), an historic *fracas* took place.

"On the evening of the 9th March a corporal and a private of the 17th, off duty, strolled out of the barracks into the city, where they met a crowd of people round a fiddler who was playing *Ça ira*. They told the fiddler to play 'God Save the King.' The mob damned the King with all his dirty slaves, and threw a shower of stones at them. The two dragoons, joined by a dozen of their comrades, drew their sabres and 'drove the town before them.' Patriot Belfast had decorated its shops with signboards representing Republican notables. The soldiers demolished Dumouriez, demolished Mirabeau, demolished the venerable Franklin. The patriots so brave in debate, so eloquent in banquet, ran before half a dozen Englishmen. A hundred and fifty volunteers came out, but retreated into the Exchange and barricaded themselves. The officers of the 17th came up before anyone had been seriously hurt, and recalled the men to their quarters. In the morning General Whyte came in from Carrickfergus, went to the volunteer committee-room, and said that unless the gentlemen in the Exchange came out and instantly dispersed he would order the regiment under arms. They obeyed without a word. The dragoons received a reprimand, but not too severe, as the General felt that they had done more good than harm."

Such is Froude's account, but portions of a contemporary letter, dated 9th March, from Belfast, may be quoted as giving another light on the subject.

It will be noticed that it states the occurrence as having taken place on the Saturday night.

"From what I can collect, a number of the Light Dragoons who arrived yesterday, getting intoxicated after their march, began about seven o'clock in the evening by attacking a sign of General Dumouriez, which a publican in North Street had put up immediately after the battle of Jemmapes, but to be continued now certainly very offensive; after pulling that down and destroying it, they sallied to Mr. McCabe's and demolished all his windows, on their route striking with their broadswords several who came in their way. From McCabe's they went to Forest Lane, and there destroyed the sign of the late Dr. Franklin, broke the windows and otherwise abused that public house, one Watson's. On returning through the main street they observed a few caps of our Volunteer light troop, with cockades in them, in the window of a milliner (Miss W——?), whose windows they broke, etc., etc."

That these roystering blades were in a certain kind of bacchanalian earnest is shown by the following:—

"A stroke made at Mr. Samuel Robinson miraculously had no other effect than cutting through the back of his coat, two waistcoats, his shirt, and only scratching his back."

Verily, Mr. Samuel Robinson was a fortunate individual.

After a while the magistrates lodged four of the principal ringleaders in barracks, and calm reigned.

They were released next day by their officers, to the dismay of the inhabitants, who formed a committee; but General Whyte promised to repress all rioting in future, took away the Dragoons' sabres, and ordered all the troops to be in their billets an hour earlier than usual.

He also promised to remove the obnoxious four troops of the 17th as soon as possible!

The exact truth will probably be found somewhere between the two accounts.

Cannon says the regiment was employed for many months in Dublin, Louth, and Meath, in suppressing the Defenders, a Catholic organisation which caused great trouble by its continual conflicts with the Protestant Peep o' Day Boys.

These worthy folk fought several pitched battles with a very respectable list of killed and wounded, and service in Ireland at that time was active service in every sense of the word.

Astonishing things were done by both civilians and soldiery, many of the latter being deliberately hamstrung in the streets or on some lonely sentry-go; and such mutilation carrying a pension of £20 with it, men sometimes cut themselves, as in later years they put lime in their eyes or blew off a thumb to procure their discharge.

In 1784, one soldier houghed himself so clumsily that it was detected; 800 lashes were ordered as a salve to the wound, and after the first 500 he was taken down—not expected to live!

Meanwhile, war clouds were rolling up in the West Indies, and the situation there was becoming serious.

A few days after war had been declared by France in 1793, we began an attack on the French possessions there, and took Tobago on the 17th April. Our next attempt was upon Martinique, where we expected support from the Royalist party, but the help failed; our force was ridiculously inadequate to the task, and reinforcements were applied for. The worst principles of the Republic had been accepted with avidity by the colonists, and some terrible scenes were enacted during the struggle. Martinique eventually taken, we next captured St. Lucia in something under fifty-eight hours, after which Guadaloupe surrendered almost without resistance, and the French West Indian possessions were ours!

But like the Russian generals, January and February, those lovely islands also possessed a natural defence against invaders which was not long in showing itself.

Yellow fever gripped our troops, and while they were dying like sheep a Republican fleet suddenly made its appearance, and, in the twinkle of an eye, landed, and firmly established a strong force.

The newcomers brought the guillotine with them, and under a *ci-devant* hairdresser's apprentice named Victor Hugues, who by some marvellous process of Republican evolution had become a naval officer, the negroes were roused, and the red blood flowed just as it was flowing in France, with the barbarities, if anything, accentuated.

Weak and ever diminishing in numbers, we made a brave struggle to retake Guadaloupe, but eventually abandoned it, and once in possession, Victor Hugues began to stir up rebellion among the neighbouring islands.

The blacks also began to give trouble in San Domingo, and many of the white planters escaping to Jamaica spread reports there that the natives would welcome British rule.

Accordingly we made an attempt, but met only with opposition, and after the British garrison had been weakened in Jamaica, and the rainy season brought the yellow fever among us in San Domingo, we again looked for reinforcements from home.

With less than 1,000 men in the first instance, we had flown in the face of a regular French garrison over 6,000 strong, double that number of Militia, and 25,000 negroes, and, though driblets arrived from time to time to our help, we could make no headway against the climate and the odds.

These reverses alarmed the Government, who were also engaged in a serious war in Flanders.

It was agreed that four dismounted regiments of cavalry should sail for San Domingo in August, 1795, but that eight troops from the 13th, 17th, and 18th Light Dragoons should go at once to Jamaica, to be at the disposal of our commander in San Domingo if he should require them.

The exact movements of these detachments are difficult to follow.

As early as the 5th May, 1794, some of the 13th had left for England, " whence they will proceed with the other cavalry lately shipped off for the Continent" —which they did not do.

Again, August 11th, 1795, "letters are received in town which mention that two troops each of the 17th and 18th regiments of Dragoons, were captured by the French on their way to the West Indies."

The date of embarkation was probably about May, or even earlier, 1795; but whether the troops had remained in England, in one of those Channel camps, since the previous spring, it is impossible to say.

Unfortunately, Cannon is most slovenly in his dates; for example, he says the 13th Light's detachment sailed in September, 1795, but we know from a letter of Lieutenant Gubbins, of that regiment, that they had reached Martinique by the 5th July—and yet Cannon's is the *official* record of the British army.

Gubbins' letter alludes to the 17th:—

"We" (that is the 13th), he writes, "came to anchor in this bay last night after a sail of twenty-four hours from Barbadoes, which island we made in thirty-seven days from England.

"We fell in with a very heavy gale of wind three days after we left England, which entirely separated the fleet.

". . . The 17th Dragoons have been most unfortunate. A ship named the *Mount Pleasant*, having on board 80 men and 4 officers of their detachment, foundered at sea, and it is supposed every one perished.

"Another ship, named the *Blenheim*, had also of the 17th Dragoons 40 men and 1 officer; she was taken by a French frigate about thirty leagues to the eastward of Barbadoes."

The loquacious lieutenant says that the *Betsy* transport, with some of the 18th, was taken at the same time, and he gives a list of officers' names of the 17th taken or lost, viz.: Captain Black, Lieutenants Werge and Johnston, Cornet Wilson, and the surgeon's mate, went down; Cornet Gorston (Garstin) taken—which list is interesting as showing the officers who accompanied the first detachment; but the report was contradicted next day, and the *Mount Pleasant* stated to have weathered the storm and reached a Portuguese port in safety.

Mr. Gubbins was rightly informed as to Cornet Garstin, as that officer was captured in June, and was still a prisoner at Point à Pitre, Guadaloupe, in October.

While the detachments were away across the billow, the regiment was suddenly summoned from Bandon to Cork, where the 105th and 113th regiments of Foot were in a dangerous state of mutiny.

They objected to be broken up and drafted into other corps, accused their officers of having sold them, elected a drunken corporal for their colonel, posted a guard at his door, and remained under arms all night.

But in the morning the 17th trotted in, followed by the 32nd, some Militia, and three vicious field pieces.

The mutinied battalions formed square against cavalry, and for a time things looked very serious; but the misguided men, feeling the futility of arguing with guns and sabres, argued it out with the general instead, who ultimately brought them to reason, and the ringleaders to the triangles!

To return to the detachments. By some mistake they touched at Jamaica, only to find that their services were required at San Domingo, and the tempest-tossed men were accordingly sent off again almost as soon as the anchors had been lowered.

The green hills had hardly receded from their eyes as they sailed against the trade winds, when a swift boat manned with oars overtook them—the Maroons in Jamaica had revolted, and they must go back!

Jamaica is a name which recalls memories of some of the most stirring episodes in our naval history.

Discovered by Columbus in 1494, during his second voyage, it became a Spanish possession.

Its shores have often re-echoed the clumsy cannon of our bold sea-rovers, in the days of Drake and Hawkins, and later when Sir Henry Morgan ranged the seas; when the Spanish main was something more than an empty sound, and galleons and pieces-of-eight were a very golden reality for those who could come across them.

Those gallant admirals of the Commonwealth, Penn

and Venables, took it from the Dons in 1655; and in 1658, when the Spaniards were finally driven out of the island, their slaves took refuge in the mountains, where they were a thorn in the side of our colonists for years.

Joined from time to time by runaway negroes, they formed two distinct communities, and their history is one of raids upon the settlers, rapine, and general lawlessness, until, about the middle of last century, when they had been united into a species of nation by a former slave named Cudjoe, they were christened Maroons, or hog-hunters, by the colonists.

Cudjoe, who seems to have been an individual of administrative and military ability, introduced a regular system of tactics, which the nature of the country rendered easy.

In the famous Blue Mountains, a magnificent chain averaging from 7,000 to 8,000 feet in height, and which traverses Jamaica from east to west, there exist natural valleys or glens, termed "cockpits," entered by narrow defiles and surrounded by precipitous limestone cliffs.

In these "cockpits" the Maroons took up their abode, establishing a system of signals by means of horns, and able to defend the narrow entrances by ambushments which commanded the narrow tracks. There they lived, quietly enough while supplies lasted, and then raiding the settlements for a fresh supply, carrying off cattle, corn, and women, like the moss-troopers of old. Eventually they took up their position in the Trelawney district, where there was good water, and a fine line of retreat in case of necessity; but so strong did they become that a treaty was entered into between their chiefs and George II. in 1738.

By this treaty they acquired absolute freedom and several privileges, undertaking to hand over runaway slaves, to help the king in war time, and to allow a couple of white residents to reside within their lines.

They remained quiet until the early nineties, when a certain Major James, who had made himself greatly respected, was deprived of his post on coming into an estate.

Eminently an athletic, hunting people, James had won their hearts by physical superiority in all their games and exercises, and the new man did not please them.

They began to kick over the traces, and eventually "ran amok" altogether.

They drove Captain Craskell, the new resident, out of the Maroon Town in July, 1795, and as there seemed no chance of their old favourite being reappointed, threw down the gauntlet of defiance on the 17th of that month, telling the whites that they were ready for them, and that if the whites did not come they would come down to them!

In April the Earl of Balcarres, colonel of the 63rd Foot, and who had been wounded at Ticonderoga, was made Governor of Jamaica, and he took strong measures to suppress what promised to be a very dangerous rebellion when one considers the spread of anarchy and Republicanism rife among the neighbouring islands.

He it was who recalled the 17th with other detachments *en route* for San Domingo, and meanwhile he had been gathering information as to the mountain passes with all the energy of an old soldier.

At the end of July there seemed prospects of a

settlement, but on the 12th August some black Militia were attacked, and the train was fired!

Balcarres' plan was this: The Maroon stronghold was to be surrounded and attacked from various points, and the 17th left Spanish Town under Mr. Bacon, who probably did not know that he had been gazetted captain-lieutenant on the 4th July.

That now obsolete rank indicated the command of the colonel's troop, and carried no particular emolument with it.

A hundred of the 62nd, under Colonel Hull, went with them, as also some Militia, and their destination was the north side of the Maroon Town.

For several days they were busy burning provisions, and then as the rains were in full force the 17th and 20th Light Dragoons went into huts.

While there a small field force was brought up with great difficulty by the gallant young colonel of the 83rd, a track having to be cut on the hillsides, the bugles of the 17th sounding to direct the workers, who were obliged to stop in the teeth of a tropical storm.

Next day the gun was got up, and placed in position, and the Dragoons found a good deal of loot hidden away among the bushes, some of them getting gaily flowered chintz nightgowns with linen and valuable plate.

Colonel Sandford had been sent previously to take possession of the New Town, and by some misinterpretation of orders, coupled with a bad map, he had pushed on to the Old Town, and fallen into an ambush.

Sandford was killed, and with him Quartermaster McBride and 6 privates of the then newly-raised

20th Jamaica Light Dragoons, 8 of the 18th Lights, and 13 Horse Militia, Colonel Gallimore's body never being discovered.

It is said that on their entry into the New Town one of the Dragoons found a copy of Wake's Catechism in a burning hut, and this he put inside his jacket just over his heart.

In the defile where they were fired upon a bullet struck the book, penetrated nearly 200 pages, and stopped three leaves from the end.

This success was not followed up by the Maroons, who, when our troops retired, came back into the Old Town and got drunk on rum.

When we finally advanced and occupied the Old Town we buried the bodies of Colonel Sandford and eighteen others, and found that the Maroons had abandoned all intention of defending the towns, and had retired into the "cockpits."

Balcarres went down to the coast early in September to make further arrangements, leaving Colonel Fitch, of the 83rd, to carry out a plan of hemming in the enemy by a cordon of troops and barricades drawn round the cockpit, and so arduous was the duty that Captain Oldham, of the 62nd, died of fatigue.

Some parleys came to nothing, and our parties were constantly falling into ambushes, in one of which Mr. Tomlinson, of the Light Infantry, was decapitated and his head hung on a tree: it was said at the time that the poor fellow had lost his spectacles and missed the way.

But a worse calamity befel us soon after, for Colonel Fitch, reconnoitring in front of an advanced post, in a striped linen jacket, with two British and two friendly Maroon officers, was mortally hit in the pit of the stomach.

His death was dramatic.

Colonel Jackson, of the Militia, the only one of the party unhurt, ran back and found Fitch on a fallen tree in great agony. Drawing a dagger, Jackson assured him that he should not fall alive into the clutches of the merciless foe—a friendly act that is far oftener performed for a brother officer than the British public is aware of—and as the Maroons cocked their pieces for another volley Jackson tried to pull him down out of danger. Fitch resisted—he could not speak—and a ball struck him above the right eye, killing him instantly. When his body was found his head was inserted in his own bowels.

He was one of the most popular colonels in the service, and deeply mourned by the 83rd (now 1st Batt. Royal Irish Rifles), which he had raised in Dublin in 1793.

On the 22nd September the House of Assembly met, when 300 dollars was offered to any person for taking or killing a Trelawney Maroon, and half that sum for the death or capture of any slave joining them.

A new commander-in-chief was appointed—Lieut.-Colonel Hon. George Walpole, of the 13th Light Dragoons, with the rank of major-general—and with his advent a better system of warfare was adopted.

He abandoned the cordon as being impracticable, and after establishing a chain of posts to cover the settlements, set the negroes to clear all cover that could harbour an ambush, and make tracks up the sides of a hill which almost commanded the interior of the cockpit itself.

The 17th now came in for a strong share of the

fighting, and their numbers were also increased, as, a few days after Sandford's mishap, the second troop was landed on the island.

They were also well mounted about this time, for it had not been the intention of Government that they should act on foot, commissaries having undertaken to horse the detachments in the West Indies at a cheaper rate. The nature of the fighting, however, kept them out of the saddle during their stay in Jamaica.

Walpole made special selection of the regiment for his bush fighting — possibly because the shabby blue jackets and dingy doe-skins were better adapted than the heavy infantry uniform for scaling precipices unobserved; or, was it because they were unusually smart?

At any rate, when the bush was sufficiently cleared, Walpole sent about 70 of the 17th, dismounted, under Lieutenant Richards, to climb the hill to the right of Guthrie's Defile, which was the entrance to the cockpit, to feel whether a descent was practicable into the basin.

After a mile march they began to mount the height, a small support of 10 men and a sergeant being sent to the left of the entrance to act as a feint if observed, or a reserve if necessary.

Up they swarmed, among the lignum-vitæ and wild cotton tree, towards the thick pimento clothing the summit, where there would be cover in plenty; but the precipitous cliffs checked them, and the Maroons opened fire.

Then crouching behind rocks and bushes they replied with their short carbines, each Dragoon marking down his man by the puff of white smoke on the opposite hillside, and then letting drive in his turn.

Neither side did much damage, it is true, but the skirmish acted as a moral check on the enemy, who saw that they were going to be fought in their own manner.

Mr. Richards, ammunition running short, sent a man down to the sergeant below, but as the little band crossed the track leading into the gorge a horn sounded loudly. Uncertain whether his officer had effected an entrance, or perhaps thinking to make a short cut, they doubled into the gully!

The other party were almost at their last cartridge; a loud shout was rolled out on the morning and then they waited!

A pause, and then a crash of muskets made stern reply. The sergeant and his Dragoons were killed to a man!

Some of the men on the hill, as their pouches became empty and their presence useless, crept down and ran towards their quarters, and were met by the general as the death-volley rang out.

"'Please, your honour,' said one of them, 'we have not a cartridge left.'—'Then what is that firing I hear?' replied the general.—'Why, your honour,' cried the soldier, 'the boys firing their last rounds, and the divil a one you will get away while he has a cartridge left.'"

Walpole was reinforced by the 13th Light Dragoons and some other regiments, but he contented himself with watching, and waiting for the rains to cease.

When they were spent, up went a howitzer to the top of the hill, and a nice time they must have had during the process—with

"A wheel on the horns o' the mornin', an' a wheel on the edge o' the pit,
An' a drop into nothin' beneath you—"

you know how the verse goes, and the gun must have gone in very much the same fashion.

Common shell in the open is a thing to be shunned, but, when plumped down from the sky into a seven-acre hollow, with mountains all round you, with the knowledge that the quickest way out is bristling with bayonets, and all the other exits are worse than going up any lighthouse ever built—it is a marvellous persuader, and the Maroons were not long in taking the hint!

They sent their women into a distant valley and moved into the next cockpit, which they barricaded strongly with old plantain trees; but next morning, when the sunrise was tingeing the mists with gold, the roar of the howitzer far up on the peak told them it was going to begin again!

They quickly abandoned their new position, and took refuge on a hill—inaccessible, to all appearances—and, growing used to the shells which now burst below them without damage, they seemed in a fair way to hold their ground.

But Lieutenant Oswald Werge, of the 17th, saw one of their women climbing the hillside with water, and creeping after her discovered a path.

Then the Dragoons stole up with sword and carbine, and the Maroons bolted down a very steep precipice to Ginger Town Bottom, from whence they sallied against us several times, only to be repulsed.

The 17th were hutted on the hill, with the 62nd in their rear, and though our movements had been successful in one way, the enemy had retired into a range of hills with an apparently never ending succession of "cockpits" among them, which might be alternately defended and abandoned until the war should become an interminable farce.

A chance conversation with a Spaniard suggested a method which, however repugnant to British tastes, certainly brought matters to a speedy conclusion and prevented the loss of many a valuable life—the employment of bloodhounds from a neighbouring Spanish possession.

After a long debate in the House of Assembly, and much opposition of that humane order which so soon degenerates into sickly sentimentality, it was agreed that trained Spanish chasseurs and dogs should be borrowed from Cuba, which was accordingly done.

The moral effect was precisely what the proposers of the scheme had hoped.

On the way up from the coast two oxen were allowed to be killed in the Spanish fashion, the dogs pinning them down and, when their throats had been gashed by a *macheto* knife, wallowing in the blood until their appearance was enough to strike terror into a less impressionable being than a West Indian native!

Negroes fled into the depths of the plantations, carrying dismay with them: slaves who might have preferred the lawless life of the mountains to the monotony of the cotton patch and rice field thought better of it; the news soon spread among the Maroons, and one of their leaders, Johnson by name, left his post and joined forces with Montagu, alarmed at the approach of the bloodhounds.

Anxious to test the new allies, General Walpole drove to Seven Rivers in a post-chaise, and the Spanish huntsmen paraded their dogs; 40 men, armed with

"SERGEANT STEPHENSON CHARGED THE FOE" (*p.* 127).

swords and fusils, and more than 100 ferocious hounds, unmuzzled, and straining at the leash.

The Spaniards fired, and shouted to encourage the animals, which, however, did not seem to need it, for they gnawed the fusil butts, and tore forward at such a pace that the general was glad to beat a hasty retreat into his chaise again, while his horses were saved with great difficulty!

It was then the dry season, and there was danger lest the enemy might fire the bush; so, with considerable forethought, when Walpole ordered an advance he instructed the leaders to offer terms if possible, and to keep the bloodhounds in the background, trusting to the report of their ferocity, which he believed would bear fruit.

There was a smart affair on the 15th December, to which Cannon and Fortescue both allude, when 30 of the 17th and 10 of an unnamed regiment, under a subaltern, were surprised by the Maroons and suffered loss.

The officer being hit, he handed over command to Sergeant Stephenson, of the 17th, who charged the foe with considerable slaughter and routed them.

The sergeant was offered an infantry commission for his gallantry, but stuck to the "Death or Glory Boys" by the advice of several of the officers (and no doubt from his own personal feelings as well), but the hoped-for promotion never came again, and the brave fellow died with the regiment in India in 1813.

On the 18th we made a forward movement against a Maroon chief named Montagu, who, unknown to Colonel Hull, was marching to join forces with another rebel named Johnson nearer to the Old Maroon Town.

The "Springers" and the 17th had only proceeded

half a dozen miles when their advance guard came upon the blacks and began a fire.

Hull sent back for his baggage, and the two parties, one on each side of a precipitous cliff with a narrow dell between them, seemed in danger of coming to a serious action.

Our men were ordered to cease fire and to take cover, and it was intimated to the Maroons that we were willing to make peace, when they sounded what we took to be a parley on their horns.

At first they were incredulous, and great activity was visible among them, but finally Mr. Oswald Werge, of the 17th, by a plucky action which he seems to have taken on his own initiative, brought things to a satisfactory conclusion.

Regardless of their muskets, he clambered down the hill, and crying, "I bring you peace," advanced towards them unarmed.

They still hung back, but at last one of them came up and shook hands, ultimately exchanging jacket and cap with him in token of amity.

An impromptu truce ensued, both sides wary and distrustful, and laying on their arms all day, but thirst conquered them at last, and the Maroons proposed a withdrawal of our sentries while they drank at the stream in the dell, afterwards withdrawing in their turn to let our scarlet 62nd and blue Dragoons fill their canteens.

There was practically no more fighting—the dogs had done their work, and neither party were anxious to prolong the struggle.

Colonel Walpole concluded a treaty by which the Maroons submitted on condition that they should not be sent out of the island.

The local government promptly violated the terms, and Walpole very rightly refused the sword of honour voted him by the Assembly in consequence.

A letter of Walpole's to Balcarres is quoted by Fortescue, and is very gratifying to the regiment:—

"I must not omit to mention to your Lordship that it is to the impression made by the undaunted bravery of the 17th Light Dragoons, who were more particularly engaged on the 15th December, that we owe the submission of the rebels. The Maroons speak of them with astonishment. Mr. Werge was particularly signalised with the advanced guard, and the sergeant-major of that regiment is strongly recommended for his spirit and activity by the commanding officer, Mr. Edwards, who is in every way deserving of your Lordship's opinion."

CHAPTER VIII.

VARIED SERVICE, 1795—1806.

Fresh Detachments for the West Indies — Hair Powder Abolished — "Admiral Christian's Storm"—Two Troops serve as Marines—Uncertainty as to Movements of the different Troops—Grenada—Yellow Jack—The 17th to the Rescue—A Smart Charge and a Great Slaughter—San Domingo — Terrible Mortality among our Troops—Veterinary Surgeons to be attached to Cavalry—Home again—Regimental Papers lost at Sea—Canterbury—Our Attempt on Ostend—Heavy Field Days and Ornamental Parades—Drafts from the 18th—Four Troops for Egypt countermanded—Deserter murders Colonel of 28th Dragoons—Riots—Manchester—Curragh—Under Orders—Again countermanded—John Hale dies—Northampton.

MEANWHILE, the regiment which we left in Ireland sent four more troops in the August of 1795 to join the cavalry camp at Netley, also destined for the West Indies.

These troops, by the way, appeared with their queues of the natural colour, hair powder having been discontinued on the 1st August in consequence of the scarcity of flour.

A tremendous fleet of 200 transports, under the convoy of Rear-Admiral Christian, had been collected to convey Sir Ralph Abercromby's army, and the 17th are said to have embarked on the 21st September.

A dispute arose about the troops on board a warship being amenable to naval discipline, and the military and naval authorities argued it out at such length that it was not until the 16th November that Christian got his fleet to sea.

Then they met the full force of the November gales before they cleared the Channel, and had to put back three times, with a terrible list of casualties.

So fierce was the tempest and so great the loss, that it was long known as "Admiral Christian's storm." Ships were driven ashore, others foundered, and the commander-in-chief did not finally sail until the following March.

Some of the fleet were more fortunate, and, by steering to southward, made the West Indies in six weeks, and with them was a part at least of the 17th.

What portion of this second detachment it was there are now no means of telling, but for a short time two troops were serving as Marines on the frigate *Hermione*, thirty-two guns, Captain P. Wilkinson. The *Hermione* was part of the fleet under Admirals Ford and Parker, at Jamaica in 1795.

Two years later a ghastly mutiny and massacre took place on the *Hermione*, when Captain Hugh Pigot commanded, which has become matter of history, when Pigot, one of the greatest martinets in the service, was stabbed and forced through the cabin windows, his voice being heard invoking vengeance as he went astern!

The 17th luckily had no part in the business, having been landed at Martinique long before.

Some writers have tried to find the origin of the term "Horse Marines" in that short spell of sea service, but their deductions are not very satisfactory; a strong bond of friendship existed, however, at a later date between the 17th and "Her Majesty's Jollies," when the former were lying at Woolwich in 1851.

A private of the regiment who had imbibed not wisely but too well was rescued from some roughs by a party of Marines, and during the short stay of the 17th in the town the greatest *cameraderie* was displayed by the two corps.

The history of the British army is full of such regimental friendships—and hatreds, too—which are kept alive, although the respective bodies may not have met for half a century or more; and there are regiments in the service which are never quartered together, for very good reasons well known to the authorities, though probably not a man is serving in them who could tell you the reason of the original feud.

The next appearance of the regiment on the scene of action is early in March, 1796, when two troops landed at Sauteur, in Grenada, where there was trouble of the reddest Republican kind.

The chances are, that the detachment consisted of the *Hermione* squadron, but I cannot say so definitely.

The headquarters and five (? *four*) troops left in Ireland were on shipboard in the Cove of Cork as early as the 10th January, 1796, lying at single anchor, and forming part of the first dismounted cavalry brigade, under Major-General Whyte, destined for the West Indies; but as the fleet did not get to sea until the 25th February it is not possible that they could have furnished the Grenada relief.

With this brigade were also the 14th, 18th, 21st, and part of the 26th Light Dragoons, all dismounted, a mounted portion of the 26th sailing round from Portsmouth to join them, only to be driven back again by those terrible winds, and to strew the lovely Cornish bays with dead horses on whose hoofs were burnt the regimental brand, D. 26.

Grenada, one of the most beautiful of the West Indian Islands, and formerly the home of the Caribs, until the French exterminated them during the seventeenth century, had been restored to Britain in 1783, but, in common with almost all the neighbouring islands, it had become imbued with the tenets of Victor Hugues and his party.

A mulatto named Fédon was the particular instrument in this case, and for pure atrocity his proceedings were hard to beat.

A French force had landed on the 2nd March, 1795, at La Bay, and massacred many inhabitants, stirring up the blacks against us, and bringing with them "Stands of Arms, Barrels of Powder, Red Caps, and other Republican Trumpery."

They captured the governor and held forty-two whites as hostages; the Militia were called out, and our planters took counsel together as to the best means at their disposal, sending off for help to Martinique, Barbadoes, and Trinidad.

A hundred and fifty rank and file of the 58th sent against the enemy at Charlottestown were unsupported by the local Militia, and had to return to St. George's in consequence.

The Militia seem to have been panic-stricken, and to have retired almost *en masse* into the ships that chanced to be lying off the shore, leaving the work to the driblets of regulars that arrived from time to time to be swallowed up by fatigue and fever.

General Colin Lindsay arrived on the 12th from St. Lucia with twenty Artillerymen, and soon after, on the 17th, attacked the rebels with a handful of the 9th and 68th regiments, and they fell back before him, but the rains came somewhat earlier than usual, and all military operations had to be suspended.

Lindsay's loss was a captain and 16 men wounded, and 2 men killed, and in a letter to the Governor he complains bitterly of the Militia deserting him, concluding with the somewhat pathetic appeal, " I must request a Supply of Blankets and Shirts for my Troops, as, when they laid down their Haversacks to engage the Enemy, the Negroes stole them."

Poor Lindsay's next requirement was a shroud, for, evidently going off his balance, he shot himself with a pistol about four o'clock next day, no one being able to assign a reason beyond fatigue, heat, and excess of anxiety.

The French party having once more full sway, plunder, rapine, and every atrocity possible stained the island.

A mulatto paraded with a white man's head, crying "*Vive la République!*" and the negroes perpetrated all those nameless horrors that inevitably ensue when the buck nigger gets out of hand.

Another little reinforcement arrived on the 1st April from Barbadoes—a few of the 25th and 29th—and Brigadier Campbell (lieut.-colonel of the 29th) with 150 tars from the ships assaulted the enemy's position with a loss of 100, being compelled to retreat in his turn.

Then came "yellow Jack," and the troops, few enough to begin with, melted away at the rate of about twenty a week, if not more.

A brother of the rascal Fédon having been killed during Campbell's attack, the infamous monster had about 50 prisoners massacred in cold blood according to one account, and heartrending reports were current as to the exact manner of their murder, one being shot five times before they hacked him to pieces.

Some of the Light Cavalry from St. George seem to have done good service, and also a Light Company of Gentlemen Volunteers, under Mr. Park, the editor of a local paper, who was unfortunately killed; but the promised aid did not come, and hope was almost extinguished in the hearts of those despairing planters, who saw what had been a veritable Garden of Eden running red as a shambles.

In March of the new year, however, solid help arrived, and a force came from Barbadoes, consisting of detachments of the 10th, 25th, and two companies of the 88th, followed a week after by some of the Buffs 8th, 63rd, and last, but certainly not least, a probable two troops of the gallant 17th.

The insurgents were now at Port Royal, or Grenville, about the centre of the east coast of the island, and Brigadier-General Nichols lost no time in marching on the position, while the available forces at St. George were ordered round by sea.

They landed on the 24th, and a battery of two 6-pounders and one $5\frac{1}{2}$-inch howitzer was made during the night under the personal direction of Major O'Mara, of the 38th, on a ridge about 1,000 yards south of Port Royal.

At daylight we opened fire, to the great discomfiture of the coloured scum that had arrayed themselves under the Tricolour; but the general yearned for an assault on their redoubt, and began by clearing some heights on our left; accordingly he sent a loyal black corps, with 50 of the Connaught Rangers, under a major, to drive them off.

The ground was so difficult that it was two hours

before they came in touch with the enemy, and then owing to the very strong position of the foe they had to fall back until Nichols sent up the 8th, or King's, to their support.

Then an alarm of fire was raised in our rear, some of the enemy having slipped round and lighted our stores, and no sooner were the flames extinguished than two French schooners with reinforcements came in and opened on us. In vain we slewed a 6-pounder round; the range was not too great, but somehow not a shot told, and the general ordered an immediate assault by the Buffs and 63rd, bringing up every man available to their support, being, as he admits, in a very tight place. The Buffs had a slight check, but formed again under a hedge, and being joined by half the 29th, which had been hurried up from Grande Bacolet, Brigadier-General Campbell led them on in person. In the meantime, the 17th, commanded by Captain John Black, and the St. George's troop of Light Cavalry, under Captain Burney, were sent to intercept the reinforcements landing on the shore. The troopers jingled down a lane, already strewn with redcoats and dead and wounded of the Sans Culotte Company, and on reaching the beach, word was given to charge. And charge they did, slap into the rascals forming up there, with the endless boom of the curling waves in their ears, and, mingling with the foaming surf, the wicked hiss of grape shot from the schooners, and the cross fire from the redoubt on the other side.

There was no quarter! It was a slashing dash of our troopers, sick of shipboard, and thankful to get astride the pigskin once again; a whirl of sabres, a whisk of those handsome bearskin crests and smart blue jackets; and, when the coral strand was black with corpses, another dash, back under cover to form up, and bandage wounds, and wait for a second chance!

That chance was not long coming.

Campbell led his men on with great *elan*, and as they breasted the ridge the enemy fled precipitately into the redoubt, hotly pursued by our infantry, the first man to spring through the embrasure being Captain Clavy, of the 29th.

Many a negro, flushed with a brief spell of lawlessness and licence, turned grey with terror at the bayonets of the Worcesters, and sprang with chattering teeth down the clefts and crannies of the hill, crashing through the dense brush while the ounce bullets rained down from above.

And then, flying madly along a little glen, they met a second Nemesis, as the 17th darted out from their cover, sabring the miscreants literally to a man!

One horse killed, with 4 rank and file and 2 horses wounded, is not a heavy price to pay for the satisfaction of ridding the earth of 300 incarnate fiends within "the space of a few hundred yards," for such is the record on the authority of Sir Evan Lloyd, another witness counting 160 bodies on the beach alone.

Poor Black, honourably mentioned for his action on that day, fell a victim to fever in July; he had joined the regiment as a cornet in 1780.

Captain Johnson, Lieutenant Werge, and Cornet Brown are also stated to have taken part in the affair, which certainly did much towards the final surrender of the island into our hands.

Fédon retreated into the hills, but his following soon surrendered, and in June the French commandant Jossey capitulated.

Fédon, with characteristic barbarity, murdered all the whites, both friends and foes, at Morne Quaquo, before he took to his heels; and though his canoe was afterwards found drifting empty off the coast, his end, like that of Nana Sahib, Balmacedo, and too many historical ruffians, was never satisfactorily accounted for.

The 17th, though engaged several times in the island, do not seem to have had any further casualties, unless from fever, and the date of their re-embarkation is not known.

While these affairs were in progress in Grenada, more serious resistance had to be faced in San Domingo.

Five troops of the 17th (four, according to Cannon) were in that island in August, 1796, quartered under General Bowyer at Jeremie, and on the 8th he sent a force against the black leader, Rigaud.

This man had been attacking the British posts, and was no mean opponent with his large following of negroes, whom the despatches designate as "Brigands" not without reason.

Lieutenant Bradshaw was sent with 22 mounted men of the 13th Light Dragoons to march on Du Centre, while Captain Whitby, with 2 subs, and 60 privates of the 17th, presumably on foot, embarked for the Caymites, reaching the post at Du Centre on the 10th.

On the 11th the enemy stormed the post at Raimond, and Lieutenant Gilman, of the 17th Foot, with 20 of the 17th Lights and some Chasseurs, repulsed them four separate times.

On the 12th the enemy kept up a heavy fire on the Raimond blockhouse, which was on a small hill, and Gilman led his mixed command in a vigorous sortie, killing 16 whites and 47 blacks, and driving the others into the woods, capturing a 2-pounder, some ammunition and stores.

Two of the 17th only were wounded, but the Chasseurs' loss was heavier, and the whites among the enemy were said to have belonged to the Emmigrant Regiment of Berwick, a corps whose history carries us back to early Jacobite times.

The 17th also assisted at the defence of Trois, besieged for eighteen days by General Rigaud in person with about 4,000 men.

Bowyer advanced with three columns on the dawn of the 19th, and seeing that several men of the regiment were killed and wounded by the enemy's fire, he mustered them for an assault on Morne Gautier, dismounting the 13th, and rallying the negroes who were wavering.

He had to retreat in the end, being bowled over by a shot in the breast; but Lieut.-Colonel Hooke, of the Leicestershires, ultimately relieved Trois, and the war gradually died out, as did also the British troops from the terrible climate, which carried them off with incredible rapidity.

Some idea of West Indian service in those bad old days of no sanitation and medical incompetence may be gathered from regimental returns.

The 22nd and 41st Foot marched through Canterbury on their return from San Domingo in 1796 with only 50 officers and men round the colours.

Of the 23rd, only 50 survived out of 800 effectives; and the 43rd was even worse—passing through Southampton on the 4th October with 5 officers, the drum-major, and half-a-dozen privates out of the original 900 that started for service, leaving 40 or 50 behind as prisoners.

Fortescue says the 17th Lights lost about 30 in San Domingo, and quotes a muster roll for March, 1797, which shows that 126 men had died during the previous year!

Government at home, heedless of their bodies, seems to have suddenly awakened to their spiritual needs, and all chaplains were ordered to either serve, or retire; but the 17th seem to have permanently dispensed with their "parson" in 1796 for good and all, as a regimental institution.

It was said that one had done duty in garrison for nine successive regiments, from which it would appear that a chaplaincy was rather a "soft thing"—it is not always a very hard one even now.

Another important innovation was made in August, 1796, namely, the appointment of veterinary surgeons to all cavalry regiments, "and as an inducement for Medical Gentlemen to pursue the Veterinary art, it is liberally purposed to make them commissioned officers, and to give them seven shillings a day"—Oh, magnanimous powers that were!

Mr. Edward Coleman, professor of the Veterinary College, and veterinary inspector to the Hon. Board of Ordnance, was gazetted veterinary-general to the army, with the patronage of appointing surgeons to the different regiments, and the step was undoubtedly a good one, sounding the knell of that bad old system of rule of thumb farriery, which in spite of pains and penalties must have cost the authorities a pretty penny in cast horses.

It was not until 1798 that the 17th benefited by the new rule, when a Mr. James Burt, an Edinburgh man, described in the College records as of the Royal Artillery, was appointed.

THE VOYAGE HOME.

In 1796 a tremendous thinning down of the strength took place, 7 sergeants, 76 men, and 2 trumpeters dying in one week, and this representing only a portion of the regiment.

In the previous year 10,000 soldiers are said to have succumbed to yellow fever in the West Indies alone, and from a melancholy list of officers now before me, I find the names of 18 killed in action, against 198 who died from unstated causes.*

The feeble remnant of our blue Dragoons must have hailed the day of departure with delight, and well might they require a draft from the 18th and 400 recruits when they landed in England in 1797.

On the voyage home they came nigh to a terrible disaster, for the headquarter ship, the *Caledonia*, foundered at sea. Luckily all the men were taken on board the *Britannia*, of Bristol, but the baggage and the records of their previous gallant service went to the bottom, leaving a gap in their regimental annals which no research can now fill up.

After going into quarters at Nottingham, Trowbridge, Leicester, Bath, and Bristol, they moved to Canterbury in 1798, starting early in March, to relieve the Oxford Fencible Cavalry, who were moving to Brighton, Lewes, and Arundel.

They were expected on the 1st April, finally arriving between the 10th and 13th, and for a twelvemonth they jingled their spurs on the flint stones of the grey cathedral city, which at that time in particular was a great military rendezvous.

* The 9th, 16th, and four other skeleton regiments of infantry, were ordered on their return to be composed entirely of boys from *thirteen* to eighteen, who were to be well fed and have walking drill merely for some time; to such shifts were we put to fill our "thin red line"!

Militia, Fencibles, and Volunteer Associations, Guards, Line, and Regular Cavalry were "thick as leaves in Vallombrosa" when the 17th marched in, and there was a little scheme afoot which was shortly to concern the regiment, and which the authorities were keeping profoundly secret.

A certain naval officer, Captain Home Riggs Popham, who had done good service during our war in Flanders and earned the goodwill of the Duke of York, was at that time in command of the district extending from Deal to Beachy Head, and very keen about the establishment of sea-fencibles. He had also a theory, and the authorities backing him up, it was decided to put it to the test—no less a project, in short, than the destruction by gunpowder of the great sluice gates at Saas, near Ostend, which confined the waters of the Bruges Canal, an engineering feat not long before completed at a cost of five millions. The canal was 13 miles in length and 100 feet wide, and by its destruction not only would the commerce be seriously injured, but it would no longer be a nursery for vessels that might be destined for our invasion.

Invasion, it must be borne in mind, was the great national bugbear of those days, and our southern counties simply bristled with bayonets, just as a few years later the coast bristled with Martello towers. So preparations were made, and Major-General Eyre Coote, commanding at Dover, was entrusted with the military part of the affair, while Home Popham was to direct the twenty gunboats and bomb ketches which assembled off Margate on the 11th May.

On Saturday the light brigade of Foot Guards marched out of Canterbury and took the Margate road without the slightest inkling of what was going forward, and they were followed by the 11th, the light companies of the 23rd and 49th, some Artillery with 6 guns, and "a sergeant and 10 privates of the 17th Light Dragoons, who took their saddles and accoutrements, although they had no horses."

Speculation was rife through the countryside, and an embargo had been laid along the coast, not a man among the troops knowing his destination or the service that was expected from him, but all of them swinging along in high spirits, and the Guards in particular giving three cheers when they went on board.

Embarking on four vessels—the *Coromandel*, *Hebe*, *Minerva*, and *Druid*—with a strong convoy, they worked round the Foreland and anchored opposite Kingsgate.

They got away on the 14th, and at one a.m. on the 19th reached Ostend, leaving the 1st Guards behind in the *Minerva*, to their ultimate benefit as it turned out.

Eyre Coote made a bold pretence of summoning the French general at Ostend to surrender, and under cover of this landed part of his men, almost unseen, on the other side of the river, where they promptly began their work of destruction. In the meantime there was a lively fire between our ships and the Ostend batteries, but the troops worked so well that the basins and lock gates were hopelessly ruined and some shipping burned, and at eleven o'clock in the forenoon Coote was ready to re-embark. So far so good, but the grey sea was foaming on the sandy shore by that time—a gale had sprung up, and the surf boiled furiously; it was impossible for the boats to live in it, and there was no other course than to take up a position among the sand dunes and abide results. The wind blew with increasing fury off the land, and 1,000 odd men gathered in hastily formed intrenchments, lay on their arms, tantalised by the British shipping beating off and on without avail, and knowing that they had raised a hornets' nest which would very shortly be about their ears. It came in the early dawn of the 20th, in the shape of demi-brigades which mustered in great force, and a smart little action was waged on that monotonous shore against odds too great for the invaders.

The thing was hopeless from the start, and, Coote wounded, the colonel of the 11th killed, 160 men down, including one of the 17th, and both flanks turned, Burrard, the second in command, did the only thing possible, and capitulated.

Next year our men were exchanged, and all the men of the little detachment of the regiment were promoted, the sergeant in charge, William Brown, receiving a commission in the Royal Waggon Train, and in 1802 becoming cornet in the "Death or Glory Boys," in which he eventually rose to be captain.

Meanwhile, the internal economy of the regiment must have been rather chaotic, and have entailed considerable labour on the officers and staff, what with 400 raw recruits to lick into shape, a new drill book, and an improved sword exercise.

On the 4th June, being the king's birthday, the garrison was marched out to Barham Downs, six miles south of Canterbury—Foot and Horse Artillery, 7th, 17th and 18th Light Dragoons, the flank companies of the 44th, and the West Kent and Hereford Militia—and there, drawn up in grand parade, they were reviewed by Sir Charles Grey, commanding the Southern District, and Prince William of Gloucester, with the usual salute, the *feu de joie*, and three hearty cheers for his Majesty; followed by "an elegant entertainment" at Sir Charles's place, Barham Court, and a ball at Delmar's Rooms.

A few days later, the 17th and 18th being both incomplete, an order came down from Government to fill up the former's gaps by drafts from the latter, which was done on the 13th June, "and that corps (the 17th) will in consequence shortly be ready for immediate service," says the local news sheet.

They were kept busy with the pipeclay and whiting, for a general parade took place on the 2nd August, in front of the new barracks, which had been completed in 1795 at a cost of £40,000, the garrison being drawn up in line and minutely inspected by Sir Charles and the Earl of Pembroke, each regiment played past the saluting base by its respective band.

The 7th Lights had gone by this time, deeply regretted by the inhabitants for the "very gentleman-like behaviour of the officers," and their place was taken by that distinguished corps, the 10th, of which the Prince of Wales was colonel.

His advent brought more work to the 17th — another ride out to Barham Downs on Sunday, the 12th, to celebrate his birthday; another minute inspection, and the march past in slow time, ending up with three cheers for the prince's prosperity—in very truth it wanted all the cheering it could get, his liabilities having been returned to Parliament not very long before at £650,000!

When the freedom of the city was presented to the prince during the following month, the 17th were again on duty and were inspected by him, while the bells rang and twenty-one guns thundered out from the Dungeon Field; in fact, the only records preserved of the regiment's doings at Canterbury are of field days and inspections, except one little matter of a certain Abraham Levi, of Holy Cross, Westgate, who was convicted in two separate penalties of £5 each for buying the leather breeches belonging to a sergeant and private—history does not state the reward of the soldiers: was it clink or triangles, or perhaps both?

On Thursday morning, the 10th May, the first detachment of four troops under orders for Egypt marched out of the city, *en route* for Southampton and Portsmouth; blue cloaks rolled over the holsters and plumes cased. The remainder followed next day, but their trouble was all for naught, and after spending more than a week with their old comrades, the 18th, the transports finally sailed without them on the 21st June.

On 5th and 6th July the rest of the regiment left Canterbury for Swinley or Windsor camp, and it was destined to be twenty-five years before the old cathedral city saw the white facings and grinning skulls again.

Little of note had happened to them during their stay there; one of the majors and the doctor had both married county ladies, and in November the regimental "vet." rode back to bear away a certain Miss Gurney in marital triumph—her dowry is not stated, but Mr. Burt's name disappears after the following year! And yet there was an incident which marred the record of their Canterbury station; it is such ancient history now that I may surely venture to tell it here.

On the morning of the 1st June, about eight o'clock, Lieut.-Colonel Shadwell, of the 28th Light Dragoons, being out of uniform at the time, saw a couple of men in Dragoon undress in the inn yard at Wrotham, and asking where they came from, was told "Maidstone."

Fancying them to be deserters, he asked for their furlough, and one pointed out his comrade, who was walking off, as having it. The colonel put out his left hand to stop him, when the other, drawing a pistol from his pantaloons, shot him in the right side, saying, "There is our pass."

The unfortunate officer cried out to his servant, staggered about thirteen paces and fell dead, the murderer calmly reloading the weapon and then bolting with his companion up the hill, pursued by the natives, who were kept at a respectful distance by the shining barrels.

Luckily for justice, a man happened to be out rabbiting, and presented his shot-gun at ten paces; the miscreant's pistol missed fire, and receiving a charge between the eyes which blinded him, the pair were secured, proving to be two Irish deserters from the 17th, named Philip Keating, from Kildare, who had come as a draft from the 18th, and John Keggans, who had enlisted for the regiment in Dublin.

Both were very young men, the eldest not more than twenty-three, and on their trial at the summer assizes Keating was condemned to death, his comrade being acquitted, and no doubt sent "back to the army again," where life would not prove very rosy, one may surmise, after that grisly tragedy!

During the summer at Swinley Camp they were joined by the disappointed detachments, and on the 5th August were reviewed, with the 16th Light Dragoons, by the king and the Duke of York, attended by a gorgeous staff; the troops brigaded in skirmishing parties, with their artillery, across Bagshot Heath to King's Reach Hill.

Then they moved into the West, and lay at Exeter and Taunton all winter, returning the following year to the Duke's camp at Bagshot.

While at Exeter, in the early days of March, 1800, two of the officers fell out over a lady of the neighbourhood, and there and then they adjusted the matter in the mess-room. At the first fire one of them received a ball in his left shoulder, afterwards extracted by Mr. Robinson, the surgeon. They were touchy gentlemen, with their "Death or Glory," and their blue and silver, when George III. was king!

But there were other things to think about when they marched for service in the Midlands, after another spell of field-days and inspections on Bagshot Heath, for the bread riots broke out, and they were called to repress them.

Part of the regiment was lying in Birmingham Barracks when the mob began to coerce the bakers, compelling them to sell their loaves at a considerable reduction, and raiding the shops of those who would not do so.

Several people were wounded and the Riot Act was read, the Dragoons dispersing the crowd, and the local Volunteers holding themselves in readiness if necessary; but things gradually simmered down, although a day or two later the regiment was again sent for, and "burst into town in full gallop."

At Duffield, in Derbyshire, they had warmer work, Captain Oswald Werge, of Maroon fame, getting a shot through his helmet, and several men having to be invalided from various causes—principally stones and glass bottles, I believe.

These disastrous civil conflicts, with which the early

years of this century were so frequently stained, were often more trying than service in front of an enemy, and reflected the highest credit on many a gallant regiment which got a bad name for generations; as a rule it is your local auxiliaries who do all the slashing—perhaps they take the opportunity to work off old scores!

During this year the captain-lieutenants in several regiments of Dragoon Guards and Dragoons, among them the 17th, were made captains of troops without purchase, and in the majority of cases the next promotion was given in the regiment.

The disturbances in the Midlands spread into the North, and a letter from Manchester, dated Saturday, 21st March, 1801, says: "This morning at three o'clock, two squadrons of the 17th Light Dragoons arrived from the inland district, and at twelve, two more under the command of Major Gore. Shortly after, a part of the 7th Dragoon Guards marched in—all is alarm and confusion, sixty people taken up here and at Bolton."

During the night between the 8th and 9th June, some troops of the regiment and part of the K.D.G.'s went through Newcastle-under-Lyme, more being expected in the evening, and the early stay of the "Death or Glory Boys" in the County Palatine was one of incessant detachment duty and night marches.

When the rioting was got under at last, the headquarters were established at Hulme, in those now dilapidated buildings known as the "Horse barracks," and upwards of 1,000 men with nearly the same number of horses paraded there in 1801, the strongest recorded muster in the regiment's career.

Manchester, so unpopular as a cavalry station in after years—partly from its situation, and partly because the peccadilloes of certain gay subalterns closed the hospitable doors of the city against them and their successors—was very different when the 17th paid it their first visit.

The Irwell was not a stream of inky hue then, and the smart blue jackets must have been familiar objects in the meadows around Throstlenest on a summer's evening, and many a pottle of strong ale did the "Dog" and the "Seven Stars" and the "White Bear" provide for thirsty sergeant-majors with little tufts of side whisker on their otherwise clean-shaven faces, when they wetted those new chevrons which were given to the cavalry in 1802.

In that year the regiment suffered a reduction of two troops on the delusive Peace of Amiens, and the horses of one of them were valued by a dealer at an average of forty guineas each.

Previously to this—in June, 1801—I find a detachment of the regiment daily expected at Portsmouth, to embark for Egypt, but they must have been again countermanded; at any rate they never went, the entire corps, after picking up its outlying troops at Lancaster, Chester, Bolton, and Preston, embarking at Liverpool on the 1st May for Ireland.

After a very bad passage they reached Dublin, and during 1804 the two disbanded troops were again added to the strength, a couple of squadrons joining the camp on the Curragh in August, under General Lord Cathcart, whom we met with the regiment at Whitemarsh in 1778.

In September, 1805, the 17th were warned for active service on the Continent, but were once more disappointed, and, sailing for England in December, spent Christmas day on board ship, and finally established their headquarters at Northampton, where, in March, they heard of the death of John Hale.

CHAPTER IX.

"SUCCESS TO GREY HAIRS, BUT BAD LUCK TO
WHITE-LOCKS." — *Old Military Toast.*

Home Popham's Little Plan—Beresford sails for South America—He takes Monte Video—Ultimately obliged to surrender—A Reinforcement under Backhouse arrives too late—Another Reinforcement under Auchmuty—The 17th to go—The Regiment completely cleared from a False Report—Colonel congratulated by the Duke of York—Sails from Spithead—New Pattern Carbines replaced by Spanish Muskets—Auchmuty has a good word for the Regiment—Monte Video stormed—The 17th thanked in Orders—Craufurd arrives with more Troops—Whitelocke arrives and takes Command—Strength of the 17th—Advance on Buenos Ayres—The 17th almost entirely dismounted—Gross Bungling of Whitelocke—Storming of Buenos Ayres—Brave Fight—Disgraceful Capitulation—Whitelocke dismissed the Service—Regiment home again and ordered to India.

IT was the early fate of the 17th to be associated with defeat, and we now come to a chapter in its history which makes very curious reading.

On the 18th January, 1806, Cape Colony surrendered to a British force under Major-General Sir David Baird.

The irrepressible Commodore Sir Home Popham (the same Captain Popham whom we have already seen at Ostend) was in command of the squadron at the Cape, and he conceived the idea of a remarkable bit of filibustering which, in the words of an official volume compiled for the express use of the Duke of York, "may be considered as the most extraordinary event that has occurred in the military annals of the British empire—the expedition to Buenos Ayres!"

Popham had been previously consulted by the Government as to the possibilities of an expedition against South America, and he had drafted out a scheme for a double descent on that country on the Atlantic and Pacific shores.

The Government does not seem to have thought much more of the matter, but Popham had not forgotten it, and, accepting the statement of an American merchant vessel which touched at the Cape, that Monte Video and Buenos Ayres were dissatisfied with their rulers and would welcome a British force, the commodore, acting on his own responsibility, prevailed upon Sir David Baird to detach some troops under General Beresford, and away they sailed on the 14th April.

Thirty-six officers and men of the Royal Artillery, a captain and 6 dismounted Dragoons of the 20th Lights, 889 of all ranks of the 71st Highland Regiment (now the 1st Highland Light Infantry), with 60 women and 40 children, was the sum total of the military element embarked on five transports under the convoy of the same number of men-of-war.

At St. Helena the persuasive Popham obtained a reinforcement from the Governor, of 102 Artillery and 174 of the St. Helena Regiment, and then they put helm up for the River of Silver, the Rio de la Plata.

Landing on the 25th June, they moved against Buenos Ayres next morning, and after a few skirmishes which cost us one man killed, and an officer and 11 men wounded, the city capitulated on the 27th and we took possession.

At first "all went merry as a marriage bell," but the

people did not want us, and about the middle of July there appeared signs of revolt.

A young Spaniard named Pueridon stirred up the city, a French captain in the Spanish navy, named Liniers, organised resistance in the country, and Beresford had to march against them on 1st August, when he killed 70 and took 10 guns.

The rains came about this time with tropical violence, and the opposition of the inhabitants increased to such a pitch that measures were taken to secure a retreat.

Liniers summoned Beresford to surrender on 10th August, and was refused; desultory firing began on our posts, and a storm dispersed the transports.

On the 12th we were attacked in force, and though Beresford held out well, such a rattling fire was poured into us from the flat-roofed houses and the church spires that the general had no alternative but to surrender.

The odds were enormous if the official account be true, 13,000 against 1,300—the losses, 150 British and 700 Spaniards; and this was only the prelude to greater and more galling disaster!

* * * * * *

The moment Buenos Ayres was captured by us, Popham had sent word to England and the Cape, announcing the victory and urging for immediate reinforcements.

Sir David Baird instantly responded, and a corps of 1,936 men, under Lieut.-Colonel Backhouse, of the 47th, sailed on the 29th August.

They were taken from the Royal Artillery, 20th and 21st Light Dragoons, and the 38th 47th, and

54th Foot, and when they arrived, 12th October, it was to find everything upside down.

Backhouse, who had seen some active service in the West Indies, at once planned an attack on Monte Video, but the shallowness of the river foiled him, so, taking possession of Maldonado—a village lying behind sand dunes about seventy-eight miles from Monte Video—and the fortified island of Goretti, which commanded the harbour, he settled down to wait for reinforcements or further instructions.

In the meantime we, at home, waxed enthusiastic over Beresford's success, and, all ignorant of his subsequent reverses, sent a force of 3,400 men to assist him, under Sir Samuel Auchmuty.

With this force went the 17th.

The regiment had shortly before, when lying at Northampton, been the victim of some unfavourable reports, and Major-General Sir Henry Warde was sent down to inspect it.

He expressed himself delighted with everything he saw, and told the commanding officer, Lieut.-Colonel Evan Lloyd, that he should "report it composed of the finest men, the best horses, and equipped with the best appointments of any corps he had inspected."

Cannon represents this as taking place in 1805, Fortescue in April of the following year.

During that month the regiment marched to London, and was reviewed on Wimbledon Common by the Prince of Wales and the Duke of York, who were loud in praise of the corps; the Duke, after the hearty, emphatic manner of royal dukes, complimenting Evan Lloyd "in very strong terms."

In September, 1806, the regiment was in quarters

on the Channel, among them being Brighton, Hastings, Romney, and Rye, and one night came a message to prepare for immediate foreign service.

Two troops were sent to form a depôt at Chichester, and the rest of the regiment marched to Portsea and Southampton, where they gave up their horses and embarked with Auchmuty's expedition at Spithead on the 5th October, clearing Falmouth on the 9th.

Putting into Rio Janeiro for water, they heard of Beresford's capitulation, and victualling for four months, Sir Samuel sailed for Maldonado, which he reached on the 5th January, 1807.

The regiments forming his force were: Royal Artillery, 9th and 17th Light Dragoons, 40th and 87th Foot, and three companies of the 95th (now the Rifle Brigade).

The 17th, for some occult reason, had been armed with long Spanish muskets at Rio Janeiro, in place of the new pattern carbine which had been previously given to them, and they were to act as infantry.

Sir Samuel Auchmuty assumed command, and at once decided to abandon Maldonado.

Leaving a small garrison in the island of Goretti, he sailed up the river, and landed nine miles from Monte Video on the morning of the 16th, and moved against that city in two columns on the 19th.

He speaks rather despairingly of the means and men at his disposal, and the odds against him.

There were only 500 barrels of powder in the fleet; he had only four 24-pounders, with 300 rounds per gun; the troops from the Cape were in want of everything; "the 47th is an indifferent body of men; the company of the 71st are mostly young boys; I need not say how fine a body of men the 17th

Light Dragoons are, as your Royal Highness lately reviewed them."

He had seen the regiment in action, by the way, in the bad old days of the American war, in which he served under Howe.

He has a good word for the Rifles, as also for the 38th, 40th, and 87th, but he says, and truly, "the equipments of our cavalry are too heavy for small horses living on grass. A Dragoon cannot overtake a native of this country; lightly clothed, without any equipments but a long musket and a sword, he approaches his enemy, dismounts, takes a deliberate aim from the back of his horse, and gallops off as soon as he has fired."

We know more to-day of those natives—the Guachos —Arabs of the Pampas, magnificent riders, adepts with the lasso, and practically living in the saddle, and it is not surprising that our fellows, tossed about on shipboard, and then pitchforked on to raw mounts, could do little against them.

Five thousand troops of the enemy were in Monte Video, well supplied and full of spirit, and Sir Samuel had word that 4,000 more with twenty-four guns were coming up from Buenos Ayres, so that what was done must be done quickly.

Rear-Admiral Stirling, who had been sent out to supersede Sir Home Popham, concurred with Sir Samuel, as did all the principal military officers, and our little force started out against the enemy, who were seen mustering strongly between us and the town.

The 17th, four troops of the 20th, and two of the 21st, all dismounted, formed the right column under the Hon. Brigadier-General Lumley, and heavy marching they must have found it, ankle deep in the loose sand in their hessian boots and tight leather breeches.

DEFEAT OF THE SPANIARDS.

They were soon fired upon from two heights where about 4,000 cavalry were mustered, and Sir Samuel's charger was killed, the 17th's colonel lending him another.

Auchmuty's orderly trumpeter Hudson also lost his horse, but the steady advance of the Dragoons, and a smart charge by Brownrigg's light battalion, sent the enemy back with the loss of a gun.

We halted eventually about two miles from the town, our advanced posts occupying the suburbs, and there we passed the night, very much on the alert until the sun rose.

With the morning came a determined attack; two strong columns of Spaniards and men of colour, numbering 6,000, marched out of the works in the same formation that we had employed on the previous day, cavalry on their right, infantry to the left, with a number of guns. Our advanced posts were driven in, and an out-picket of 400 men was so hotly pressed that Colonel Browne, commanding the left, ordered up three companies of the 40th, under Major Campbell, to support them.

The Somersets, wearing those tall felt shakoes known among our men as " smoke jacks " charged the Spaniards with the bayonet, meeting a most gallant resistance, and just about the moment when British valour was weighing the balance to our side, the dark green 95th and the Light Infantry attacked the flank of the column.

The Spaniards then broke, left a gun in our hands, and fled towards the town, pursued by our men, whose blood was up; the slaughter of the enemy being given by our general at 1,500—a proof of the gallantry displayed on both sides.

The other column, seeing the repulse of their comrades, drew bridle and galloped back into Monte Video.

Many of the natives retired after this to their homes, and we sat down, to use that very expressive military phrase, before the town, to take it as best we might, the obvious manner being to storm it!

Our total loss between landing and the affair just narrated was 18 killed and 119 wounded, among the latter figuring 4 rank and file of the 17th.

In the actual storming of Monte Video, the regiment played no active part, forming a portion of the reserve, under Lumley, with the 20th and 21st Light Dragoons, the 47th (John Hale's old corps), a company of the 71st, and 700 seamen and Marines.

Various batteries were constructed under difficulties, and on the 2nd February a practicable breach was reported to the general, in a wall near the south gate.

Orders were quietly issued for the storming to take place an hour before daybreak, and in the evening the governor was summoned to surrender, but made no reply.

Then, on an intensely dark night, the troops mustered, and for more than 100 of them, it was to be the last muster of all!

Colonel Browne was in command, and under him were the Rifle Corps, the Light Infantry, Grenadiers, and 38th, with the 40th and 87th in support.

The head of the advance had almost reached the breach when the enemy discovered them, and a concentrated fire of guns and musketry was poured down from the walls.

Rolled hides had been packed into the breach, and

it was a quarter of an hour before it was detected by Captain Renny, of the light company of the 40th, who was one of the first to fall as he led his men on.

The regiment passed it twice before they saw it, and the 87th, posted at the north gate, which the others were to open for them, would not wait, but scaled the wall and dropped into the town, with bayonets fixed and an Irish yell!

Monte Video was built of brick, the houses two-storied with flat roofs, and heavily grated windows in the Spanish fashion.

At the head of the unpaved streets, cannon had been planted; the housetops bristled with long muskets pointed over the parapets, and a gallant resistance was made; but, with loud cheers, our men took gun after gun, overthrew them, scored the regimental number upon them with the bayonet point, and chased the Spaniards, and creoles, and mulattoes, and all the half-hundred cross-breeds of which the garrison was composed, up streets and down streets, through gardens where a little later the orange and the cactus would be aflower; and then the dawn came, and the town was ours!

Early in the morning everything was quiet, and the women in their black mantillas were walking about as though nothing had happened.

They must have found it but a ghastly promenade, for 800 of their own people lay dead, to say nothing of 500 wounded, and there were plenty of redcoats dotted here and there in their last sleep, with sombre corpses of the Rifle Corps.

We lost some valuable officers that night, and others died of a mortification peculiar to the country; but Governor Heridobro and 2,000 men remained in our hands, and Home Popham's fiasco seemed in a fair way to be righted after all.

During the siege, the 17th were personally thanked by Auchmuty and Lumley for good work done in bringing up provisions and taking prisoners; and when the town fell, a portion of the cavalry were mounted.

Four troops of the 17th, and two of the 20th and 21st, seem to have been provided with chargers; but whether they had brought their trappings with them, or rode with the cruel Spanish bit and curious little Guacho stirrup, is not clear; in either case, it must have been rather heartrending work for the riding-master.

South American horses, good as some of them are, are not ideal mounts for a British cavalry regiment of the Line; and the spectacle of our bearskin-crested men astride long-maned, switch-tailed pintos, of all sizes and colours, may have been picturesque, but hardly up to the regulation.

Forage being difficult to obtain in the neighbourhood of Monte Video, Lieut.-Colonel Lloyd was sent up country on outpost, the rest of the regiment remaining in cantonments about the town.

According to Cannon, the regiment had 224 mounted men, and 371 dismounted, on the 1st May.

But another phase of that expedition was about to set in, the coming of Craufurd with reinforcements, and the arrival of John Whitelocke to command the whole.

* * * * * *

Brigadier-General Craufurd—the same who afterwards fell so gallantly at Ciudad Rodrigo—had sailed from Falmouth on the 11th November, 1806, with the intention of making a descent on the coast of

Chili, and, if successful, of opening up communications with Beresford across the South American continent.

Failing to find the admiral who was to accompany him, he put into the Cape, where he received the news of Beresford's surrender and orders to sail for the Rio de la Plata without delay.

His force consisted of two squadrons of the 6th Dragoon Guards, then dressed in scarlet with cocked hats, some Artillery, the 5th, 36th, 45th, 88th, and five companies of the 95th Rifles, in all about 4,311 men.

In the meantime the Government, wishing to concentrate these various forces under one leader, selected Lieut.-General John Whitelocke for the command, who, with Major-General Leveson-Gower, and the 89th Regiment, 1,000 strong, of which Whitelocke was colonel, sailed from Portsmouth in the *Thisbe* frigate, and reached Monte Video on the 10th May.

In the February previous to his arrival the 9th Light Dragoons had landed, dismounted, under the convoy of the *Nereid* frigate, and, Craufurd joining on the 15th June, the general had a very respectable army under him, which he proceeded to handle in such a manner that we lost everything in a few days and he himself his commission!

While awaiting Craufurd, sloops-of-war had been sent up the river to reconnoitre Buenos Ayres and find a suitable landing place for the troops.

The Rio de la Plata is more properly an estuary; its width at Maldonado is 150 miles; opposite Monte Video it is 80 miles from shore to shore, and at Buenos Ayres, 200 miles from its mouth, it still measures 30 miles across! Not only is it full of rocks and sandbanks, but the terrible *pampero* suddenly tears along its waters—the wind from the Pampas, which is as dreaded as the sirocco, or the typhoon of Chinese seas.

With the lead continually going, our tars sounded the treacherous shoals and little inlets until word was brought to the general that the only safe anchorage for the ships was the Bay of Ensenada de Barragon, about 30 miles east of Buenos Ayres.

The 17th and the guns were embarked at Monte Video about the middle of June, the rest of the army taking ship from Colonia, and though the passage was delayed by head winds, we eventually disembarked in small divisions on the 28th.

From the subsequent court-martial on the general commanding, it is possible to give the exact strength of the regiment at the disembarkation in the words of Lieut.-Colonel Evan Lloyd, who was called in evidence.

In reply to a question asking for the effective strength in men and horses, equipment, etc., he replied:—

"I was desired to send a detachment with the advance under Major-General Gower. The regiment consisted of 3 captains, 9 subalterns, 8 sergeants, and 187 horses; 2 horses died in the village, and several were lost in disembarking. The dismounted consisted of 4 troops, 461 rank and file, with a field officer. Forty men of the mounted and the dismounted were not disembarked till the next day. Of the mounted cavalry 2 troops were ordered to be dismounted, their saddles sent back to the ships, and ordered to put themselves under the direction of the Commissariat to carry provisions, or sick or wounded, as occasion should require. The remainder, about 30 mounted, joined at the heights of Barragon, and I believe I saw no more of them after."

The 47th, the St. Helena Militia, and the detachments of the 20th and 21st Light Dragoons were left at Monte Video. The rest of the army was divided as follows, according to the official return.

Royal Engineers, Artillery, and seamen attached to the guns, 530; Craufurd's Light Brigade—Light Battalion and 95th, 1,280; Auchmuty's 1st Brigade—5th, 87th, 7 companies of the 38th, 1st Battalion 47th, 1,990; Lumley's 2nd Brigade—17th Light Dragoons (dismounted), 88th, and 36th, 1,800; Colonel Mahon's 3rd Brigade—6th Dragoon Guards and 9th Light Dragoons (both dismounted), 40th, and 45th, 2,185; Lieut.-Colonel Lloyd's two mounted squadrons of the 17th, 156 men: total, 7,941, of which, after allowing for a reserve and various details in hospital and on detachment duty, 5,680 went in to the attack.

One of the first errors Whitelocke committed was that in connection with the mounted men of the 17th.

Two of the troops had to give up their horses to the commissariat, 30 were put in charge of the provisions, 10 rode as orderlies, and 12 were attached to an infantry brigade, and the remaining 48 formed the general's personal escort, thus effectually depriving the army of its only cavalry force at the very moment when the sandhills were full of hard-riding Spanish horse, who snapped up a staff officer in our very teeth, and otherwise hampered our advance over a difficult country. Even Evan Lloyd, the leader of the 17th, and a cavalry officer of experience whom we have seen in the American war, was retained to look after the provisions. It is said that those horses given over to the transport service broke loose when the pack-saddles were put on them, and the probability is that many were lost, as the animals of that country possess a singular instinct for finding their way to their native place, even swimming rivers and traversing hundreds of miles with unerring certainty.

In a tempest of rain the troops began their march; Mahon, with the dismounted portion of the 17th and the 40th Foot, acting as rearguard, Gower leading the advance.

Both officers were attacked, but on the 1st July Gower cleared the enemy out of the village of Reduccion, and next day passed the River Chuelo by a ford.

At the Coral de Miserere Craufurd made a brilliant charge, took nine guns and a howitzer, and penetrated into the suburbs of the city itself, afterwards falling back about a mile by Leveson-Gower's orders, and standing to arms all through that soaking, miserable night.

Next day, the 3rd, Whitelocke joined with the main body, having been misled by his guide, and on that morning Leveson-Gower sent Captain P. K. Roche of the 17th to General Liniers, who, while willing to treat, declined the terms offered.

On the 4th, Whitelocke again tried to "bluff" his adversary, who returned a manly answer on the same lines by Captain Whittingham, who afterwards distinguished himself in Spain.

There was then nothing left for it but to issue orders for the assault of the city, which was accordingly done.

Buenos Ayres was built of white stone for the most part, the houses standing in their own gardens with the usual flat roofs. The streets were unpaved, except for the sidewalks, and the centre of each thoroughfare was consequently mud in rainy weather.

Perfectly aware—from his own letters—that each housetop would be vigorously defended, and having the stern object lesson of Beresford's disaster to guide him, Whitelocke's conduct of affairs admits of no palliation.

He and Leveson-Gower drafted out a scheme between them, and the scheme was briefly this:

The whole force was cut up into wings and ordered to advance in detail by more than a dozen different routes to the far end of the city—practically three miles of march through hostile streets—*and every musket to be unloaded !*

At the far end they were to seize the houses, load, form, and at a given signal return, presumably by the same ways, and upset all opposition.

A triumphal progress, in short, through a city, every house of which was a separate fortress ! Instead of the subsequent court-martial on Whitelocke, there should surely have been an inquiry into the state of the general's brain, and into that of his major-general, who submitted the plan to him.

At half-past six on the morning of the 5th July, 1807, the troops began their march, soaked by the rain.

Auchmuty led the left, Craufurd the centre, and two 6-pounders escorted by the Carabineers and 9th Lights formed a reserve to the latter.

Among the principal reserve at the Coral de Miserere were 83 dismounted men of the 17th, armed once more with short carbines.

Auchmuty was perhaps the most successful, as he took the Retiro and Plaza de Toros, together with 32 guns and 600 prisoners, but the success was short-lived.

The town was silent as the grave as our columns entered it; not a soul was to be seen and every door was closed.

But, suddenly, above the tramp of the marching men,

and the rumble of the field pieces, they heard a few detached shots, and, as if by magic, the housetops became alive with a horde of Spanish soldiery.

Musketry, tiles, aloes in heavy boxes, furniture, and every conceivable missile was rained upon our men, and across the streets were deep trenches with cannon beyond them which poured grape shot into the columns!

Corporals preceded each wing with implements for forcing doors, but the doors were so strongly barricaded that there was nothing for it but to push on, our men rendered powerless to reply by the iniquitous order that had sent them into the midst of the enemy with empty firelocks!

Some indeed did load, but for the most part the only relief was afforded by several bayonet rushes on the guns beyond the trenches, which were overthrown and scored with the numbers of the regiments that took them.

Struggling on under the withering fire from above, the doomed columns pressed forward, and seizing on various positions—churches, convents, or private houses—tried manfully to hold their ground, while they waited in vain for the promised orders that were to reach them!

Meanwhile, 16 mounted men of the 17th, and 30 dismounted of the 9th, under Torrens and Whittingham, charged an attack on our rear and dispersed the enemy, and the same 16 men of the regiment, with 50 infantry, penetrated later on into the city and opened up communication with Auchmuty.

Ten other horsemen of the 17th kept touch with Mahon at the village of Reduccion, but it was all useless; the streets were sprinkled with British corpses; the inhabitants, black and yellow, fought with incredible ferocity; and it all ended in surrender, on terms dictated by the Spanish commander.

The treaty was signed on the 7th July, by Whitelocke and Rear-Admiral Murray on our part; all prisoners taken by the Spaniards were to be given up, and we were to embark from Monte Video in two months' time.

Our loss in killed, wounded and missing during the fiasco at Buenos Ayres amounted to more than 1,100 officers and men, the 88th. alone having 70 rank and file killed, with 3 officers, and 12 officers wounded.

Many of the shot holes made by us in the steeples of Buenos Ayres were painted black by the Spaniards, and in some cases the balls were left in the masonry as mementoes.

An interesting relic of the campaign came into the possession of the Highland Light Infantry as recently as 1881, in a faded pipe-major's banner taken from the 71st in 1806!

After a trial of more than thirty-one days by court-martial, on which sat Lord Lake (who died during the proceedings) and Sir John Moore, among other distinguished officers, Whitelocke was dismissed the service, and "Success to grey hairs, but bad luck to White locks," was a popular toast in the army for many years.

A Marlborough boy, and son of Lord Aylesbury's steward, he had entered the 14th Foot in 1777, through Aylesbury's influence; married a daughter of Mr. Lewis, Chief Clerk of the War Office, and received rapid promotion in consequence, establishing some reputation as a "parade officer," and seeing a little service with the 13th Foot in 1793, after which he was on the Home Staff, and held commands at Portsmouth and Carisbrooke.

He might have been seen in the late "twenties,"

driving in a one-horse chaise about Kensington, attended by a coachman in very shabby livery—what ought to have been an honourable career closing thus in dishonour brought about by the most unaccountable incompetence.

At the same time it is difficult to see why his second in command did not share some of the obloquy!

As late as 1830, when he went down to purchase an estate in Somersetshire, and, putting up at a village inn, invited the landlord to drink a bottle with him, mine host flung the price of the wine on the table on learning his identity, in such execration was the unfortunate man still held.

In November, the 17th, with the rest of the army, left South America, and, driven into Cork by the weather, the regiment mustered there on Christmas Eve, 1807.

In January of the new year they sailed for Portsmouth, and, disembarking on the 17th, joined the depôt at Chichester after a hard and unfruitful campaign.

Furloughs were granted up to the 20th February to all who wanted them within a hundred miles of London, and every man but one—detained through sickness—joined on the appointed day.

Nine days later, the boys in blue, 800 strong, marched for Portsmouth for their first taste of Indian service—a formidable business in those times, as we shall narrate in the following chapter.

CHAPTER X.

EARLY INDIAN SERVICE, 1808—1822.

Regiment thanked by Corporation of Chichester—Embarkation—Inspected at the Cape—Strange Coincidence—Calcutta—Bombay—Well horsed—Fanatic Rising—Mission to Persia—Cantonments at Ruttapore—New Lieut.-Colonel commanding Expedition to Cutch — New Uniform —Pindari Troubles—The Fourth Mahratta War—Gallantry of Sergeant Hampson —Pursuit of the Pindaris— Officers thanked in Orders— Another Expedition into Cutch — Regiment Turned into Lancers— Leaves for Home.

FEBRUARY, 1808, was a stormy month; the mails were snowed up; the roads, like most roads in those days, in vile condition; and as the driving rain whistled about the old walled city of Chichester, it seemed as if Nature were weeping over the departure of the 17th.

Nowadays it is not an unusual thing for drafts and regiments on the eve of foreign service to get a little out of hand, and wreak a farewell vengeance on obnoxious publicans, and "paint things pretty red" before they go; but the 17th seem to have had a soul above that kind of folly, and it is on record that they were thanked by the mayor and corporation, "who stated that they had spent £3,000 in the town in six weeks, without a single Dragoon misbehaving himself!"—the £3,000, by the way, representing arrears, which in those times often grew to an enormous amount.

On the 1st March, the China fleet of eleven sail, under convoy of the *Lion*, was ready for departure at Portsmouth, and the 17th were expected that morning, a deputation of the Court of Directors of the East India Company, with a secretary, coming down from London to superintend their embarkation, and presently the blue and white column of men, 800 strong, marched in on foot, under command of Major Lynch Cotton, an officer who had joined them the previous year.

The transports, *Hugh Inglis*, *Preston*, *Lord Nelson*, and *Calcutta*, were the ships destined for the Indian ports, and, the despatches finally closed and delivered to the pursers, the fleet dropped down stream, and Old England became a dead letter in the fullest sense of the word to most of those 800!

On the 1st June they reached the Cape, where they were inspected by Major-General the Hon. Henry George Grey, one of their own lieutenant-colonels, who had come to them from the 18th Light Dragoons in 1796, and who spoke in high terms of their condition.

On the 4th they fired a *feu de joie* in honour of the king's birthday, in connection with which event there is a curious coincidence, as on four successive years the regiment celebrated that loyal anniversary in the four different quarters of the globe, namely, at Canterbury, in Europe, in 1806; at Monte Video, in America, in 1807; at the Cape of Good Hope, in Africa, in 1808; and at Surat, in Asia, in 1809.

They reached Calcutta on the 25th August, not without incident; a fire broke out on the *Hugh Inglis* in the Hoogli, and next day a squall carried away the three topmasts, with 15 men, all of whom were rescued except one; but, landing at last, 790 strong, they were marched to Fort William, where they did garrison duty until December, losing Major Cotton, the regimental quartermaster, and 62 non-commissioned officers and men by way of a start.

Placed on the Bombay establishment, the regiment again embarked, and, sailing round the Indian peninsula, landed at Bombay, 1st February, 1809, afterwards moving up country to Surat, 153 miles north of Bombay, and about twenty from the mouth of the River Tapti.

Surat was a place of considerable importance in those days, and was the site of the first of the Company's factories, which had been established there by permission of the Mogul emperor in 1612.

The regiment was now well horsed, principally on Persians, by a well-known native dealer, named Soonderjie, each animal averaging from 450 to 500 rupees, and two galloper-guns were added to its establishment, after the then fashion, which we see in process of adoption once more in our own time.

And now, scanty as details have been for some of the earlier periods in the regiment's history, there comes a bald gap in its annals which no amount of delving in Indian journals can fill up; it is only here and there that stray mentions occur—changing of quarters, fresh officers gazetted, and the like—until towards the close of their stay, when they were engaged in the war against the Pindaris.

In the romantic background of that gorgeous East the 17th are almost lost, only coming out at rare intervals into the picture when there is a bit of fighting to be done, leaving one to regret that no record has been kept of that old time service and the interesting social side of the regiment's sojourn.

About a year after their arrival at Surat, there

was trouble with a kind of local Mahdi in Mandavi, and among the force sent out to suppress him were four troops of the 17th under Major Supple, who reached the insurgent village (Burhodun?) at dawn on the 19th January.

The fanatics, assembled on the plain before the village, declined to surrender their leader, who masqueraded as an earthly embodiment of Adam and Christ, and various other Biblical personages, and yelled defiance at the 17th, who made a feint attack, which only provoked more derision and clouds of dust.

The Dragoons then went in with a will, sabre *v.* spear, and axes fixed to a 12-foot bamboo shaft, and any amount of wild religious fury.

We had to kill 200 of them before they sought shelter in their village, and even then they were game to the last against our infantry and guns, which had come up in the meantime.

The 17th eventually burned them out, but the regimental loss was heavy : a corporal and two privates killed ; every officer with the detachment and several privates and many horses wounded, Lieutenant Adams' helmet being cut to pieces on his head.

On the 11th of the same month, a detachment under Lieutenant Charles Johnson had sailed from Bombay for Persia, to escort Sir John Malcolm's mission to that court, whither he was going to secure Persia's aid against any Russian or French attempt on the North-West.

They rejoined in December, and Sir John Malcolm sent a letter to Lieut.-Colonel Evan Lloyd, quoted at length in Cannon.

It is very laudatory of the conduct of the escort, mentioning the officer, Sergeant Willock, and the two corporals, Carrigan and Batson, and concludes with the observation "that the impression which the appearance, discipline, and private behaviour of your men has made upon all ranks in the countries through which we have travelled, is such as must do honour to the name of a British soldier."

Seventy-eight years after, according to Fortescue, the name of Sergeant Willock was found scratched among the ruins of Persepolis, with the regimental crest and motto above it, by Lieutenant Anstruther Thomson, now Major Anstruther, of the 17th; and, on the wall of Xerxes' house, "Pte. M. Cloyne, 17 L. D.s, 1810"!

The years 1811 and 1812 seem to have been years of peace, though the latter was certainly not one of plenty.

In December, 1811, the regiment had left Surat, with its green and yellow paddy fields, and moved to Ruttapore, in the northern division of Gujerat, where new cantonments had been specially constructed for them by the Bombay Engineers; and while there —in September, 1812—famine and fever broke out in the province.

The natives died by thousands, of sheer starvation, the rains having failed them for two years; and the epidemic fever that accompanied the drought carried off 4 officers and 73 men of the regiment in four months.

Those were drinking days, and days of European clothing under an Indian sun, the only difference being that the jackets were lighter blue in colour, cap-covers were worn if the headdress allowed of it —which the crested helmet certainly did not—and white trousers were also permitted: marvel is it that the mortality was not greater.

On the 1st January, 1812, they received another lieut.-colonel from the 16th Light Dragoons, the Hon. Lincoln Stanhope; Evan Lloyd, the last of the American war officers, retiring from the command on his promotion to the rank of major-general, though his name is borne on the list until 1837.

During 1813 and 1814 the 17th were constantly engaged on active service, but where, or against whom, is not clear, though they are known to have served under Sir George Holmes at that period, and where that muscular giant led his men on there was sure to be hard fighting.

As a rule he went into action with a thick stick, but when he *did* draw his sword the result was terrific; and he is known, when major with H.M.'s 75th in 1803, to have killed his man with a blow, which almost cut him in half!

In 1813 three troops repressed the Pindaris, of whom more anon.

In December, 1815, the regiment went with a force under Colonel East against the Rajah of Cutch, the ruler of a wild, volcanic country north-west of Gujerat.

The natives of Cutch were credited with every species of vice and villainy, and their land was a barren, unproductive tract of mountain and plain jutting out into the Indian Ocean, and separated from Gujerat by a curious sandy desert, called the Ran, partly submerged at certain times of the year, and white with patches of salt, left by the evaporation of the sea.

Across this desert, dangerous in some places from quicksands, the 17th marched, and for three hours they wound through the monotonous waste, seeing nothing but wild asses, which frequented the islets that here and there dotted the surface of the sandy sea; and theirs was the privilege, if indeed it was a privilege, of being the first British troops to enter the region.

Contrary to expectation, there was no opposition on the part of the natives, until they reached the town of Anjar, which was besieged, breached, and duly taken.

A couple of marches farther on was the fort and town of Bhooj, the capital of Cutch, and though our advance against it was retarded by the discovery that the wells had been poisoned with arsenic, the place eventually surrendered, and a treaty was signed.

Bhooj was destroyed by the earthquake of 1819, which so altered the channel of the Indus.

Beyond the fact that Lieutenant Oliver de Lancey was severely wounded in the arm at Anjar, nothing has been recorded of the actions of the 17th, who returned across the Ran with the new year to root out brigand chieftains on the Gulf of Cutch, a treacherous inlet where the tide boils and bubbles, and the bore rushes roaring in from the sea.

After raiding a band of pirates and capturing their fort at Dwarka, on the Gulf, the field force was broken up, and the 17th returned to their cantonments at Ruttapore in May, 1816.

It is probable that by this time they had undergone the external transformation laid down in the orders of 1812 for the uniform of the Light Dragoons—those changes which roused the ire of the Marquis of Wellington, as he then was. The crested helmet and smart laced jacket were done away with, and a flat-topped felt shako with lines introduced, making

Wellington's Peninsular Light Horse mighty like the French *chasseurs-à-cheval* at a little distance. The blue jacket gave place to a coatee, with narrow, white, lancer facings from collar to waist for the 17th; worsted epaulettes, white welts to the seams, and grey overalls with white stripes. A lancer girdle was given to them, white, with blue lines for the privates, and a white sheepskin covered the saddle in certain orders. It was a pretty dress, certainly, but not so smart as the old jacket, and the shako was in bad taste. When the 17th received the change, it is not possible to tell; it was a far cry to India in those days, and it may have been a couple of years, or even longer, before they appeared in the new rig.

And now the Pindaris, whom we have casually mentioned in 1813, began to give serious trouble, and a greater set of rascals it was never our lot to engage.

The etymology of their name, as given by Sir John Malcolm, and confirmed by the most intelligent of the people themselves, was derived from their habit of frequenting the shops of the sellers of an intoxicating liquor termed Pinda; and, assuming that to be true, it is an index to their nature.

The name occurs in Indian history as early as 1689, when they were obscure freebooters; but latterly they became a powerful community, helping the Mahrattas in their warfare, and, though banded together for the common pursuit of plunder, they were luckily recruited from all classes and creeds, with no real tie but loot and licence, otherwise they would have been more formidable.

Carrying nothing but a few cakes, and grain for their horses, they moved in bands of 2,000 or 3,000, with their women also mounted, and they would march at the rate of forty or fifty miles a day, until they came to some fertile but unprotected district, which they proceeded to harry in a manner that would have gladdened the heart of an old moss trooper.

Silently wending their way through pathless jungle, they fell on a village like a scourge of locusts, destroyed what they could not carry away, ravished, murdered, burned—their women excelling them in atrocities—and before help could be summoned they were off again, back through the almost impenetrable tangle, laden with spoil, to their fastnesses, where, while the men got drunk, the women quarrelled over the loot until it was time to start on another raid.

They were regularly employed by the various Mahratta sovereigns in the capacity of scavengers rather than fighting men, joining Scindiah *en masse* in 1804, and eventually came to have a species of headquarters, in the eastern part of the fertile Malwa district, an immense tract practically divided from Gujerat by spurs of the Vindhya range.

From this place they raided the neighbouring territory, and were taught a smart lesson by the 17th and some native infantry in 1813, but there were other interests at stake which delayed their annihilation a little longer.

Holkar and Scindiah, the two rival Mahratta leaders, had been both pulling the strings, and it was not until 1817 that we finally commenced a war during the course of which the power of the Pindaris was broken.

The Gujerat Field Force, commanded by Sir William Keir Grant, K.M.T., consisted of the 17th, under Stanhope, a native flank battalion, H.M.'s 47th, 2nd Battalion 7th Native Infantry, a Grenadier battalion, and the 1st Battalion 8th Native Infantry, to which was to be attached a contingent of two thousand of the Guickwar's Horse; and their primary object was to protect the frontier, keep an eye on the Lower Narbadá, and make themselves generally useful in case of need.

Part of the infantry of this force was despatched to Pahlanpoor at the end of October, rejoining a month later, and I find that a party of the 17th, under Lieutenant de L'Etang, suffered shipwreck in the Gulf of Cambay the same month; possibly they were a draft from home; but at any rate they were all saved, though they lost 15,000 rupees' worth of baggage.

A general advance was begun on the 4th December, along the road to Oojein, and on the 8th December, three marches from Baroda, the force entered the dense Burreeah jungle, the lurking place of the Bheels, where during the first day's march those diminutive rascals attacked the rearguard.

Two troops of the 17th went back under Stanhope, and there was a dashing fight, for the Bheels were no mean opponents, despite their appearance, and the colonel, Captain Benjamin Adams, and Cornets Smith and Marriott particularly distinguished themselves, Marriott and his horse being severely wounded.

Sergeant-Major Hampson was shot in the spine by an arrow which entered his mouth, but he wrenched it out, drew his pistol and shot the Bheel who fired it, before a gush of blood suffocated him, and he dropped dying to the ground.

The squadron was thanked in field orders next day for their spirit and steadiness, and on the 10th, the line of march led them through open country to the Dawud Ghat, in the hills that separated Gujerat from Scindiah's country, the force encamping at Dawud, where a message recalled them to a spot sixteen miles from Baroda.

Back they went through the ghat again, and had reached Jerree, two stages on the journey, when a discretionary order came to Keir Grant from the Resident, by virtue of which he sent a detachment of infantry and guns back to Baroda, and returned with the rest of his command again to Dawud.

On the 24th December the force reached Rutlam, where it was practically in touch with the armies of Sir Thomas Hislop and Sir John Malcolm, who on the 20th had inflicted a crushing defeat on Holkar at Mehidpoor.

The Mahrattas had been broken by that battle, and the next thing was to pursue them, and annihilate their allies the Pindaris.

On the 26th, a light detachment was formed under Sir John Malcolm to follow up Holkar's beaten legions next morning, and of the Gujerat Field Force the flank battalion and two squadrons of the 17th were ordered to join at Koondla on the 27th, if possible.

They came up with the general at Seeta-Mhao, where, learning that the enemy had fled in a north-westerly direction, he followed to Narghur, which he reached on the 30th, only to find that the foe had counter-marched.

Eventually, after twisting this way and that, the pursuit was stopped by orders from Hislop, who had joined with Keir Grant at Mundisoor on the 2nd January, 1818.

Holkar, seeing the game was up, came to terms, and our men were free to follow the Pindaris and wipe them off the face of the earth—if they could find them.

The Pindari *durra*, or division, which the 17th pursued was that of Cheetoo, a notorious chief, who, having betrayed his friend Kurreem Khan into the hands of his enemies, had set up as a Pindari Napoleon on his own account.

It may not be uninteresting to note here that the Mahratta war of this period was undertaken under the governor-generalship of the Marquis of Hastings—the same Lord Rawdon who had raised a memorial to Corporal O'Lavery of gallant memory.

At ten o'clock on the night of the 7th January, Keir Grant set out on a forced march with the 17th, 6 companies of the 47th, and some picturesque Mysore Horse, moving along until nine next morning.

Five guns and some baggage was all the harvest they gleaned, for the Pindaris had decamped, and it was not until the 19th that the regiment had a slap at them at the village of Mundapie.

Keir Grant marched from Parlee with 4 squadrons and some infantry, and after a twenty-mile ride came in sight of the rascals, who tried to escape.

Then the 17th galloped forward, drove some, who seemed to have stood, from their guns, and, pursuing them uphill, sabred about 100, with only one casualty, a private wounded.

After that a part of the regiment was in action at Fort Pallee, and the rest of the 17th engaged night and day in harrying the broken Pindaris without mercy.

It is a thousand pities that no records exist of what must have been a very romantic service, in a wild rolling country teeming with jungle and fordable streams.

Tiger and leopard and pig abounded at that period,

LINCOLN STANHOPE AND THE PINDARIS (*p.* 181).

and many a mysterious rustle in the bamboo must have halted the night march, and made hands tighten on the clumsy flintlock carbines.

The *joúr* was just harvested in those districts where Cheetoo's ruffians had not spread rapine; the nights were often icy cold and the daytime heat intense, but the dogged determination of the Briton was too much for the native in his own land, and the net gradually grew closer and closer.

There is mention of a fierce fight between a detachment of the 17th, under Lincoln Stanhope in person, and a body of Pindaris led by Cheetoo himself, but beyond the fact that it was in March, there is no definite information as to time and place.

The detachment, after a thirty-mile "trek," formed and charged the robbers—gay with turbans and fragments of chain mail of great antiquity. There was a short stand and a hasty flight, and again the curved sabres were plied with a will, and 200 of the enemy went to whatever kind of Paradise the Pindari thought was in store for him.

Adams, Marriott, Thompson, and, of course, the colonel, were all thanked in orders, and the work being done, the 17th returned to Ruttapore for a while.

At the end of 1818 they were in the saddle again, this time in the province of Candeish, eastward of Surat, which was ceded to "John Company" in 1819; and a detachment of 86 convalescents, presumably recovered by that time, joined Keir Grant in Cutch.

The whole regiment seems to have reassembled at Ruttapore after this, and set out under Lincoln Stanhope in May, 1820, for a final visit to Cutch, his force being generally supposed to have the invasion of Scinde for its object.

They encamped at Keyrah, between the then ruined town of Booge-booge and Mandivie, but after lying there for six months the project was abandoned, and the regiment returned to its old quarters.

Stanhope destroyed the pirate nest at Dwarka on his way back, and though the 17th were not then with him, they had to deplore the death of a popular former officer, Mr. Marriott, then lieutenant in H.M.'s 67th, aide-de-camp to the Honourable the Governor in Council, and acting brigade-major to Stanhope's force, who was mortally wounded in the affair.

From Ruttapore the regiment marched to Cambay in November, ignorant that on the 20th August they had been officially constituted a Lancer corps, and embarking in boats for Bombay, which they reached in December, bade adieu to the land of Ind, where they had spent fourteen years, and sailed for home on the 9th January, 1823, only learning the change in their designation on touching at St. Helena, according to Fortescue.

A veteran of the above campaigns, Paymaster Stephenson, was still serving with the 17th in 1856. He had joined as a private in India, in 1814; became cornet in 1844, and went through the entire Crimean War, acting as adjutant at Inkerman. Was he a son of that gallant Maroon fighter, Sergeant Stephenson, who died with the 17th in India, a disappointed man, in 1810, one wonders?

CHAPTER XI.

THE COMING OF THE LANCERS, AND THE HOME SERVICE OF "BINGHAM'S DANDIES."

Landing in England—Small Numbers but Fine Condition—Moustaches—Losses during Indian Tour—They receive a Waterloo Colonel—A Glance at the Lancers—A Waterloo Lancer and his Weapon—An Experiment by the 9th Light Dragoons—Tight Uniforms—The Lancer Dress and its Absurdities—London Duty—Canterbury—The Regiment decidedly popular there—Regimental Races—Staghounds purchased—Their Colonel's High Opinion of them—Lord Bingham—Changes in Uniform—An Officer's Outfit in the "Twenties"—Another Waterloo Colonel—William IV.'s Alterations—Regiment to be clean shaven—Cholera—A Royal Review—Prince George of Cambridge appointed.

ON Sunday, the 18th May, 1823, the first batch of the 17th came to anchor off Gravesend in the *Upnor Castle*, a free trader, and on the same day they disembarked and marched into Chatham, looking remarkably well, and the men wonderfully healthy, to quote from a contemporary account.

They arrived home only 200 strong, and when time-expireds had been dismissed, and others invalided, there remained a pitiful remnant of about 50!

At Chatham the flat-topped shakos were given up for ever and a day, the flintlock carbines sent into store, and they set about growing moustaches, and recruiting hard, and so successfully that by the end of the year they numbered 311 rank and file.

Their lieutenant-colonel, Stanhope, and Captain

Adams, who had journeyed overland, *via* Egypt—rather a feat in those days, by the way—joined the regiment at Chatham, and it is a little curious to note that of all the officers who went out with them in 1808, Benjamin Adams, then a lieutenant, was the only one who returned. Evan Lloyd was still on the list, but he had been detained on embarkation to give evidence at Whitelocke's court-martial.

In those fourteen years of Indian service the 17th had received 929 officers and men from home, and, not counting those killed in action, its losses had been 822 of all ranks!

Oliver Delancey, of American war fame, having died two months before they left Bombay, they received a new colonel in the person of Lord Robert Edward Henry Somerset, K.C.B., who had led the Household Cavalry at Waterloo and done some good Peninsular service before that; but there was shortly to come into the regiment another officer, destined to leave a strong personal mark upon its history, George Charles, Lord Bingham, who gave it the sobriquet of "Bingham's Dandies," and in after years, when third Earl of Lucan, helped to send it to death *and* glory in the Balaclava charge!

And now, having reached that period when the 17th had become Lancers, after sixty-two years' gallant service as Light Dragoons, it is proper that we should look somewhat minutely into the new weapon and its wielders, and the causes that led to its reintroduction into the British army.

For about a century and a half before the battle of Waterloo the lance had been an obsolete weapon in the British service.

In the old heroic times it was of great repute, but

with the decline of the pike in military favour the lance also passed into disuse and the sword took its place in our cavalry, as also in that of most European nations.

During the civil war between Charles I. and the Parliament there were regiments of Lancers on both sides, and some of the Dragoon regiments were armed with the weapon.

The lance of those days was 18 feet long, with a thick butt, and a leathern thong for slinging it to the arm, and, like the modern British Lancer until a recent period, its user carried sword and pistols, but no carbine.

During the eighteenth century we had no Lancers; but the wars that followed the French Revolution brought us into intimate contact with the weapon once more.

In 1807, Napoleon raised a regiment of Poles for his Guard, and in 1810 added another, known to fame as the "Red Lancers."

These *Lanciers rouges* were very gorgeous gentlemen, dressed in scarlet from head to heel, with dark blue plastrons like our present 16th, and had formed part of the army of Holland under Napoleon's brother, Louis.

In 1808, three regiments, also of Poles, were serving with the French forces in the Legion of the Vistula, and when six regiments of Light Horse Lancers were added to the Line in 1811, these three figured at their tail as the 7th, 8th, and 9th.

All these corps fought against us, either in Spain or during the Waterloo campaign, and their valour, and, one regrets to add, their brutality, were well known.

Again, there was a regiment of Uhlans among the

Black Brunswickers, and our Spanish allies had various Lancer corps, either regular or partisan.

But the Cossack seems to have finally opened the eyes of our authorities to the existence of a military something previously undreamed of in their philosophy.

When the Hetman Platoff visited this country in 1814, in the train of the allied sovereigns, an escort of his snub-nosed warriors accompanied him and were quartered at the old Portman Street Barracks.

They were Lancers of the Russian Guard; red coated, blue breeched warriors, with brown Hussar busbys, and pads of grey fur on each shoulder; the shafts of their lances painted red.

There are possibly people yet living who can remember those barbarians solemnly escorting their chief to the ball, and then, dismounting at ease, lying down with their backs against the railings in the centre of a London square and smoking the hours away until they were once more called to horse.

It was decided at last that we must have Lancers, and Lieut.-Colonel Hervey de Montmorency, a Peninsular officer of more than usual intelligence for those times, is credited with having been a prime mover in their introduction.

If the idea of the arm itself was taken from association with our allies, the actual weapon was a direct legacy from Waterloo, for Captain Mercer, of "Mercer's Battery" — so famous for the mound of dead and dying that lay before its position — was indirectly responsible for the type of lance ultimately adopted by the British army. His language is so good —indeed, his journal is by far the most picturesque book yet written on the Waterloo campaign—that I have transcribed his account of the affair.

It was the morning after the battle, and the gallant captain was strolling over the field.

"I had satisfied my curiosity at Hougoumont, and was retracing my steps up the hill, when my attention was called to a group of wounded Frenchmen by the calm, dignified, and soldier-like oration addressed by one of them to the rest. I cannot, like Livy, compose a fine harangue for my hero, and, of course, I could not retain the precise words, but the import of them was to exhort them to bear their sufferings with fortitude; not to repine, like women or children, at what every soldier should have made up his mind to suffer as the fortune of war, but, above all, to remember that they were surrounded by Englishmen, before whom they ought to be doubly careful not to disgrace themselves by displaying an unsoldierly want of fortitude. The speaker was sitting on the ground, with his lance stuck upright beside him—an old veteran, with a thick, bushy, grizzly beard, countenance like a lion—a lancer of the Old Guard, and no doubt had fought in many a field. One hand was flourished in the air as he spoke, the other, severed at the wrist, lay on the earth beside him; one ball (case-shot, probably) had entered his body, another had broken his leg.* His suffering, after a night of exposure so mangled, must have been great, yet he betrayed it not. His bearing was that of a Roman, or perhaps of an Indian warrior, and I could fancy him concluding appropriately his speech in the words of the Mexican king, 'And I, too—am I on a bed of roses?' I could not but feel the highest veneration for this brave man, and told him so, at the same time offering him the only consolation in my power—a drink of cold water, and assurances that the waggons would soon be sent round to collect the wounded. He thanked me with a grace peculiar to Frenchmen, and eagerly inquired the fate of their army. . . After a very interesting conversation I begged his lance as a keepsake, observing that it never could be of further use to him. The old man's eyes kindled as I spoke, and he emphatically assured me that it would delight him to see it in the hands of a brave soldier, instead of being torn from him, as he had feared, by those vile peasants. So I took my leave, and walked away with the lance in my hands. Ever since,

---

* It is more than likely that they were from Mercer's own guns.—D. H. P.

my groom (Milward) has been transformed into my lancer-orderly; and I propose, if ever I return to England, consecrating it to the memory of the interesting old hero." (In a footnote Mercer adds) "During the remainder of the campaign Milward carried it; and on returning to England I even rode into Canterbury followed by my lancer—a novelty in those days. Whilst in retirement on half-pay, it was suspended in my library, but on going to America in 1823 I deposited it in the Rotunda at Woolwich. On my return in 1829 the lance was gone. In 1823 or 1824 it seems Lieut.-Colonel Vandeleur, of the 9th Lancers, came to Woolwich to look for a model. Mine pleased him, and he took it to St. John's Wood Riding-house, where it was tried against others in the presence of the Duke of York, and approved of as a model for arming the British lancers. After a long hunt I at last found it at the Enfield manufactory, spoilt completely, the ironwork and thong taken off, and flag gone. It cost me a long correspondence with the Board before I succeeded in getting it restored and put together. When I received it from him who had so long wielded it, the flag was dyed in blood, the blade notched and also stained with blood; inside the thong was cut 'Clement VII.,' probably the number of his troop."

This interesting relic afterwards passed into the possession of Dr. Hall, another old Waterloo man, who has now joined the great majority; and it would seem only in accordance with the universal fitness of things that the 9th Lancers, as the senior regiment of the arm, should possess the trophy if it be still in existence.

The following account appears in the *Sun*, 22nd April, 1816, and is headed, "Improvements in Military Tactics—a new corps."

"The commander-in-chief, ever indefatigably alive to the important duties which His Royal Highness has to fulfil, means to introduce that powerful auxiliary to the military system, viz. a Corps of Lancers, constituted upon Polish principles. They are to be attached to each regiment of cavalry, for the express purpose of operating in a similar manner to the rifle corps belonging to the infantry. The idea of this measure had been some time in agitation, when the Earl of Rosslyn tendered his admirably appointed legion, the 9th Light Dragoons, to effect the desired innovation. Arrangements were made about a month since; and Captain Peters (a young, active, and, perhaps, one of the most intelligent officers of the British army, who had seen much service) was selected to drill 50 picked men, all under 30 years of age, and 5 feet 8 inches in height.

"The utmost diligence was exercised to perfect this little force, and they had arrived, about a week since, at such an *acme* of perfection as to receive the almost unqualified approbation of their master. Things being thus speedily accelerated, a day was appointed for the review, and on Saturday (April 20th) it took place, in the Queen's Riding-house, at Pimlico, in the presence of but very few spectators, and those only were admitted by ticket.

"The men were drawn out in line, at eleven o'clock precisely, dressed in blue jackets, faced with crimson, grey trousers, and blue cloth caps or bonnets. Each man, mounted on a high-bred charger, carried a lance 16 feet long; about 21 inches from the point appeared a flag, with the *Union* colours. The opposite extremity was confined in a leathern socket, affixed to the stirrup. They also had sabres by their sides, and holster-pistols in the saddle-bow. The lance was supported near the centre by a loose string, through which each man thrust his arm, and then the lance reclined in the rear, which it always did after the sword was brought into use.

"The arrival of the Earl and Countess of Rosslyn, and

a party of distinguished fashionables, was the signal for the commencement of operations. The different cavalry modes of attack were resorted to with the sword and lance alternately; when the latter was used, some very original and pleasing manœuvres were practised with complete success, particularly when the figure eight was formed by the different bodies, within a very narrow space; it was managed with an adroitness and facility astonishingly clever. The spectators were delighted with the scene, which lasted for an hour and a half.

"The object of the figure was to show how quickly a line might be broken in any direction, and formed again without any apparent disorder.

"It is thus confidence will be given to the soldier, and prevent his ever being at a loss to regain his position, should a sudden impulse for the moment overwhelm him.

"The purpose of the flag is to throw the enemy's horse into confusion, which would be the case almost invariably."

The authorities were so satisfied with the result of that old time "musical ride" that, instead of a troop being attached to each corps as originally intended, four entire regiments, the 9th, 16th, and 23rd Light Dragoons in 1816, and the 12th in 1817, were armed as Lancers, and a special uniform, as *nominally* Polish as our Hussars' was Hungarian, was given to them.

At that period, as is well known, the Prince Regent had considerable influence on the fashions, and it is recorded, on the authority of a Lancer colonel, that when the eventful moment arrived for the prince's uniform to be tried on, an officer of rank was summoned to attend with the tailor.

The soul of the royal George abhorred a crease; the new jacket must fit him like a glove or he would have none of it; so that what with seams and oversewing, the model those great minds produced was a marvel of the genus "skintight," and, in common with the rest of our cavalry, the Lancers could hardly go through the sword exercise; how they ever managed to clear the tops of their caps with the lance remains a mystery to this day. Perhaps they did not try—possibly they knocked them off, for strange things were done at that period when the Dragoons lost their helmets at the trot, and a commanding officer had to ask permission to be inspected in forage caps because there was a breeze on Brighton Downs!

The Light Dragoon jacket, with its plastron, as adopted in 1812, was preserved almost unaltered, and the four regiments kept to their existing facings with the exception of the 12th, which changed from bright yellow to scarlet.

The trousers were hideously ugly, and called "Cossack"; very full, and narrowing over the boot, pleated at the hips and waist like a modern dancer's accordion skirts.

Large epaulettes weighed down the shoulders—the men had brass scales; a mammoth aiguilette, after the fashion of an exaggerated bell-pull, cumbered the freedom of the left arm, but the crowning glory was the *chapska* or helmet.

It was of cane, covered with cloth, not unlike the modern pattern, but larger, taller, and terribly uncomfortable.

Lieutenant-Colonel John Luard, who wore it at Bhurtpore, tells us that it was nearly the worst headdress ever invented.

The aiguilette, he says, was done away with by 1824, in which case, if he is correct, Salisbury's drawings so admirably reproduced by Fortescue are wrong; certainly there are errors to be found in some of them.

In June, 1824, the regiment moved to Regent's Park Barracks, and took the London duty for the first time in its history.

Very smart no doubt they looked, with their drooping plumes of scarlet and white, and long pennons—an unaccustomed spectacle to the Cockneys, used to the giant Lifeguardsmen, with their huge bearskin crested helmets and high boots, and the then recently re-adopted cuirass.

The Lancer privates of that day wore black leather sabretasches, and white sheepskins over their blue saddle-cloths, the hind flaps of which were looped up below the valise when in marching order; while the officers, when *en grande tenue*, presented a glitter of silver lace and embroidery that must have created a sensation even in Bond Street, where gorgeous uniforms were not uncommon.

After being reviewed, on the 9th July, by the commander-in-chief, with the 8th Hussars, the regiment left Regent's Park on the 10th for Canterbury, where they arrived on Wednesday, the 14th, bag and baggage, and proceeded to make themselves very popular.

In looking through the local records of a military centre like Canterbury, whose walls had scarcely ceased to echo the blare of trumpets and the roll of drums for five-and-twenty years, one is struck by the different manner in which the advents and departures of regiments are mentioned.

In many cases, one finds the simple announcement that "On Friday last, the —th Light Dragoons marched in, and are to occupy quarters in this town"; and, perhaps a year later, "This morning the —th Light Dragoons left in two divisions for Coventry," or John O'Groat's, or where you will, and never another allusion to them for the whole of their stay; with others it is different, and it is possible to gauge the measure of a corps' good conduct, or the reverse, by these signs and tokens.

The 17th, as Lancers, seem to have stood high in local esteem with the Canterbury folk; there was evidently money in the regiment, and it was laid out to advantage.

The first thing we hear of them is, not unappropriately, their music—on the occasion of the laying of the foundation stone of a new corn market, when a dinner was given at the Rose Inn, and "the evening was spent with a great deal of hilarity, not a little hightened (sic) by some excellent airs played by the band of the 17th Lancers." As a matter of fact, the entire town seems to have got drunk at the expense of the mayor and corporation; but that was a mere detail in the "twenties."

The following month witnessed the Canterbury races, held on those Barham Downs where the regiment had been so often paraded during their previous stay; and it was announced with considerable flourish of trumpets that the officers of the 17th were subscribing a stake of £50, besides other matches, "it being impossible to bestow too much praise on them for their spirited encouragement of sport," etc., etc.

On the last day of the meeting, Friday, August 20th, these old time regimental events were run, amid a tremendous concourse of spectators, in spite of bad weather.

The first was:—

A MATCH. Last half-mile for Fifty Guineas. Owners to ride.
12 stone each.
Major Luard's chestnut gelding, VOLUNTEER.
Captain Locke's bay gelding, KNIGHT ERRANT.

Captain Locke won, and the strains of the regimental band heralded the contest for

THE GARRISON PLATE OF £50, for horses bona-fide the property of the officers of the 17th Lancers. One mile heats. 12 stone each. Gentlemen riders.
Major Willington's chestnut gelding, RED GAUNTLET, by Morie Bell.
Lieut. Robbins' chestnut gelding, SILVER TAIL.
Lieut. Clarke's chestnut gelding, SWORDSMAN, by Swordsman.

Mr. Clarke's horse came in first, and one is led to wonder, from the prevalence of chestnuts, whether that colour may not have been affected by the regiment at that time.

In October the officers bought a pack of staghounds from a Mr. Sawbridge, of Olantigh, the local gentry giving them permission to hunt over their ground, and I find a meet fixed for the 20th, and another on Monday, the 22nd.

Lincoln Stanhope seems to have been a considerable sportsman, with elements of the gay and festive in his composition, and his name occurs at most of the neighbouring races and convivial assemblies; he did not disdain even to secure the services of Mr. Flemmington, the ventriloquist, for an entertainment at which he and the officers were present, as also "the excellent band of the regiment," which seems to have had no dearth of engagements; but in the meantime, the more serious round of duty was not neglected, and on the 30th October Lord Edward Somerset reviewed them—in the mud—putting them through a variety of evolutions, and expressing himself in the highest terms of the advanced state of discipline at which the regiment had arrived, though "they are nearly all recruits," says a reporter.

At last, in June, 1825, they received orders to move, and leaving Canterbury on the 9th, took the London road once more, and found themselves at Albany Street for a short time, until they were moved to Brighton and Chichester, from whence they went to Exeter and Topsham the following year, when Lord Bingham joined them.

He was then a major of twenty-six, with ten years' service, and on the 9th November succeeded Stanhope as junior lieut.-colonel.

It might be supposed, from the regimental nickname associated with his tenure of command, that dress and drill were Lord Bingham's ruling passion; he certainly brought the 17th to a wonderful pitch of perfection at a period when pipeclay and parade seemed the sum total of a soldier's calling; but the new lieut.-colonel had higher aspirations, and like his contemporary, George Cathcart, sought active service with the Russian army, which they were both destined to fight in the Crimea.

He obtained leave to join the camp on the Pruth in 1828, and served as a volunteer under Diebitsch against the Turks at Varna, Schumla, and Widden; commanding a cavalry division under the walls of Adrianople in 1829, and returning to his regiment with the decoration of a Knight of St. Anne, and, no doubt, some new and original ideas about the lance exercise from a close acquaintance with the Cossacks.

He is said to have paid £20,000 for his lieut.-colonelcy, in his desire to secure the actual command of the 17th.

In 1827 they were at Hounslow and Hampton Court, and did duty at the funeral of the Duke of York, marching to Liverpool the following spring *en route* for Ireland.

In 1829 the uniform of the regiment shows another change, the white plastron disappearing for a time, the plume being now black, and the trousers of light grey becoming a curious shade of slate colour, known as the "Oxford mixture."

A detailed list, with the prices, of a Lancer officer's dress and undress uniforms for the year 1829 may not be uninteresting in this place, showing that there was evidently a tendency towards economy in the closing years of George IV.

DRESS.

	£	s.	d.
Jacket	19	11	0
Overalls with lace	5	8	6
Spurs	0	10	0
Cap and feather	18	9	3
Girdle	3	3	0
Sabre and knot	12	6	0
Waistbelt and tasche	12	12	0
Pouch and belt	11	9	0
Dress overalls	4	11	6

UNDRESS.

	£	s.	d.
Shell jacket	8	3	6
Overalls with cloth stripe	2	12	0
Sword-knot and scabbard	3	15	6
Waistbelt and tasche	3	13	6
Greatcoat	9	4	0
Cap	3	7	0
Forage cap	2	10	3
Cloak	7	1	7
Horse appointments for one horse	37	8	0
Total	165	15	7

In November of this year, Somerset was removed to the 1st Royal Dragoons, and a very interesting soldier became colonel of the 17th in his place—Sir John Elley, a veteran of Flanders, Spain, and Waterloo, and whose story will be found in the appendix.

While the regiment was in Ireland the king died, and another great alteration took place in their costume with the accession of the new monarch.

When William IV. came to the throne he set about clothing the army in scarlet, and so fond does his majesty appear to have been of the national colour that he even substituted it for the facings of the navy, in place of the historic white, which George II. is traditionally believed to have adopted for the sea-service from the Duchess of Bedford's blue and white riding-habit in 1748.

A great wave of red went over our forces, and the Lancers did not escape; in fact the 16th retain their scarlet tunics to this day.

The new changes were embodied in an official regulation dated 18th May, 1831, a copy of which is in my possession, and from it I extract a few details to illustrate the Lancer of the "thirties."

The coat was to be double-breasted, with two rows of gold buttons, nine in each row: a Prussian collar 3 inches deep, and a 7-inch skirt, with plenty of gold embroidery plastered here and there.

Bright bullion epaulettes, $2\frac{1}{2}$ inches deep, adorned the shoulders; blue cloth trousers fitted tight to the legs and had two gold stripes down each outer seam for full dress, scarlet ones for undress.

The helmet, or lancer-cap, as it was called in those days, was a colossal affair, with a trencher top 10 inches square, covered with white cloth for the 17th, and having gold cord running up the angles and crossing transversely over the top.

A large gilt plate in front bore the royal arms and the regimental device, and a plume of black cocktail drooped from the bullion rosette, 16 inches long in front and 9 inches at the back.

The spurs, 2 inches long, were of yellow metal; the sword steel mounted, with a blade of $35\frac{1}{2}$ inches.

A round scarlet stable-jacket was also ordered, "with small gilt studs quite close down the front," steel spurs for undress, and a blue forage cap with a gold band.

Another change was made at the same time by the abolition of moustaches, which were only to be retained by the Hussars; so that the regiment was completely metamorphosed before they had done with it, in all but its proverbial smartness.

Some idea of the alteration effected by the razor may be gathered from the fact that when, in the "twenties," a "gentleman ranker" and another private deserted with their officer's mufti, and shaved themselves, their sergeant was in their company for a quarter of an hour before he could recognise them!

After four years of Irish service—and some of it was rough work in Clare—with a touch of Asiatic cholera that carried off three men in Dublin, they returned to England, and were isolated in country quarters for fear of infection, eventually going to Gloucester, and in 1833 to Hounslow.

While there they were reviewed at Windsor by the king, who told the colonel and Lord Bingham that he considered the regiment "perfect"; afterwards inviting the officers to dinner in St. George's Hall, where he reminded them that he had reviewed them at New

York when he was a young naval midshipman, at the same time recalling some particulars of their uniform and services.

The next twenty years were comparatively uneventful: colonels died, and new ones were appointed—in 1842, Prince George of Cambridge, the present duke, now colonel-in-chief. In 1840 they went back to blue clothing, and from that time their history is one of parades, assisting the civil power, and the usual change of quarters, until the eventful year 1854 which brought them to a very important participation in the famous Crimean war.

CHAPTER XII.

THE 17TH IN THE CRIMEA, AND THE REGIMENTAL STORY OF THE BALACLAVA CHARGE.

Under Orders—The Band—Embarkation and Enthusiastic Send-off—A Little Joke in the Dardanelles—Cholera—Bulganak—Alma—Mackenzie's Farm—Exact Crimean Uniform—Balaclava—Butcher Jack—Officers of the 17th—Dress of the Light Brigade—Nolan and the Order—The Word of Command—Death of Nolan—The Charge—Morris—Jack Penn—Berryman and Captain Webb—O'Hara—France to the Rescue—Lances Shattered—Total Losses—Wounded of the 17th—Narrow Escape of Captain Morris—Wooden's Nickname—"Blood" Smith—Strange Memento—The Balaclava Bugle—"Siamese Twins"—Cornet Cleveland—Drafts for the 17th—Winter Quarters at Ismid—Home Once More.

THE causes that led up to the Crimean war are too well known to need more than a passing word here.

The original "cloud in the East," old as the Crusades, was the custody of the Holy Sepulchre; and the thousand and one political considerations to which it gave rise may be found in a thousand and one histories; suffice it for our purpose to record that we formed an alliance with France to help the Turk against Russia, and that the spring of 1854 saw us busy with military preparations on a larger scale than had been necessary since the days of Waterloo.

The 17th were then lying at Hounslow, with D troop taking the Hampton Court duty, and the six troops of which the regiment then consisted were at once formed into four for service, and two for the depôt at Brighton, the first-named being 314 strong, of all ranks; the latter 72.

By the middle of April, those destined to remain behind had been carefully weeded out and the band broken up.

It had consisted of some 20 performers, many of them foreigners, who claimed their discharge, while about 3 were turned into the ranks.

Two brothers named Deakon—1st cornet and trombone—deserted; were traced to the orchestra at the notorious Argyle Rooms, but, eluding pursuit, were afterwards heard of travelling with Wombwell's Menagerie.

Through Godalming and Petersfield the regiment marched for Portsmouth, the advanced portion being billeted at Emsworth and Havant, until the five merchant vessels hired by Government for their conveyance were ready to receive them.

At last, on Tuesday, 18th April, the *Ganges* and *Pride of the Ocean* were alongside the dockyard; the former, officially known as Transport No. 20, being a rapid sailer of about 950 tons; the other, Transport No. 21, a beautiful American clipper ship of 1,400 tons.

The weather was magnificent, the town full of Easter holiday-makers, and the whole place agog to witness the embarkation, the band of the 79th Highlanders marching up the London road to meet the first division and play it to the waterside.

About a mile out, the head of the blue column came in sight, and to the strains of "Cheer, boys! cheer!" and "Oh Susannah, don't you cry for me," the gallant lads, with their red and white pennons fluttering gaily from the lance shafts, rode in through streets thronged with onlookers, who cheered them to the echo, and dismounted near the quay somewhere about ten o'clock.

It was the first time for 46 years that they had left for active service, and only the second occasion in the whole of their history that they were taking their own horses with them.

The mounts were very restive, and the process of slinging them on board the *Pride of the Ocean* was an exciting one, performed under the eye of their colonel—Lawrenson—and a fashionable gathering.

One man, Housden, was badly kicked on the head, but, in reply to the colonel's inquiry, said it was nothing to the cuts he expected to get before long, and the whole of the 80 horses were eventually stalled in less than three hours, leaving the coast clear for the advent of the second division, which arrived about 3.30, and transferred themselves on to the *Ganges*, both vessels dropping down to Spithead the same evening.

On the 23rd, 24th, and 25th, the remainder of the regiment went on board the *Eveline* (headquarter ship), the *Blundell*, and the *Edmundsbury*.

An idea had gained ground that our cavalry was to be shipped across the Channel, and from thence to make a triumphal progress through Paris to Marseilles, a wag in the French capital going so far as to perpetrate a huge hoax on thousands of the Parisians, who assembled at a Paris terminus to witness their arrival on that very significant of dates—April the First! But a long sea voyage was before them, and, after a variety of experience, they reached the Dardanelles about the middle of May.

On the 18th, the *Ganges* anchored astern of the *Pride of the Ocean*, waiting for steamers to tow them up, and the tug, by some mistake, taking charge of the hindmost ship first, a little pleasantry was indulged in as she passed her consort, Captain Winter, of E troop, on the *Ganges*, telling his trumpeter to sound "revallay"—a kind of "Now then, you fellows, wake up!"

The skipper of the other vessel was not to be outdone, though, and, shaking loose his foresails, forged ahead and passed the *Ganges;* whereupon, Captain Webb, of D troop, ordered his trumpeter, Landfried, who still survives, to sound the "Trot!"

It is said that while waiting the arrival of the tugs, Captain Winter and Cornet Cleveland were rowed ashore in a boat, and, making a bet who would land first, both jumped over in shallow water and splashed their way towards the beach, Winter, a very tall man, winning, and so enjoying the honour of being the first of the Cavalry Brigade to touch Turkish ground. Alas! neither of them was destined to set foot on English soil again!

The regiment walked its horses ashore at Kulali—twenty-six had died on the voyage—and on the 30th May it was inspected by the Sultan, Abdul-Medjid, at Scutari, and, re-embarking on 2nd June, sailed for Varna, where it swam its cattle from the ships, and there became part of Cardigan's immortal Light Brigade on the 4th.

On the 8th it marched to Devna, eighteen miles off, encamped there until the 28th July, and moved on to Yeni-bazar, where cholera came into its ranks and carried off 12 men.

It was back in Varna at the end of August, and, embarking on the 2nd and 3rd September, sailed for the Crimea, losing 2 more men on the voyage, and landed on the 17th at Kalamita, or, as our fellows called it, "Calamity" Bay.

The regimental strength was then only 247 of all

ranks, and on the 19th the allied army set out on its march towards Sebastopol.

The infantry was in close column, the 17th being in rear of the left flank, from which position it was hurried up with the 8th Hussars to support the advance guard, which came in touch with the Russian cavalry across the Bulganak River, in the afternoon.

There was some carbine firing, and a few horses were killed; our Horse Artillery galloped forward and let fly, but the enemy declined to attack us, and after a little booming of guns on both sides, we bivouacked in battle array, and so spent the night that preceded Alma.

Alma was an infantry fight, but the 17th followed the Highland Brigade without orders, incurred the forcible displeasure of fiery Sir Colin Campbell, and were capturing prisoners on the heights when Lord Raglan stopped pursuit.

There were early complications with the French commanders, and one of the first was a two days' wait before we again advanced, but on the 24th our cavalry went forward as far as the Belbec River, to find all quiet in that direction.

On the 25th we began a flank march through woods and swamps to gain the south side of Sebastopol, against the wish of Lord Raglan, who had intended to attack the city from the north, and on the march we fell in with the Russian baggage and rearguard at the Khutor Mackenzie, or Mackenzie's farm, as our men christened it, named after a Scottish admiral in the Russian service.

There was a bit of a scrimmage, the Greys dismounting to skirmish, and some Rifles hurrying up on gun limbers, one of the enemy on the other side of a marsh potting us with so much success that Lord Cardigan is said to have offered £5 to the first man who would shoot him.

"Jack" Berryman, of the 17th, captured three prisoners, and we took some waggons, the army afterwards bivouacking on the Tchernaya, and eventually coming to a halt on the plains of Balaclava, where the real business of war commenced.

In common with the rest of the British forces, the 17th had landed in the clothes they stood in, and were destitute of everything; even their round-ended valises had been left on board ship and were not forthcoming.

Their uniform was a blue double-breasted jacket, with white collar, cuffs, and turnbacks to the tails, but no "butterfly" on the breast, which was not adopted until the tunic of 1855 was served out.

Their dress caps were worn cased the whole time; their trousers of lightish grey with two white stripes were strapped with cloth up to the fork, the booted-overall being adopted afterwards, and the saddle was placed over a white blanket folded to eighteen thicknesses, or plie, the blue cloak being folded in front over the holsters, and a black sheepskin above all.

On the shoulders were the circular brass pads and scales, and below the red and yellow girdle at the back was a little ornamental tuft of white wool, old as the regulation of 1812.

Water bottle and white havresack completed their appearance; all these details being here placed on record from the mouth of one who wore the dress.

And now began an arduous spell of patrol and outpost duty, which severely taxed our weak cavalry regiments, who suffered too from the cold, and who had also to put up with a considerable amount of chaff from the rest of the army, which made them the more resolved when *their* time came.

Colonel Lawrenson having gone home invalided, Major Willett took command of the 17th, and the major dying on the 23rd October, Captain Morris, hearing of a probable attack on Balaclava, threw up his staff appointment and returned to the regiment on the 24th, still wearing his staff-undress, frock-coat and forage cap.

It must be borne in mind that Balaclava, straggling along the edge of the deep, land-locked harbour, was our base, and the spot from whence our supplies— when any could be drawn, which was not often— were obtained; and Sir Colin Campbell, with the 93rd Highlanders and some Turks, was charged with its defence; Lucan's Cavalry Division, which consisted of Scarlett's Heavy and Cardigan's Light Brigades, being encamped close by.

As is well known, Cardigan and Lucan—the 17th's former Lord Bingham—were brothers-in-law, and there was bad blood between them, which was not appeased by the stirring events that followed.

It was the custom of the cavalry to stand to their horses an hour before dawn, to await the staff-officers' reports from the outlying pickets, and then, all being reported quiet, to dismiss for breakfast; but on the morning of the 25th October, as, indeed, for two or three mornings, there was no breakfast for them; Lord Lucan, with the first grey streak of daybreak, espying a signal on the flagstaff of the Causeway Heights that warned him that the enemy were coming on in force!

Lord George Paget, commanding the 4th Light

Dragoons, at once galloped back to his men, and as Lord Cardigan was still on board his yacht *Dryad*, on which it was his habit to sleep the night, Paget got the Light Brigade into the saddle, Lucan sending down an order immediately after for the cavalry to advance.

Later in the morning they were retired a little out of gun-shot, and waited in that position, with their faces to the foe, until the arrival of the famous order that sent them to glory and the grave!

With the "thin red line" of Highlanders (and about thirty Guardsmen) we have nothing to do in this place, nor yet with the immortal "three hundred" and the rest of Scarlett's horsemen; their exploits took place in the south valley, and constitute one of the reddest and most lustrous pages in British history; our mission is with the Light Brigade, and more particularly with the 17th Lancers.

Picture two grassy valleys, running roughly east and west, and divided by the Causeway Heights.

South of the southernmost valley, Sir Colin's Highlanders, barring the way to Balaclava, and a dense mass of Russian cavalry pouring over the heights towards them, only to be repulsed by their magnificent steadiness and withering fire, and afterwards by the daring dash of Scarlett's men.

At the western end of the north valley—spectators of the fight and burning to take part in it—the Light Brigade, with Cardigan at its head, glittering in his brilliant 11th Hussar uniform, and cursing the bad luck that kept him inactive.

At this time the Brigade was drawn up with three of its five skeleton regiments in the first line: the 11th Hussars on the left, the 17th Lancers in the centre, and the 13th Light Dragoons on the right, with the 4th Light Dragoons and 8th Hussars behind them; when the moment for the advance arrived the 11th were formed in a second line, thus leaving the 17th and 13th in front.

Captain Morris, whom we have seen return to his regiment on the eve of action, was senior captain of the 17th, and had seen considerable service in India, although he was only thirty-four; having been at Maharajapore, wounded at Aliwal, and present with the army of the Sutlej; and earlier in the day he had urged Cardigan to let him go in with the 17th to help the Heavies, without avail.

The regiment mustered only 139 strong, but at the last moment it received a rather gruesome addition in the person of the regimental butcher, John Veigh, who rode up in a canvas smock, blood-stained from the shambles, selected the better of two spare swords, and with a short black pipe alight took his place in the ranks.

Like Morris he scented a fight and meant to be there; and it is on record that two butchers of the Heavies had done the same thing with their brigade.

The officers with the 17th that morning were:— Morris, commanding; Captain Robert White, of C troop, who led the 1st squadron; Captain John Pratt Winter, of E troop, who led the 2nd squadron; Captain A. F. C. Webb, who led D troop; Captain the Hon. Godfrey C. Morgan (now Lord Tredegar), who led B troop; Lieutenant J. H. Thompson, of C troop; Lieutenant Sir W. Gordon, Bart., of E troop; Lieutenant J. W. Cradock-Hartopp, serrefile; Lieutenant and Adjutant J. Chadwick; and Cornet Archibald Cleveland, serrefile—Cornet Wombwell riding on Cardigan's staff.

With the exception of the brigadier, who was a perfect demon in the matter of dress and equipment, there was very little show in that group of 670 odd horsemen, drawn up at the mouth of the north valley.

Their uniforms were stained and patched, their shirts, to quote the words of one of them, " were simply rotting off their backs"; the Lancers' caps and the Light Dragoons' shakos were covered with oilskin cases, the Hussars wore no plumes—the smart dangling pelisses of the 11th had been put on as an extra garment, but the three weak troops of the 8th had to dispense with the luxury, their pelisses having been lost in transit between ship and shore.

It was essentially a blue brigade, save for the crimson overalls and busby bags of the 11th, the touch of faded scarlet on the head-dress of the 8th and the collars and cuffs of the 4th Lights, and the white facings of the two remaining regiments, which had probably forgotten the taste of pipeclay for many a day.

But a flash of colour darted up to Lucan as Captain Nolan, of the 15th Hussars, in full uniform, brought the order whose misinterpretation caused such harrowing slaughter and subsequent discussion; and properly to understand the facts, it is necessary to glance at the position of the ground and the forces of the enemy in and about the north valley.

The Causeway Heights, which we have spoken of as dividing the two valleys, had been taken by the Russian cavalry when they encountered the Heavy Brigade earlier in the morning, and though Scarlett's charge had driven them back, the heights themselves, bristling with the Allied redoubts, remained in the enemy's hands.

Lord Raglan from his position had a clear view of

the field, and seeing that another body of Russian Horse was approaching, escorting artillery with lasso-tackle, he concluded that their object was the removal of our guns from the redoubts, and at once took steps to prevent it.

The final order is historically known as the "fourth," following as it did on three previous ones to advance the cavalry, and it was brought by Nolan, in writing:

> "Lord Raglan wishes the cavalry to advance rapidly to the front, follow the enemy, and try to prevent the enemy carrying away the guns. Troop of Horse Artillery may accompany. French cavalry is on your left. Immediate.
> "(Signed)   R. AIREY.'

This order was misinterpreted by Lord Lucan, though he shows in his subsequent despatch that he knew well enough which guns were intended; there were circumstances, however, that seem to have upset his judgment at a moment when it ought to have been calm.

He questioned the advisability of the order to the aide-de-camp, who, a mighty believer in the efficacy of cavalry under any conditions, ventured to observe in reply, "Lord Raglan's orders are that the cavalry should attack immediately."

"Attack, sir! attack what?—What guns, sir?"

It is only fair to add that the redoubts were not actually visible from Lucan's position, though that really matters very little when his despatch is considered.

"There, my lord, is your enemy, there are your guns," said Nolan, waving his hand, largely, towards the valley and speaking with some warmth: it was not for him to particularise, he was evidently chafing at the delay, and his tone has been deprecated as conveying something in the nature of a rebuke.

It was the younger school impatient with one whose traditions dated back to the Georges, and the earl was not unnaturally angered.

Choosing to accept Nolan's waving arm as indicative of the true direction, he trotted back alone to Cardigan, and ordered him to attack the Russians at the other end of the valley, Cardigan saluting in reply, and suggesting difficulties, as the enemy had batteries in front and on both flanks.

Lord Lucan shrugged his shoulders, saying that "There was no choice but to obey," and the rest of the affair lay in Cardigan's hand, Lucan simply ordering the 11th Hussars back into second line.

Cardigan, two lengths in front of Wombwell and Maxse, and about five from the first rank of the men, after giving instructions to Lord George Paget, turned his head and said, "The line will advance, right squadron 17th will direct," and moved forward at a trot.

Survivors question the sounding of any trumpet!

Scarcely had the Light Brigade traversed a hundred paces when Cardigan's military instincts received a severe shock, for Captain Nolan, who was riding with them, swept across his front from left to right, pointing wildly with his sword towards the redoubt on the Causeway Heights, and shouting, "Threes right!" in a vain endeavour to alter the direction which he knew to be absolutely wrong.

Captain Morris shouted, "That won't do, Nolan; we've a long way to go, and must be steady," and Cardigan, boiling with anger at what he thought presumptuous interference, cried with great vehemence, "No, no! Threes back into line!"

Then the first shell burst, a splinter striking Nolan in

the heart, and the advancing troopers saw a strange sight.

The sword fell from the upraised hand, but the arm remained in the air. The legs still gripped the saddle, and the body was yet erect, as his horse turned and galloped back along the line, and one agonised shriek burst from his lips, never to be forgotten by those who heard it!

It was not until the animal had carried him through the 13th Light Dragoons that his grip relaxed, and he fell dangling by one stirrup iron, the first man killed in that bad business.

But Cardigan kept on, only turning once to check Captain White, of the 17th, who was trying to force the pace, and although they were now under a fearful fire, it was only by degrees that the speed was increased to a gallop.

Straight in front of them the Cossack battery of 12 guns was ploughing along the historic "half league," full in their faces, and behind the battery were mustered dense squadrons of Russian Horse. Jabrokitsky's infantry and artillery thronged the Fedioukine Hills on the left, and the Causeway Heights on the right, along which wound the Woronzow Road, swarmed with infantry and guns, from all of which three separate points the deadly fire was kept up on the doomed advance, which became frightfully decimated as it drew nearer and nearer.

When about 80 yards from the main battery the Russians discharged almost every gun of the 12, and the first line of the brigade, then going at the estimated rate of 17 miles an hour, was cruelly shattered.

One of the 17th, a private named James Melrose, and known in the regiment as a Shakesperean reciter, had a moment before exclaimed, "What man here would ask another man from England?" The next instant, and the iron hail whanged into the squadron and he fell, with scores of his comrades.

It is hardly possible to convey an idea of the slaughter of that ride. "Steady there; close up, close up!" was the constant cry as man and horse went down, and not the least heartrending part of it was the inevitable trampling on the wounded by the three other regiments which came pounding in the rear.

Part of the left squadron of the 17th outflanked the battery, passing it in the blinding smoke; the rest of the regiment followed Cardigan through and over the brass guns.

Morris was with that portion which went by comparatively unscathed — about 20 men in all—and suddenly coming upon a squadron of Russian Hussars, he turned to his following, and crying, "Remember what I have told you, men, and keep well together!" rode straight for the Russian leader, running him through with such force that he toppled him over on the off side of his horse, and, unable to disengage hand from sabre-hilt, was actually fastened to his adversary without the power to do anything.

The enemy, closing round him, sabred him severely about the head, cutting through his forage cap and rendering him unconscious, in which condition we will leave him for a while, and ride in fancy with the rest.

Among them was a veteran of Afghanistan and India, still affectionately spoken of by the handful who survive as "Old Jack Penn," though he himself has long joined the majority.

Penn volunteered out of the 3rd Light Dragoons into the 17th immediately on his return from India, in 1853, and came out to the Crimea with a draft that left Portsmouth in June.

On reaching the battery he drove his lance into a gunner and left it there, and when the regiment opened out after passing the guns he rode at a Russian Hussar officer, who turned to fly.

Penn pursued him on his near side, and with "cut six" nearly severed his head from his body!

The Lancer's horse receiving a ball in the shoulder, he dismounted, and cut off the Hussar's pouch belt, also taking possession of his clasp-knife and sword, which he used with effect on the return ride.

It is believed to have been somewhere about the moment when the bulk of the battery was discharged—reducing the first line to a possible 50 or 60 men—that Goad and Montgomery, of the 13th, and Winter and Thompson, of the 17th, were killed, and Webb and Sir William Gordon wounded.

Winter was last seen among the guns laying about him with a will; and his horse, badly hit with grape, was one of the first to gallop back to our own lines.

Troop Sergeant-Major Berryman, on reaching the guns, felt his mare stop dead, and, himself slightly wounded, he got down to find her off hind-leg broken, and while debating whether to shoot her, Captain Webb rode up to him, hit in the leg, and asking what he had better do.

"Stick to your horse, sir, and get back as far as you can," said Berryman, getting on a riderless charger and going in again; but his new mount was struck full in the chest, and the sergeant-major went down in a moment. All was smoke and confusion, and there seemed nothing for it but to make his way out, which

"ON REACHING THE BATTERY HE DROVE HIS LANCE INTO A GUNNER"
(*p.* 214).

he did, passing through the 11th Hussars, who closed in to let him by as they tore on their road to glory.

Berryman saw that Captain Webb had halted, unable to ride farther from the agony of his wound— the shin was completely pulverised—and running to him he lifted him out of the saddle, Lieutenant Smith, of the 13th, holding the horse meantime, and then riding off for a stretcher, Berryman remaining under heavy fire with the wounded officer, although he urged him to save himself.

Later on he was joined by Sergeant Farrell, also of the 17th, whom he called over to his assistance, and the two remained by the popular captain until help came in the person of Private Malone of the 13th, when they made shift to carry him in among them, Farrell's cap being taken off by a round shot as they went, and all three earning the Victoria Cross for their bravery and self-devotion.

The rest of the 17th, with the Light Dragoons, were meanwhile busy among the guns, sabring at the gunners, who made a gallant stand, and "Butcher Jack" was seen to cut down *six* with his own hand, still smoking the black pipe, which was alight when he returned without a scratch!

An attempt was made by the gunners to draw off their pieces, and a small body of the 17th, rallied by Sergeant O'Hara, were doing their best to prevent it, when the brigade-major, Mayow, shouted "17th, 17th, this way!" to warn them of the approach of the cavalry which was preparing for a dash on the broken remnants.

Thinking from the direction of his pistol that he ordered an advance on the left front, O'Hara and a handful went on, leaving about 15 of the 17th with

Mayow, who led them into the Russian Horse beyond the battery.

Just as the Hussars opposed to Morris's outflanking band had fallen back before their rush, so did the grey-coats whom Mayow charged retreat up the valley, although there were squadrons upon squadrons all about them who might simply have ridden our entire brigade to pulp had they been properly led.

Our first line was by this time broken up into groups and driblets, fighting independently, or making their way back among the *débris* of dead and wounded; of horses in every attitude of hideous agony; of torn and trampled men, with faces crushed by iron hoofs out of all human semblance, or lacerated beyond hope of recovery, yet still living, still sentient!

And over this mass of misery and crumpled valour came the "Cherry-pickers" and the Royal Irish, and Paget's Light Dragoons; into the guns, through and beyond them, dropping units at every stride, and accompanied by a surge of riderless horses that added to the chaos of it all.

Everything becomes confused and uncertain, but everything is heroic; "glimpses through the cannon smoke" of personal combats, always unequal; of Morris, recovering consciousness to find himself sorely beset by the Cossacks who prodded him with their lances as he lay, and he vainly whirling his sabre round to keep them off, until he was fain to surrender to an officer; of Chadwick, whose bright bay with the four white legs had come to a stand from wounds and loss of blood, leaving the lieutenant still in the saddle, warding off enemy after enemy, until a lance in the neck threw him stunned to the ground; of Cardigan himself, first at the guns, and then charging alone on to a squadron of the foe who tried to capture him; turning his thoroughbred chestnut and riding back through the now silent battery, almost unhorsed by a right-rear-point from a Cossack spear, and then, mistaking some retiring men in front for the relics of his first line, heading straight back to the starting-place as proudly as he had left it.

Nor must the French aid be forgotten; the gallant dash of the 4th Chasseurs-à-cheval on to the Fedioukine Hills to silence the guns in the scrub there; a scamper of grey horses, whose blue-coated, red-breeched riders rolled up the Russians and left 2 of their own officers and 8 men dead and 28 wounded.

The bulk of the 17th—and what an insignificant bulk it was—after penetrating some distance up the valley, retired before an overwhelming mass of cavalry; picked up O'Hara's handful on the way, and drove through Cossacks and Dragoons obliquely across the battleground until they gained the vicinity of Scarlett's Brigade, while the rest of the regiment, after furious slaughter among the guns, rode back as best they could by twos and threes.

Penn returned with a portion of the second line, charging through a body of the enemy that tried to stay them, and, using the sword of the Russian officer he had killed, at the seventh guard he snapped off 10 inches of the point, ultimately getting safely back, to receive the distinguished service medal, and be afterwards invalided home from a touch of sun when on outpost at Baidar, in reality the result of a severe roll under his horse at field drill in India two years before.

He has left it on record that the 17th's lances, with the gay pennons fluttering, were much shattered by grape-shot during the advance.

Twenty-five minutes after the order to charge was given, the remains of the Light Brigade were back again, and of the 140 who went in with the 17th, Captain Morgan numbered off *thirty-four* survivors.

Six hundred and seventy-eight men, worn with service, had disorganised and defeated more than 5,000 of the enemy's Horse on an empty stomach in something under half an hour, and it says much for our men and very little for the foe that a solitary survivor lived to tell the tale.

Of the entire brigade 113 were killed, 134 wounded, while the mortality among the horses amounted to 475 killed or afterwards shot as unserviceable, and 42 more or less seriously hurt.

Of the 17th Lancers, Captain Winter and Lieutenant Thompson, with 22 men, never returned from the "Valley of Death"; Captains White and Webb were wounded, the latter mortally; Sir William Gordon's head was terribly gashed by five sword cuts; Chadwick and 13 men were wounded and taken prisoners; Hartopp escaped, as did also Wombwell, after losing 2 horses.

Captain Morgan's charger, "Sir Briggs," was slashed over the eye, and the regiment lost altogether 99 mounts. Captain Morgan* had a narrow shave at the battery, a gun being discharged apparently full at him, the ball, however, striking his right-hand man in the chest!

A great number of the men were killed by

---

* Afterwards Lord Tredegar. Mrs. Duberly, wife of an officer of the 8th Hussars, tells how he won a regimental pony race at Devna on an animal for which he had paid fifty shillings, and while these sheets are passing through the press Lord Tredegar has set a soldierly example to his country by placing eighteen horses of his private stud at the disposal of the Government.

lance wounds, one having thirteen through chest and stomach; another six; the latter—he was of the 17th, and he came out alive—losing 2 horses under him, getting several sabre cuts and bullet holes through his cap, his sword bent double in the sheath by a minié ball, five bullets in his saddle, one in his lance staff, and sword wounds innumerable. Truly about as satisfying a feast of glory as the greediest could desire.

The experience of Captain Morris was dramatic; we left him a prisoner, badly wounded and in great pain, and chance brought him to the side of Wombwell, also a prisoner. "Look out and catch a horse!" he said to the captured aide-de-camp, and several riderless mounts passing at the moment, Wombwell suddenly made a dash for freedom, and luckily succeeded, returning safely with the 4th Light Dragoons. Morris soon lost sight of the officer to whom he had surrendered, and, being menaced by the Cossacks, mustered strength to run into some thick smoke, caught a spare horse by the rein, and after being dragged some distance fell and swooned away again. Coming to, he saw that he had attracted the unwelcome attentions of another mounted Russian, who looked at him with murder in his eye; so, scrambling to his feet, he again sought shelter in the powder smoke, and, almost run down by another loose horse, managed to secure him and get into the saddle, spurring up the valley to escape the cross-fire, which, however, caught the animal, and brought him down, dead, with the captain's thigh pinned beneath him! Once more the wounded man became unconscious, but sense returning—he had three deep wounds in the head, a fractured right arm, and some broken ribs—he worked his leg clear and started running, stumbling on to his face several times, until, utterly exhausted, he recognised the body of his friend Nolan, and lay down beside it.

Strange coincidence; they had exchanged letters in the event of anything happening, and as they lay there, the dead Hussar with the torn heart, and the unconscious Lancer, Nolan's uniform contained a message to Morris's wife, and in Morris's pocket was a letter to Nolan's widowed mother!

Troop Sergeant-Major Wooden, of the 17th, went out to the captain's aid with Surgeon Mouat, of the 6th Dragoons, and, after a rough dressing of wounds under fire, they got him in to the lines, both winning the V.C.

Although so desperately hurt, Captain Morris recovered, and died in India in 1858, Wooden, who was of German extraction, ultimately becoming quartermaster in the 104th, and, sadly enough, blowing his brains out many years after at Dover.

Speaking with something of a German accent, Wooden was one dark night challenged by a sentry, and for the moment could not recollect the password.

"Hush. *'Tish me!*" he whispered, as the man brought down his lance.

"Who?"

"*'Tish me! 'Tish me!*" came the answer; but the sentry either could not, or, what is more likely, *would not*, recognise the voice, and wanted to know "who the blankety blank *'Tish me* might happen to be."

"*'Tish me, the devil!*" cried the angry Wooden.

"Pass, 'Tish me the devil!" and for the remainder of his service with the "Death or Glory Boys" Wooden went by that *sobriquet*.

Kinglake implies that Sergeant O'Hara was instrumental in the captain's rescue, having been told of his whereabouts by Private Smith, and of Smith, Mutiny men of the 17th tell a good story.

Nicknamed "Fighting Smith" by an admiring public, this veteran died recently in St. Pancras Workhouse—that last abiding place of far too many old soldiers—being also accorded the honour of a military funeral, but in the regiment he was known as "Blood Smith," and this was how he got the name.

He was always getting into trouble, and one day when in India, after the Crimea, he paraded with only one spur, which was quickly noted by the commanding officer.

"Where's your spur, Smith?" said the colonel.

"Lost it, sorr."

"Where did you lose it, pray?"

"Up to my knees in blood, fightin' for my counthry, sorr," was the unabashed reply, and the name of "Blood Smith" stuck to him ever after.

A remarkable relic of the Balaclava charge was discovered on the ground a few months ago, when some boys removed a large boulder to get the honey from a bees' nest beneath it.

There was a mouldering helmet, lying as it had undoubtedly lain for forty-five years, and on its front, grinning through the tarnish of nearly half a century, was the grim badge of the 17th Lancers!

Another relic which not long ago created some sensation was the bugle of Trumpet-Major Joy, who was Lucan's orderly trumpeter on that day of days, and for many years private messenger to the Duke of Cambridge at the Horse Guards.

Whether there *was* any trumpet note at all I

cannot say; as I have mentioned before, survivors are dubious on the point, but in the honest belief that the instrument was one whose call had launched the Light Brigade on its death ride, Mr. Middlebrook, the patriotic landlord of the well-known "Edinburgh Castle," bought it for the enormous sum of 750 guineas under the hammer, and, with a fine feeling that does him honour, the bugle at his death will pass once more into the possession of the regiment.

Douglas, of the 10th Hussars, gives some interesting reminiscences in his book of Balaclava and its survivors—there are about nine of the 17th still on the roll (1899)—and he narrates how the first anniversary of the charge was celebrated in the Crimea, in a store-hut cleared for the occasion, with bran sacks for tablecloth, and how Sergeant Reardon, of the Royal Dragoons, recited Tennyson's "Charge of the Six Hundred" for the first time.

He also tells of two trumpeters—who shall be nameless, as one of them is still living—one belonging to the 17th Lancers, the other to the 8th Hussars, and how as provost-sergeant he came upon them one Christmas night under laughable circumstances.

"Both were short and stumpy," he says, "and both in a marvellous degree were partial to a 'dhrop' of anything—no matter what, hard or soft, mixed or 'nate,' it was all one to them. They were the most inseparable of chums, so inseparable that we named them the Siamese twins.

"If you wanted B——, look for D——, and you could not miss him also should D——'s presence be needed, find B——, and you secured the other too, so they were fitly named.

"And what connived at this Damon and Pythias

feeling was this peculiarity—that D——, when drunk, was able to walk, but could not sound a note upon his trumpet; while B——, on the contrary, could do anything in the sounding line, but was unable to walk a step. So this was how they managed it: D—— carried B—— on his back round the quarters both of the 8th and 17th, at each corner B—— winding out the 'First and last posts.'

"It was their particular fortune that, however drunk they might be, they could not be confined, as there was no one to relieve them; so they got drunk when they liked, and kept up the carrying game, and it was this I had a laugh at on leaving our Christmas party that night on provost duty."

The sadly diminished Light Brigade was ordered up to support the French cavalry at Inkerman, and the 17th had three casualties to report—one man killed, another wounded, and Cornet Cleveland struck in the side by a shell splinter, from the effects of which he died next morning.

He was only twenty-two, a fine young fellow of grand physique, the only son of a Waterloo officer of the Inniskilling Dragoons, and nephew to Major Willett, of the 17th. Succeeding to a large fortune at twenty-one, he was contemplating selling out, when the war came, and he went to the front instead, very popular with the officers and men of the regiment.

At Balaclava his horse was hit twice before he reached the battery, and while Cleveland was engaging a dismounted gunner the animal was run through the leg, and could hardly be brought to a trot.

Three Cossacks attacked him, thus handicapped, but he wounded the first, received a lance thrust through his cartouch box, and a prod in the ribs from the third, which bruised him, coming out otherwise unhurt, only to fall a few days later in that useless advance of our Light Brigade which we owed to the express solicitation of the French general.

And then came the horrors of the Crimean winter; when all the criminal mismanagement at home began to tell with such cruel effect on "Horse, Foot, and Dragoons."

The remnant of the 17th suffered severely in common with every other regiment out there; their chargers died of starvation, and the ragged, bearded men bore very little resemblance to the smart fellows who rode laughing through the dockyard gates on that smiling April morning.

When the 10th Hussars arrived in the following spring from India, 700 strong, they found the mounted strength of Heavy and Light Brigades combined was not more than *thirty files!*

During April and June drafts came out to the 17th, and 100 men were sent up the Baidar Valley in July, but the regiment, like all the others who had braved the winter, was in curious case, and wanted careful nursing to bring it up to a semblance of its former self.

After the battle of the Tchernaya, at which the 17th was present, there was little more to be done: the war was coming to a close, and as the weather set in cold, the cavalry was sent into winter quarters.

With the 8th and 10th Hussars, the regiment embarked for Ismid in Turkey, under Brigadier-General Shewell, leaving Balaclava on the 13th November, with many a lingering look at the magnificent coast line of that Crimean peninsula and a sigh for the brave fellows who had landed with them, so full of hope but fourteen months before, and who were then sleeping their last sleep in the "Valley of the Shadow."

The 17th sailed in the *Candia* and *Etna*, 15 officers, 291 men, 224 horses, and two days later reached Ismid, occupying the centre of the town, which is terraced on the side of a steep hill overlooking the gulf.

Sergeant Temple was appointed deputy provost-marshal, with a regimental provost from each of the Hussar corps under him, and the Brigade seems to have spent rather a pleasant time in the quaint old Turkish town, with its mosques and minarets, and Missouri's music-hall on the quay, where there was an inter-regimental sing-song every night.

The spring of 1856 saw the regiment *en route* for home again, a sergeant's party leaving in the *Oneida* on the 27th April, and the rest on the 29th in the *Candia*; 18 officers, 442 men, and 171 horses, some of their mounts having been turned over to the 10th Hussars, who had made matters very lively in the cavalry lines with their Arab stallions.

On the 14th May, 1857, they reached Queenstown, with the proud consciousness of having added a fresh laurel to their honours, and one which it would almost seem must remain the brightest of them all; for with the altered conditions of modern warfare it is a million chances to nothing that there can ever be another "Balaclava Charge."

There is something of sad coincidence to be recorded for the 25th October in the year of grace 1899, for, on the 44th anniversary of the day when the thunder of the Russian guns rang in the ears of the Light Brigade, the solemn rattle of the funeral volley rolled over the grave of John Swiney, one of the last of the 17th Lancers, who was reverently laid to rest in the

P

picturesque cemetery at Chingford, a few short hours before his remaining comrades met at their annual dinner.

The old veteran had written signifying his intention of being present, little thinking that his name would be coupled with that toast which is drunk standing, and in silence, "To the memory of the dead."

CHAPTER XIII.

THE 17TH IN THE MUTINY, AND THEIR SECOND TOUR OF INDIAN SERVICE, 1857–1865.

Reduction of Strength—Outbreak of the Indian Mutiny—Regiment Augmented—Off to Bombay—Captain Sir William Gordon—General Michel—The Hot Season in India—Tantia Topee, the Mahratta Brahmin—The Lancer of the " 'Fifties"—Flogging—Recruiting—The Trials of a Draft—Lieutenant Evelyn Wood—Tantia's Flight—The Highland Camel Corps—The Cholera March of 1860—Khaki—Sudden Death!—A Well-won V.C.—Home Again.

WHEN the regiment landed in Ireland headquarters were stationed at Cahir, the depôt coming over from Brighton, various detachments being quartered at Clogheen, Clonmel, Fethard, and Limerick, and after some rough work at Nenagh on the Shannon side, and Christmas spent in Portobello Barracks, Dublin, they were transferred to Island Bridge Barracks in March with a reduced establishment of 6 troops, of 28 officers, and 442 men.

Two months after they had settled down there strange things began to happen in India.

The terrible sepoy rising suddenly broke out, and for a moment seemed as though it would carry all before it. Horrible rumours found their way to this country—unhappily destined to be confirmed—of murder and massacre, of nameless outrage on British women and defenceless little ones; of gallant men betrayed and outnumbered; and a state bordering on chaos as native regiment after regiment revolted and joined the rebels.

Britain was probably never more thrilled to its very core than by the news that slowly—all too slowly for those who awaited tidings of their kith and kin—filled the papers and carried anguish through the length and breadth of the land, and instant measures were taken to reinforce our garrison out there.

The earlier stages of the rising and suppression were over before the 17th received orders to go, but the regiment was prepared for active service and raised to ten troops, receiving 132 volunteers from the 3rd, 4th, and 13th Light Dragoons, the 11th Hussars, and the Scarlet Lancers to bring it up to strength, and there was plenty of work for it to do when it finally "got the route."

Cawnpore had been captured and the siege of Delhi was in full swing when the regiment was warned on the 2nd September, 1857; Delhi had fallen into our hands, and the first relief of Lucknow was matter of history before they entrained for Cork to join the 8th Hussars, who were going out with them in the *Great Britain*.

On the 8th October they sailed, reaching Bombay on the 17th December, both regiments wearing their European clothing, a rational dress for our troops in India being one of the outcomes of the Mutiny campaigns.

It will hardly be credited a century hence that our Carabineers and, I believe, Queen's Bays, wore *brass* helmets through that broil and moil; that the 93rd marched and bled in feather bonnets—the kilt is by no means to be despised either in heat or cold—and that practically all the difference made in the dress of most of our cavalry regiments was a white cap cover!

The 17th had lost their jackets in 1855, and received a blue tunic instead, with the top of the lapels turned back and showing a white "butterfly," as they called it, but during the Mutiny they wore it buttoned up, blue, and had a white curtain to their peaked forage caps.

The lances of that day were made of lance-wood, and a new attachment was adopted for the pennons which fixed with a spring—those in the Crimea had been tied on with white tape—and in addition to the sling they had an iron guard for the hand, now long since done away with.

The colonel, three officers, and four roughriders had gone out by the overland route, and when the regiment landed on the 19th and 21st December they took train to Campoolee, *en route* for Kirkee, where they were to be horsed, and where they arrived about Christmas Day. Horsing was a slow and gradual process, all sorts and conditions of mounts arriving— Arab stallions, Australian walers, a few Cape mares, and a varied assortment of long-tailed, long-maned nondescripts, which were put through their paces as fast as possible, it being the 27th May before the first squadron—A and E troops—were sent up to Mhow under Captain Sir William Gordon, who had been so badly cut about at Balaclava.

All the old 17th men I have spoken to on the subject are unanimous in proclaiming Sir William Gordon one of the smartest officers who ever held her Majesty's commission, and Fortescue has embalmed some of his methods in his excellent history of the regiment.

He tells how Sir William brought his squadron into Mhow, five hundred miles of hard marching, and not a day's halt, without one sore back; inspecting every horse himself, and shifting the stuffing of the saddles with a two-pronged fork where the coat appeared ruffled.

They had done away with the rolled blanket, and used a pannel saddle and numnah then, by the way.

The object of the march of that squadron was to join the command of General Michel, who was on the trail of Tantia Topee, a Mahratta Brahmin, one of the wiliest, and to a certain extent one of the best, of the rebel leaders, from a military point of view. The rascal, who was hand and glove with Nana Sahib, had commanded the Gwalior troops, and been through the thick of the rebellion. He had beaten Wyndham, been thrashed by Colin Campbell, failed in an attempt to relieve Jhansi, sustained two defeats by Sir Hugh Rose, and, about the time that the squadron reached Mhow, he had been again worsted by Sir Robert Napier, and was retreating westward with his following. He was almost of European complexion, with grey hair, and there was still plenty of fight in him, for he kept us busy until the ensuing spring, and was even then only taken by treachery, when deserted by his troops and worn out by the undeniably gallant struggle he had made.

John Michel (gazetted major-general October, 1858) was an active, spare-built man of great energy; warm hearted but impetuous, and a keen sportsman, he proved himself the very officer to cope with the slippery Tantia. He had seen considerable regimental duty with the 57th, 27th, 64th, 3rd, and 6th Foot, ample means enabling him to secure promotion in the palmy old days of "purchase," and after commanding a brigade in the Kaffir war of 1846–7, he saw further service with the Turkish Contingent in the Crimea, and died Field Marshal Sir John Michel, G.C.B., in 1886.

A good deal of the pursuit took place on the 17th's old fighting ground, Malwa, where they had harried the Pindaris in the Mahratta war, one of General Michel's first moves being an advance of two columns to cut Tantia off from Indore, on which he was marching.

Tantia fell back towards Rajghur, and Michel moved up to Nulkeera, where he joined the columns, and had then 1,100 men and 4 guns under him, to oppose 10,000 rebels and 40 pieces of cannon.

His little army was composed of the squadron of the 17th, 80 strong, 180 of the 3rd Light Cavalry, 600 of the 71st Highland Light Infantry and 92nd Gordons, the rest native infantry and Bengal gunners.

On the 14th September General Michel started for Rajghur in the rain, his cavalry splashing through the black mud, and the infantry toiling after them, to halt about half-way, and march again at four o'clock next morning.

September is the unhealthy, steamy month of the Indian season, and the rain was succeeded by distressing heat, when men fell out, and horses died in their tracks, the cavalry outdistancing the infantry, and thus compelling the general to halt from sheer necessity.

Finding, when the march was resumed about half-past two next morning, that the rebels had fallen back, he sent his slender band of horsemen after them, under Sir William Gordon, while he hurried on the rest, and before long they came in touch of Tantia Topee drawn up in battle array, with 8,000 men and 27 guns, formed in two lines.

Sir William prudently halted for the supports to come up, but when they made their appearance the rebels broke and bolted, our cavalry pursuing on the spur, capturing all the guns and only drawing rein from absolute exhaustion.

An officer of the native cavalry dropped dead from sunstroke when they halted; the 17th had one horse killed; and after a day's rest the little column again started on its avenging mission, only to be stayed by the tropical rain which flooded the country and allowed Tantia to wind his sinewy course through the jungle to Seronge, where he lingered for eight days and then pushed north to storm Esaughur, which done, and seven guns captured, he and Nana Sahib's nephew, Rao Sahib, parted company for a time.

A few days later we again came unexpectedly upon him near Mungrowlee, while pitching our camp after a thirty-five-mile march, one of the 17th dashing in from the picket to report that the rebels were close by.

With 1,091 men of all arms the general instantly went out to meet them, 5,000 men and 6 guns posted on a strong position, rendered still more secure by a dense jungle, through which some of the rebels crept round to our rear and killed a wounded Highlander. Sir William Gordon galloped up with his troop on the alarm being raised, and, detecting the whereabouts of the cowardly rascals, charged into the jungle in open order.

The "Death or Glory Boys" did tremendous execution among the trees, and gave the rogues a very "bad quarter of an hour," pursuing them singly or in twos and threes, until every point and butt was red, and more than 80 of the Velliattees slain.

Sir William slew 4 himself, and bowled over as

many more—his own life being saved by Sergeant Cope, who killed a rebel in the act of shooting him in the back—while every one of the 43 men who went in with him is credited with a couple apiece.

Tantia, after a bold show of outflanking us with his horsemen, bolted, leaving his guns in our hands, and while he is flying into the east to join the Rao again, we will glance back as far as Canterbury, returning to India in time to follow the fortunes of the squadron in their next encounter with the rebels at Sindwaho.

At the period of the Indian Mutiny, life in the 17th Lancers was very different to our own day, and we will take a rough page from the experience of one of them, who went out sergeant in charge of a draft a few months after he enlisted.

He walked down to Westminster to join the 16th, but in the sanded bar of a well-known recruiting public-house he chanced upon Sergeant Nibbs, of the "Death or Glory Boys," who took in the position at a glance.

"16th no good for you, my boy; 17th's the rigiment; no work, shoot tigers all day in India, be an officer in six months"— and almost before he knew what it was all about a shilling was slipped into his hand, and, subject to the doctor's approval, he found himself committed to the 17th for fourteen years' peace service or seventeen years' war, at the munificent rate of one and threepence a day, with a bounty of five pounds.*

On our recruit's arrival at the Canterbury depôt, where he was quartered in the old Artillery Barracks, the

---

* Sergeant Nibbs told one of the "Six Hundred" that he had enlisted 1,700 men for the regiment, and had received 19s. a head, besides —as my informant naïvely put it—" what he got out of them himself!"

first thing that struck him was the small size of the men, accustomed as he had been to the stalwart Lifeguards; and, placed under the hands of Sergeant-Major Cattermole, he was soon immersed in the mysteries of squad drill, riding-school, and the complicated old sword and lance exercise.

The sword, lance, and pistol of that period were supposed to remain in wear for twelve years, the lance pennon for two years; the lance, without the flag, cost 12s., the light cavalry sword £1 2s., and the new pattern, side-lock, pistol, £1 16s.

Those were flogging days, and every Saturday afternoon the farriers had flogging-drill in the riding-school, where they practised on stuffed sacks, the great art being to make the cat fall on the same spot at each stroke.

Stealing, and striking a "non-com." were the most prevalent crimes, and fifty lashes the usual punishment; no one was thought any the worse of for a spell at the triangles, and it was not an uncommon thing for six infantry men to be whipped before breakfast.

About the fifth stroke the blood flowed, at the tenth the sufferer's back turned blue, and while some men fainted, others would put on their shirts and jackets afterwards as though nothing had happened.

The new recruit had not been long with the depôt when he was made corporal, and before he had been passed out of the "ride," Sergeant-Major Cattermole—whose sandy "Dundrearies" were afterwards well known for many years at the portals of the Admiralty—took him before the colonel and advised his promotion as sergeant.

He owed the step less, as he modestly says, to any particular smartness, than to the fact that he had some education, and it is hard to realise to-day that of the thirty-two men composing the draft under his charge, he alone could read and write, only a few of the others being able even to sign their names!

Doubts having arisen as to the accurate badges for the various non-commissioned ranks, an order had been issued from the Horse Guards, 22nd May, 1850, regulating the matter for the Heavy and Light Dragoons, and the Lancers, and henceforward regimental sergeant-majors were to sport four chevrons with a crown over them; troop-sergeant-majors, three chevrons and a crown; stripe-sergeants three chevrons simply, and corporals two, the badges to be carried on the right sleeve only.

The young sergeant had not much time for "peacocking about" in his new rank, for stern responsibilities quickly followed on his promotion, and on the 11th December his draft sailed from Gravesend in the *Bloomer* transport, with details of the 7th, 8th, and 14th, and various other regiments destined for India.

The trials of the draft were many, and to begin with the ship lay off Deal for a week, breaking away from two anchors on Christmas Day.

When they were passing the Isle of Wight in a slight fog, the sergeant, who was down below, reading "Peter Simple," was roused by a terrific crash, and rushing on deck found that a Boston whaler had run into them.

The tug *Napoleon* towed them into Portsmouth Harbour on New Year's Eve, and as they came to anchor in rear of the *Victory* the ship's bells rang out the Old Year; their next fortnight was spent on the convict hulk *Victorious*, until the *Bloomer* was repaired, when they resumed their voyage, making five feet of water a day, and only sighting one ship the whole time.

The draft met with a mishap on board, which very nearly resulted in trouble for the sergeant in charge.

Captain Steel, of the 3rd Dragoon Guards, ordered their cloaks to be brought up and hung in the rigging to get out the creases, and a squall coming on they all went over the side.

When they landed, the editor of a Poonah paper got hold of the story and made copy of it, to the disgust of Sir Hugh Rose, who held that someone had been talking, and was within an ace of "breaking" the sergeant over the business; as a matter of fact, he did lose his stripes later on through the kind offices of Colonel Crawley—of Mhow Court Martial fame—but was reinstated by Sir William Gordon, and enjoyed considerable popularity as an impersonator of female parts at ten rupees a night in the regimental theatre.

The draft had taken train from Bombay to Campoolee, and from there proceeded to the Queen's depôt at Khandellah, where it lay for three months.

Meanwhile the task of mounting the regiment continued, the 2nd squadron leaving Kirkee for Sholapore on the 11th June, under Major White; the 3rd on the 11th September for Mhow, under Major Learmonth, and headquarters on the 22nd; but before they were all united again Sir William Gordon's squadron had seen some more sharp fighting, and was still hustling the rebels.

After the defeat at Mungrowlee, Tantia Topee had rejoined forces with Rao Sahib, and General Michel came up with the latter at Sindwaho on the 19th October, by forced marches.

They were still in the hilly jungle country, but the rains were over, and the motley costumes of the rebel army peeped, half hidden, through the rank green

"SEEING SOME RED-COATED REBELS FORMING INTO SQUARE, LIEUTENANT
EVELYN WOOD SPURRED AT THE CORNER MAN ABSOLUTELY ALONE"
(*p.* 237).

growth—so concealed that Michel could not tell their numbers, which were afterwards estimated at 10,000.

Michel's force had been augmented, and consisted of rather more than 1,700, among whom were 118 of the 17th's old Balaclava comrades—the 8th Hussars, in their new blue tunics with white wicker helmets, and 4 Royal Horse Artillery guns.

The rebels made a bold start, their infantry advancing downhill on our centre, their horsemen threatening our troopers on the flanks, and their guns plumping some shot into the 17th, who were sent off to the right in anticipation of the usual flight.

We were hotly pressed at one time, and had to mow them down with grape from the grey-painted guns, but once repulsed, their nerve left them, and the 17th, the Hussars, and the 1st Bombay Lancers chased them for nine miles, spearing and cutting them down wholesale.

With Michel's column was a young lieutenant of the 17th Lancers—now known to fame as General Sir Evelyn Wood—who, after winning golden opinions for his courage as a midshipman with Peel's Naval Brigade in the Crimea, had joined the 13th Light Dragoons in 1855, purchased a lieutenancy in the same regiment, and exchanged into the 17th in 1857.

He was the only officer of Gordon's squadron who could speak Hindostani, and at Sindwaho was doing duty with the 3rd Bombay Light Cavalry, a party of which escorted two guns on Michel's left, when they were fired upon by the mutineers.

Seeing some red-coated rebels of the 36th Bengal Native Infantry forming into square, Lieutenant Wood spurred at the corner man, absolutely alone, until a brave trooper of the 3rd rode up to help him, and killed the mutineer, after "having narrowly escaped a cut from a two-handed sword which shore through his saddle into his horse's spine."

Lieutenant Bainbridge, of the 17th, hurried up a knot of the 8th Hussars under Adjutant Harding to Wood's assistance, and as the rebels broke, Harding cried out to Wood to engage one, riding for another himself, and to his death as it proved, the man waiting until he was close upon him, and shooting him dead.

Wood's sepoy also faced his pursuer with the bayonet, but by a fatal error of judgment for himself clubbed his musket at the last moment, and was promptly run through.

The losses of the 17th were a sergeant and 4 men wounded, 3 horses killed, and 4 wounded, while of the enemy 500 were killed, and 6 guns taken, the squadron having very materially helped in the adding up of that total.

But the wily Mahratta was as full of resource as a horse is of bones, and after retreating north he suddenly retraced his steps, and, heading southward, slipped past Michel within four miles of his outposts.

Michel was soon after him, but had to make a detour, sending off a message to Brigadier Parke to warn him of the new movements; and coming on the rebels near the village of Kurai, our cavalry divided Tantia's two wings, Tantia and Rao Sahib escaping with the right while we were breaking up the left wing.

Sir William Gordon pursued for six miles with the 17th and 3rd Bombay, and, checked for a moment by a nullah, saw his men safely over, joined them, and calling out that the first man up with the flying cavalry should loot the leader, led them in open order at full gallop.

He was first man in himself, slew the rebel commander, and divided his gold bracelets and costly trinkets among his troopers, and thus brilliantly closed the independent adventures of A and E troops; for the time was approaching when the rest of the regiment was to have its chance. Meanwhile Tantia fled towards Rájgarh, losing forty of his followers at the hands of Colonel Becher, who attacked him near Bagrod, but he crossed the Narbadá River, and pushed on for Nágpúr.

Learning that two forces under Hill and Roberts were advancing against him, he turned north-west, hoping to recross the Narbadá and gain the territory of the Gaikwar of Baroda, and on the 19th November he reached Kargún, where he gathered up two guns, a couple of troops of cavalry and a company of infantry belonging to Holkar, and hurried on westward, crossing the Agra road at the moment when a convoy of stores was rumbling along.

Promptly looting the carts, cutting the telegraph wires, and carrying the native escort with him, he quickened his pace for the river, hotly pursued by Major Sutherland with some of the 92nd Highlanders and 4th Bombay Rifles, whom he had improvised into a camel corps, and who came up with the rebels near Rájpúr.

Tantia's force was then between 2,000 and 3,000, the Major's about 200, but he charged up the road on to the guns under a hail of grape shot, captured them, and put the rest to flight, his men being so exhausted by the efforts they had made to come up with the enemy that Sutherland encamped on the battle ground, leaving Tantia to gain the broad river and cross in safety.

When Sutherland reached the bank next evening it was to catch a glimpse of the rebel camp out of reach beyond the waters just as the sun sank behind the horizon and the swift Indian night came down.

Tantia did not linger long, and before dawn he was far on his way towards Baroda, marching with that marvellous celerity so peculiar to the natives, unaware that Nemesis was on his heels in the shape of a flying column under Brigadier Parke, who had been sent after him by Michel.

When news of Tantia's course reached the general his forces were at Chárwah, south of the Narbadá, and crossing with his own column he marched on Máu, leaving the squadron of the 17th at Hoshángábád, and despatching Parke in hot haste with some Bombay troops, 50 of the 8th Hussars, some of the Southern Mahratta Horse under the gallant Kerr, of Kolapore fame, a camel corps of the 72nd Highlanders, Moore's Aden Horse, and some Gujerat Irregulars, who made one of the finest marches on record—241 miles in nine days, the last twenty being through dense and difficult jungle.

Tantia was only 50 miles from Baroda when Parke surprised him on the 1st December at Chhotá Údaipúr, and fought him on broken ground among his own tents.

The rebels made a stand with 3,500 men, trying to turn our left flank where some of the Southern Mahratta Horse in blue tunics and scarlet turbans were posted, but Kerr, a well-known horseman—riding eight stone at that time—changed his front and led his sowars on in a dashing charge, killing 60 of the enemy, and crumpling them up.

Bannerman, of the same corps, charged from our

right flank, Parke's two Bombay 9-pounders played on Tantia's centre, and the affair ended in an universal pursuit towards the jungles of Bánswárá.

This happened on the 30th November; on the 22nd September the fourth squadron of the 17th with the headquarters, leaving a depôt at Kirkee, had marched with D troop Royal Horse Artillery and some infantry for Máu, or, as we know it better, Mhow, under Colonel Benson; and proceeding from Mhow towards the Betwah river, Major Learmonth's squadron had joined them at Bhopal, and Sir William Gordon's at Hoshángábád, where all three squadrons were again united on the 6th November, leaving only Major White's out in the cold.

While they were there news came that Tantia was moving on Indore, on the great trunk road, and they were ordered up to Mhow in haste, crossing the Narbadá in boats, and accomplishing the fifty-two miles in twenty-six hours.

Tantia, in his jungle fastnesses, was cheered for the moment by intelligence that Mán Singh (who afterwards betrayed him) and Prince Firuzsháh were coming to his help, but he lay low for some time longer, while Benson watched for him at Rutlam, an old halting-place of the 17th in the Pindari war.

At last, at four o'clock in the afternoon of Christmas Day, 1858, Tantia, with his elephants and following, issued from the jungle near Partábgarh, forced his way past Major Rocke, who had not sufficient men to stay him, and headed away for Mandesar and Zirápúr, having practically broken through the cordon and got a fair start.

But Benson was equal to the occasion, and was after him like the wind; 210 men of the 17th, and 37 of the

R.H.A. with a couple of guns; thirty-six miles the first day, twenty-six the second, and so on; bivouacking in the intense cold in sight of the rebel camp-fires, resuming the march to find them gone, until, on the 29th, pushing cautiously forward in the "darkest hour before dawn," they saw their prey at last, and drew up to wait for daylight.

There was still a two-mile trot before them, but when they eventually cleared a wooded lane the rebels were visible about 4,000 strong, arranged in order of battle on some rising ground, with a ravine and jungle behind them, at Zirápúr.

Benson attacked in columns of divisions, and when Tantia's men opened fire he uncovered his own guns, which replied at 400 yards with grape and shell.

They soon broke and were driven into the jungle, the Lancers following them across the ravine; but the rebels fought well, and took up another position, which we attacked in line, with two guns in the centre, Sir William Gordon's squadron charging them a second time into the jungle and over the hollow.

A few more attempts were made to face us, but the lesson had been too sharp, and Tantia's force fled, still further demoralised and now struggling only for escape, with very little real fight left in it.

Captain Drury Lowe, who had joined the 17th in the Crimea, captured four of Tantia's elephants, and the regiment still possesses their ornaments as trophies of Zirápúr.

The 17th and the R.H.A. had each a man wounded and 2 horses killed; the losses of the rebels do not seem to have been estimated, but they must have been severe, and moreover their troubles were not at an end.

Next day Colonel Somerset arrived with 2 guns, Major White's squadron, and 150 Gordon Highlanders on fast Sandney camels.

It is said that the Highlanders suffered severely from the gait of their steeds, and that, being in the condition of John Gilpin when "the snorting beast began to trot," it was with some difficulty that they were induced to remount after a halt, and they had to be constantly bribed by the promise of an action at the end of the next stage.

Benson's gun horses were done, so filling up the limbers and transferring the animals from the ammunition waggons to Benson's 9-pounders, Somerset started off in hot haste.

He did not allow the grass to grow under his feet, but raced along over vile, unmetalled tracks and ploughed fields at an average of forty miles a day; the Lancers lying down to snatch a brief sleep at their horses' heads, and then up again to escort the clattering guns at a trot, leaving baggage and camels in the rear until they came to a village which the guns negotiated alone, the Lancers passing it on either side in consequence of the narrowness of the road.

A body of the rebel Horse was drawn up beyond the village, and it advanced at a walk as if about to annihilate us; but Somerset ordered the battery forward at the gallop, and, dashing out of the village in gallant style, they unlimbered and let fly, the first ball unhorsing the rebel leader and checking the rest.

A handful of the Camel Corps was hurried up, but the finishing blow was dealt by the 17th, who came galloping into view, brought their lances down to the "engage," and charged with a yell that spread terror among the rebel cavalry.

The dark-skinned sowars did not wait, but turned and broke, and the next moment the 17th were into them, dealing death right and left, prodding and piercing the lives out of them for seven miles of scampering slaughter until they pulled in from absolute physical incapacity to keep it up any longer.

Our men had done 147 miles, the last seventy in forty-eight hours, with hardly any sleep, and practically destroyed Tantia's cavalry at the end of it, yet—and it strikes one as a most unaccountable omission—in the whole of Colonel Malleson's narrative of the pursuit the 17th is not once mentioned!

Cold and rain; halting only to feed the horses; their own rations taken anyhow, and none too often at that, the pursuit of Nana Sahib's agent must be ever regarded as a magnificent piece of work on the part of the men who planned it and the men who carried it out.

It lasted for nine months; it covered over 3,000 miles; it meant the passage of rivers, and the threading of trackless wilds; jungle, nullah, mountain pass; night marches through the terrible Malwa mud, and always a handful against a horde.

Had Tantia Topee possessed the old Mahratta courage and been able to infuse it into his men, even our British grit would not have saved us on occasion from the tremendous odds; but the man, while as wily as the serpent, was also as harmless as the dove when it came to a fight, and so he trailed along with his followers and his banners, and his patient elephants; beaten every time, yet still hoping against hope with true Asiatic pertinacity.

"THE NEXT MOMENT THE 17TH WERE INTO THEM, DEALING DEATH RIGHT AND LEFT" (*p.* 244).

The horrors of his flight must have been great, and one is not surprised to read that "many a well-bred charger was left standing by the roadside, its back swarming with maggots and its hoofs worn to the sensible sole."

Yet, of Sir William Gordon's squadron, with the exception of those killed or wounded, every horse was returned fit for duty, thanks to their captain's unremitting attention.

Tantia never recovered his defeat at Baród on the 1st January, and, though many rebels still adhered to him, his numbers were fast diminishing.

Michel was on his heels once more with the whole of the 17th, marching at the rate of 256 miles in eight days; and while he trended northwards, Brigadier Smith was jostling Firuzsháh towards the south.

Showers, with a light column from Agra, fell on Tantia and beat him again at Dewassa on the 16th; Holmes carved him up on the 21st at Sikur; Rao Sahib and Firuzsháh left him to his fate, and were severely mauled in their turn; and it must have been pretty evident to Tantia Topee that the game was up at last.

Still he struggled gamely on, and plunged into the jungle with two pandits, a groom, two horses and a pony, meeting Rájah Mán Singh, who upbraided him for leaving his force, to which Tantia replied that he was tired of running away, and would remain with him.

He made an attempt to communicate with Rao Sahib and Firuzsháh, but they were in no condition to reopen the ball, Rao Sahib having indeed been badly beaten by Honnor on the 10th February at

Kusháni,* and Firuzsháh a great deal too anxious about his yellow skin to risk it any further.

It was a final effort of Brigadier Somerset's, with seven troops of the 17th immediately after Kusháni, that seems to have led to Tantia's desertion of his weary followers, when the "pipeclay boys" ran them down after 230 miles in six days and a half, and 300 rebels surrendered.

After that came a spell of hiding in the Paron jungle, negotiations between Meade, of Meade's Horse, and Mán Singh, who for certain considerations promised him betrayed the exact whereabouts of the hunted outlaw.

It is said that he was finally taken in the early morning of the 8th April, 1859, by a party of the 9th Bombay Native Infantry; but there is a tradition in the 17th that Sergeant "Nobby" Clark, while walking in the camp, was approached by some natives, who led him to a tamarind tree, under which he found Tantia sleeping, and that, consequently, the honour of his capture belongs to the regiment.

Be that as it may, one curious fact remains to be told: when Tantia—after the court martial had sentenced him to be hanged—was turned off a bullock hackery and died like a lamb, some of the officers cut

---

* There is an incident narrated of the Kusháni fight which we may be pardoned for introducing here; the story of a lucky shot. Lieutenant Stourton, of the 8th Hussars, was pursuing a rebel chief who was mounted on a swift Sandney camel, and though he was doing all he knew to get at him, his horse always swerved as he came within striking distance. A sergeant called out, "Why don't you try him with your revolver, sir?" and Stourton, who had forgotten all about the weapon, took the hint and fired, camel and man falling at his first discharge. On examination the ball was found to have passed through the rider's body into the back of the camel's head, killing both outright!

locks of his white hair to send home, and, there not being enough to go round among the men, who also wished for mementoes, they paid Jack Porter, a regimental greyhead, at the rate of a pint a lock, until he was well nigh bald, so that any hirsute relics of Tantia Topee that may hereafter come into the market must be received with considerable suspicion!

At last, on the 13th May, to be absolutely precise, the "Death or Glory Boys" went into quarters at Morar, in Gwalior, with one squadron under Captain Taylor at Jhansi.

May is the hot month in India, and the sudden change from the fatigues of the campaign to comparative inaction in bad quarters proved terribly trying to officers and men.

There were many deaths, and the usual monotony of Indian service in peace time; with its early morning drills, its loafing through the burning hours with the thermometer 100° in the shade, and the church parade on Sunday, to which the band invariably played them to the tune of "Star of the Evening," and always brought them back to "Old Dog Tray."

While on the subject of church parade, it may be worth while to recall a good story which went out with the draft from Canterbury of a well-known chaplain of the Established Church, who used to minister to the spiritual needs of the men at the depôt very much after the fashion of the late Rev. Joshua Brooks, whose strange vagaries are still remembered in the North.

This particular chaplain had a peculiar knack of interlarding the service with a running commentary on the behaviour of his martial congregation, and so well did his remarks fit in with the "authorised version" that it was often difficult to tell which was one, and which was "t'other."

There was no "dearly beloved bretheren" for him; he always began with "Soldiers!" in a voice of thunder.

"Soldiers!" he would commence, "the Scripture moveth us in sundry places to—wake that 17th Lancer up, provost-sergeant, will you?"

Or, again, "I heard a voice from heaven saying—7th Dragoon Guards, don't make such a noise with those scabbards!"

There was no intentional irreverence in it, for the old fellow was quite serious, and it certainly had the effect of increasing his flock, as many a man paraded with the Church of England party on purpose to hear him.

Apropos of music, there was little singing on the march, but one song, "My Village Home," was exceedingly popular with the 17th in the Mutiny days, and was introduced by the sergeant in charge of the draft, of whom we have spoken, the bandmaster taking it down from his whistling.

On the 10th January, 1860, the 17th were ordered to Secunderabad, in the flat territory of the Nizam, and their route thither has become known as the "cholera march," from the terrible mortality they experienced.

They wore khaki then, with blue piping on the sleeves of their stable jackets and up the back, with those white tuft buttons, constructed to defy as far as possible the destructive efforts of the *dhobie*, or native washer.

Their khaki pantaloons were adorned with two blue stripes, and worn with a Wellington spur, and an alteration was made in headgear at this period, forage-cap peaks being abolished in April, and in 1861 the entire regiment was put into helmets of new construction, made by Saddler-Sergeant Lewis, who had come from the 12th Lancers, of leather, covered with white dungaree.

Men of the regiment still speak solemnly of that cholera march, which cost them thirty-eight lives, and the sudden snapping of old ties of comradeship; for death came with appalling swiftness, and the man with whom you had ridden the last stage was often buried before you saddled up again.

Veigh, the Balaclava butcher, died in that way, and, strangely enough, was actually buried in a grave he had been digging for another man!

Often was some poor fellow consigned to the sandy soil, yet warm, while his squadron waited, impatient to be gone before the dawn should come and bring the chances of death more closely to them all.

It is a gruesome subject, yet I am tempted to give one actual instance of the lightning rapidity with which a smart private left a gap in the muster roll of the regiment.

He shall be nameless, for he was the younger son of a noble family, who had enlisted from motives which did him honour, but upon which it is not necessary to touch here, and he walked into the bazaar one day with another man of his troop with whom he had struck up a friendship. In the bazaar the other man purchased some native sweetmeat, and the gentleman ranker, whom we will call X——, expostulated with him.

"For heaven's sake, my dear fellow, don't eat that rubbish; you'll die to a moral certainty!"

"Not a bit of it," was the reply, and while "the

other man" was still munching his confection, X——stopped before a dramshop and ordered some arrack.

It was now "the other man's" turn, and he implored his comrade to come to the canteen and leave the rank poison, without avail.

"I know what I'm doing, old man. I'll meet you after stables"; and they parted.

A few hours later "the other man" was sitting in his tent, when a shadow fell across the opening, and a sergeant appeared carrying a piece of board in his hand—the "other man" had some skill in ornamental writing.

"I know you won't mind painting the skull and marrow bones and an inscription for us," said the sergeant.

"All right," said the "other man." "Who's it for?"

"Poor X——; we're burying him at sunset!"

While the regiment lay at Secunderabad there appeared in *The London Gazette*, 4th September, 1860, a notification that the Victoria Cross had been granted to Lieutenant Evelyn Wood for two deeds of bravery.

The first, already mentioned above—the charge on the rebels at Sindwaho—was performed in all the excitement of action; the other was one of those silent heroisms, done in the dark and almost alone, which are possibly the greater heroisms of the two.

The broken mutineers had captured a potail and haled him away into the jungle to hang him in their own good time, and, the man being loyal to us, Wood determined to save him if possible.

He was then doing duty with Beatson's Horse, and, although fagged by the long pursuit, he set off with a duffadar and four sowars of the corps, and a naik and six sepoys of the Bareilly Levy.

They had ridden twelve miles through the scrub when the glow of a camp fire shone above the jungle top still farther ahead, and, leaving the rest of his party with the horses, he went on with the duffadar and a sowar on foot for three miles.

At one o'clock in the morning they were crouching at the edge of a nullah, peering down on the rebels' bivouac, where nearly seventy rascals lay sleeping round the blaze in fancied security, while five others kept sleepy guard over the wretched potail.

The odds were tremendous, but Wood did not hesitate, and, whispering to his two followers to fire with him, sprang boldly into the nullah on the heels of the volley. Surprised out of their sleep and their very lives, the rascals stampeded with a chorus of howls into the midnight jungle, though not before several of their number had fallen victims to the dashing gallantry of the young lieutenant.

He had been previously recommended for the V.C. by Captain Lushington in the Crimea, as a midshipman with Peel's Naval Brigade, and his subsequent career is too well known to need allusion in this book.

After five years at Secunderabad the 17th left on the 14th December, 1864, and marched dismounted to Sholapore, taking train from that place to Poonah, from whence it proceeded on the 20th January to Bombay, and went aboard the *Agamemnon* next day.

The second tour of Indian service was at an end, and it landed at Tilbury in April, 1865, having lost 38 officers and 373 men during the previous eight years from death and a variety of causes, and leaving, moreover, 122 who volunteered into other regiments.

CHAPTER XIV.

GREAT BRITAIN AND ZULULAND.

Inspected by the Commander-in-Chief—The last Balaclava Officer—A V.C. Myth—Scotland—Horse Guards' Order against Smoking—The Black Plume and the Pet Bear—Ireland—The Smartness of their New Uniform—New Regimental Title—Carbines for the Lancers—Lieut.-Colonel Gonne Shot—Off to Zululand—Their Fighting Dress—The Prince Imperial—Ulundi—Charge of the 17th—Reduction—India—A Lost Chance of Service—Home Again—The Drum Horse—"Lizzie," the Pet Bear—Their Recent Stations.

IN October the regiment was inspected at Colchester by H.R.H. the Duke of Cambridge, Commander-in-Chief, and for the next fourteen years the history of the "Death or Glory Boys" is comparatively uneventful.

The last of the Balaclava officers, Lieut.-Colonel Robert White, retired in 1866, and in March of that year the regiment lay for the first time at Aldershot.

In 1867 John Brown was promoted cornet, having been a trumpeter in the "death ride," and their quartermaster at this time was John Berryman, whom we last saw at Balaclava, winning his V.C. in company with Sergeant Farrell, who had died in India.

Berryman, who left the regiment in 1880 for the 5th Lancers, from which he subsequently retired as major, was one of the first batch of recipients who were decorated by her Majesty in Hyde Park in 1857, and the only one of the regiment represented on that occasion.

It was generally believed that he had received an extra bar to his Cross, and the myth was kept alive in several successive histories of the decoration, but I have a very interesting letter from him, written shortly before his death, in which he denies the granting of a V.C. bar to *any* recipient.

They kept the "Gentlemen Dragoons"—to use one of their old nicknames—very much on the move for the next few years; in 1867 they were at Shorncliffe and Brighton, in 1868 at Woolwich, and later at Hounslow and Hampton Court—their old quarters before the Crimea—and in July, 1869, they paid their second visit to Edinburgh.

Very different was their appearance now from those days when, as scarlet-clad Light Horse, they filed over the old Berwick Bridge, with John Hale in command.

Everything changed but facings, badge, and motto; no longer Light Dragoons even, but gay Blue Lancers, in booted overalls, with smart white "butterflies" turned back under their chest belts, and red and white banneroles fluttering from the bamboo lance staves.

I do not know whether any of Peter Ker's descendants were in being to listen to the muffled thunder of the kettledrums that heralded the approach of the newcomers, but it is certain that Colonel Balders and his officers stormed no tollhouses this time!

Apropos of this allusion to the change in the habits and customs of the British officer wrought by the passage of a century, one may be pardoned for introducing in this place an order, gravely promulgated by the Horse Guards as recently as November, 1845 :—

The Commander-in-Chief has been informed that the practice of smoking by the use of pipes, cigars, or cheroots, has become prevalent among the officers of the Army, which is not only in itself a species of intoxication occasioned by the fumes of tobacco, but undoubtedly occasions drinking and tippling by those who acquire the habit ; and he intreats the officers commanding Regiments to prevent smoking in the Mess Rooms of their several Regiments, and in the adjoining apartments, and to discourage the practice among the officers of Junior Rank in their Regiments.

I do not know what effect this had on the morals of the 17th, but I do know that the late Laslett J. Pott, on the eve of the Crimean War, found Lieut.-Colonel Darby-Griffith, who commanded the Greys at Balaclava, not only sucking a short black pipe in Nottingham Barracks, but found him also in his shirt-sleeves. Truly, grandmotherly legislation had not affected that gallant soldier over much!

In 1868 they received bamboo lance shafts, and during this year 1869 their plumes were altered from white to black, an innovation that did not last long, and the "squadron organisation" was tried until April, 1870, when the troop system was again reverted to, and continued in use until 1892.

It was laughingly stated in the regiment that the black plumes were adopted as mourning for "Mick," the bear, who had been brought from Secunderabad, and died in 1868.

He was a popular pet, and his particular chum was a man named Gillett, who could do anything with him, but he scared the bandboys, and was a terror to the sentries when he shuffled noiselessly alongside one of them in the silent watches of the night, and stood up on his hind legs!

In April, 1870, the regiment moved to the Royal Barracks and Arbour Hill, Dublin, occupying quarters in Ireland for the next five years, and four months after its arrival its numbers were increased to 540 men and 350 horses.

In 1871 various changes were adopted in the Army, all of which affected the 17th sooner or later; the purchase and sale of commissions very properly "went by the board"; "short service"—on the true merits of which there will probably always exist a difference of opinion—was introduced, and in November the time-honoured rank of cornet was abolished.

The farriers' churns disappeared in 1872, and jack boots came into use; but perhaps the greatest alteration of all was in 1876, when, returning to the white plumes again, they also received the full white plastron for the front of their tunics—a change that carries the mind back to their dress regulation of 1812 again.

There is no doubt that the uniform of the regiment from this time forward became one of the handsomest in the British army; that of the 11th Hussars runs it very close, and the Scarlet Lancers have a claim to consideration; but, without making any invidious comparisons, there is something unusually striking about a "Death or Glory Boy" in whatever "order" one meets him; whether mounted, with white plumed helmet and fluttering pennon, his pipeclayed chest swelling with pardonable pride under the yellow festooned lines, or walking out in the now doomed stable jacket—smartest garment that was ever devised to show off a fine shoulder and a hollow back—round forage cap—also soon to be a thing of the past—set over one ear, with well-curled "quiff," and trousers so creaseless that it is a marvel to the uninitiated how they are put on and off.

The same year that witnessed the adoption of the plastron saw a change in the title of the regiment. H.R.H. the Duke of Cambridge, who had held the colonelcy from 1843 to 1852, was now made Colonel-in-Chief, and the 17th became "The Duke of Cambridge's Own."

Another change of some importance, effected also in 1876, was the issue of six carbines to each troop, the Lancers having previously carried no firearm but a pistol, and in 1878 carbines of the Martini-Henri pattern were given to the entire regiment, the pistols being sent into store, and sergeant-majors and trumpeters armed with revolvers.

After ringing the changes between Longford, Athlone, Ballinrobe, Castlebar, and Gort (1871), Ballincollig, Limerick, Cork, Fermoy and Clogheen (1872), a month on the Curragh the following year, and back to Island Bridge again in the autumn, the regiment moved in August, 1874, to Dundalk, Belfast, and a troop in December to Belturbet; returned once more to Island Bridge, Dublin, in June, 1875, and the following June sailed for England, where it took part in the manœuvres in Somersetshire, and afterwards proceeded to East Cavalry Barracks, Aldershot, for a course of Long Valley and Laffan's Plain.

In August, 1877, headquarters marched to Leeds, and in May, 1878, detachments were acting against the cotton strikers in Lancashire, charging down Castle

AN UNFORTUNATE ACCIDENT. 257

Hill at Clitheroe, and upholding law and order in the disturbed districts of Burnley and Blackburn.

After another visit to Aldershot they took up their quarters at Hounslow and Hampton Court, where, on the 10th February, 1879, warning came to get ready for active service once more.

An unfortunate accident marred their wild enthusiasm. The lieut.-colonel commanding, Thomas Gonne, a very smart officer and fine "drill," was shot at revolver practice, and so seriously injured that he lost his chance of the campaign.

He was standing close to Troop Sergeant-Major Paul, and the command was given to fire "right and high," when by some mischance Lieutenant Russell, the musketry instructor, reloading his revolver, lodged two bullets in the colonel's groin.

The sergeant-major, who had narrowly escaped the shots himself, galloped back to Hounslow on the colonel's horse for the doctor, and Mrs. Benson, daughter-in-law of General Benson, who had led them at Zirápúr carried the stretcher down.

The doctor's horse was lame, so he exchanged with Paul, whose mount took him to the spot at top speed, and the wounded man was conveyed to his house at Heston, three miles off.

Colonel Gonne, who had entered the service in 1855, had been with the regiment in the Tantia troubles, as acting interpreter and staff officer with the 2nd Cavalry Column, and it is not possible to imagine harder luck on the very eve of going to the front again.

As a result of this mishap, Drury Lowe, who had retired in 1878, was appointed supernumerary lieut.-colonel to take the regiment out.

R

Sixty-five men and horses from the 5th Royal Irish and the Scarlet Lancers brought the regiment up to fighting strength, and their own band was turned into the ranks.

The duke came down to inspect them at Hounslow on the 22nd, and on the 24th one wing under Major Sam Boulderson, A, D, E, and F Troops, embarked on the *France* at Victoria Docks, the other wing, B, C, G, and H Troops, under Drury Lowe, embarking on the *England* at Southampton on the 25th.

They had given in their sheepskins, shabraques, and lance caps, and received white helmets, which, with their tunics buttoned over blue, and their usual breeches and jackboots, formed the regiment's dress for the campaign; a dress destined to be very much the worse for wear before they had finished, one man— this on the authority of the sergeant-major—patching his pants with a piece of tin, the exact locality not stated!

The strength on embarkation was 570 of all ranks and 522 horses, five of the latter dying on the *England* during the voyage, and six on the *France*.

The voyage was uneventful; both ships were detained at St. Vincent and again at Table Bay to coal, but reaching Durban early in April the regiment was ashore by the 14th, and encamped for a few days at Cator's Manor, Drury Lowe's right wing marching to Landman's Drift on the 17th, Boulderson's left wing on the 21st to Dundee, a place which has now such a tragic interest for us all in view of recent events. The 17th practically came in for the fag end of the Zulu War.

The horrors of Isandhlwana, the heroism of Rorke's Drift, Gingihlovo, Inhlobane Mountain, Kambula, and many a now forgotten fight; these were all past and gone, but the regiment landed in time to take part in the final advance after the rearrangement of the British forces.

Brigadier-General Wood's "Flying Column" (the 17th's old officer, Evelyn Wood) was to bear down from the north upon the king's kraal at Ulundi, while the 2nd Division, under Major-General Newdigate, C.B., was to march upon it from Landman's Drift on the rapid Buffalo River, and to the 2nd Division was attached the Cavalry Brigade—the K.D.G.'s and the 17th Lancers.

The two regiments marched up to Rorke's Drift under Major-General Marshall, and a party of the 17th helped to bury the dead at Isandhlwana on the 21st May, and to bring in some of the waggons, joining the 2nd Division at Landman's Drift on the 23rd, and finally crossing the Blood River into Zululand on the 1st June.

On the 5th they had a skirmish with the enemy at Erzungayan Hill, where they lost their adjutant, Mr. F. J. C. Frith, who was shot by the Colonel's side.

When news came of the death of the Prince Imperial, the 17th and the 1st Dragoon Guards furnished the escort that went up to the spot, and the hope of the Bonapartes was brought in on a stretcher improvised from a horseblanket and two lances of G Troop.

The late Alphonse de Neuville, greatest of all military painters, depicted the regiment in more than one picture of this period.

A good deal of hard work fell to its share during the next month, outpost and reconnaissance duty;

and on several occasions they came in touch with the enemy, but never very seriously.

A squadron was sent to Fort Marshal on the line of communications, the rest continuing with the 2nd Division on its march towards the headquarters of Cetewayo, which it neared in company with Wood's column on the 3rd July, hearing the war songs of the Zulus in their kraals, and expecting to be attacked that night.

At four o'clock next morning the force crossed the White Umvolosi River, the three squadrons of the 17th acting as rearguard, and the advance, 4,166 Europeans, 958 natives, 12 field guns, and 2 Gatlings, formed a huge hollow square, the sides of which marched in fours, the front and rear faces being deployed.

Inside were the Natal native contingent, the ammunition, and hospital bearers, the Dragoon Guards and Lancers covering the whole until the surrounding hills began to swarm with Zulus, when the square was halted, and the cavalry trotted in and dismounted.

A huge circle of savages was closing round us; magnificent fellows, black and brown, with shields and assegais, feathers and floating leopard skins; a grand barbaric horde of foemen worthy of the British steel, which they were about to taste with a vengeance, after the Gatlings and field guns and Martinis had played the prelude.

A little before nine, on a fine morning—blue sky and rolling cloud, and the rugged outline of cleft and cliff for a background—the Zulus began their attack, and in spite of a murderous fire from the square, it was nearly three-quarters of an hour before they showed symptoms that they had had enough.

"UP HILL AND DOWN DALE THE 17TH HARRIED THE FLYING NATIVES" (*p.* 261).

Our colours were uncased and flying; men fell and were passed into the centre of the square; the Lancers were lying down when a bullet cut the back out of Trumpeter Connor's jackboot, within an inch of the nose of Sergeant-Major Paul, of G Troop, who was lighting his pipe at the moment.

A cross-fire told heavily on the square, and Lieutenant Jenkins was shot in the jaw, but outside, within a radius of 100 yards, we were piling up black and red heaps of Zulus, and the impis began to waver at last.

Then three British cheers were called for and given with a will; "Up 17th and at 'em!" followed; Chelmsford ordered Drury Lowe to engage, and through an opening in the rear-face the "Death or Glory Boys" filed out, Captain Wyatt Edgell and his troop farrier being killed at the same moment—had the Captain lived a little longer, he would have succeeded to the title of Lord Braye!

Forming up in echelon of wings, rank entire, with a front of something over 300 yards, the lance points came down and the squadrons charged!

They were fired on heavily from front and flank as they got under weigh, but there was no resisting the impetuous rush of eager men and horses, and the Zulus, hidden in a grassy donga, broke and fled before them!

Old Indian officers must have read the account with a quickening pulse, for it was Tantia Topee over again, and the "pig-sticking" pursuit of two miles was also a revival of ancient memories.

Up hill and down dale, through the waving Tamboukie grass, the 17th harried the flying natives, and

Cetewayo's army melted away before them, Buller's men sallying out in their wake.

The colonel was hit by a spent ball, and Private Waite stuck pluckily to his saddle for ten minutes after he was wounded and bleeding freely; the day was not won without casualties, and the 17th had their share.

Drury Lowe, Mr. James, of the Greys, attached to the 17th, and Adjutant H. C. Jenkins were wounded, with 5 men; Wyatt Edgell and 2 men were killed, and 26 horses were returned either killed or wounded.

Next day the 2nd Division set out on the march back, reaching the Upoko River on the 15th, and, after handing over its horses to the 1st Dragoon Guards at Dundee, the regiment went down on foot to Pinetown, *en route* for its third tour of Indian service.

In September it was reduced to 6 troops; 198 time-expired men and invalids returning to England under Lieutenant Kevill-Davis; while, on the 1st October, Major Boulderson assumed command in place of Colonel Drury Lowe, the left wing sailing in H.M.S. *Serapis* on the 8th, the right wing in H.M.S. *Crocodile* on the 20th, landing at Bombay and uniting at Mhow once more in November.

Lieut.-Colonel Gonne arrived on the 4th December, and took command, which he retained until his appointment as Military Attaché at St. Petersburg in April, 1881.

The regiment suffered a severe disappointment in 1880, being unable to proceed on active service in Afghanistan, as desired by General Phayre, through the bad state of the saddlery it had taken over, but

20 non-commissioned officers and men went up on transport duty in July, and were afterwards thanked in orders.

The 17th lay at Mhow until January, 1884, and in February relieved the 10th Hussars at Lucknow, where they were destined to remain until they got the route for home in 1890.

Few incidents of importance happened in the meantime: Lieut.-General H. R. Benson succeeded to the colonelcy in 1884, and in December a squadron acted as escort to General Sir Frederick Roberts, the Commander-in-Chief in India, at the camp of exercise; but there is nothing further to record, beyond the sad death of Lieutenant Dyer, whose pony ran him under a tree, with fatal results.

On the 9th October, 1890, the regiment sailed in the *Serapis* once more; lost Captain Butler, who died at sea; left a squadron at Suez for duty with the British army of occupation in Egypt, and landed on the 3rd November at Portsmouth, from whence it went to Shorncliffe to be acclimatised, the detached squadron rejoining the following year.

On the regiment's arrival from India it took over the drum horse of the 11th Hussars, and the stately, piebald creature has done duty at the head of the "Death or Glory Boys" ever since, in spite of its age, which must be somewhere about twenty years.

Another member of the corps who merits a place in this record was brought home from Lucknow— "Lizzie," the pet bear.

Her mother was shot in Cashmere by Prince Adolphus of Teck, who gave the cub to his troop, but one day the little animal mysteriously disappeared, and was "absent without leave" for a whole year, until she was recognised in the company of a travelling showman, and claimed by her old comrades.

From their arrival in England their stations have been as follows:—

1891.—Shorncliffe.	1895.—Leeds.
1892.—Hounslow.	1896.—York.
1893.— ,,	1897.— ,,
1894.—Preston.	1898.—Ballincollig,

where they remained until the end of 1899, watching with the keenest interest the events taking place on the scene of their last campaign, ready for "The route" if it should chance to come their way!

An attempt had been made in 1897 to get horses of a uniform colour for the various squadrons—C squadron, in particular, having two troops of chestnuts; but an outbreak of pink-eye in the Scots Greys afterwards rendered the attempt abortive.

The 17th's mounts were requisitioned for the Greys, and replaced by registered horses.

Later on, these in their turn got pink-eye, and when the regiment moved, it moved dismounted.

CHAPTER XV.

THE LANCER BRIGADE IN SOUTH AFRICA.

Aldershot—" Old 25th Light Horse"—Ready for Action—Cape Town—Bloemfontein — 3rd Cavalry Brigade — Grootfontein — Dewetsdorp—Thabanchu—Condemned to Death—The Advance on Pretoria—Death of Fortescue—Diamond Hill—A Remount Party—Gordon succeeded by Herbert—Lawrence, V.C. — Elands River— Murder of Greenwood—Lancer Brigade Broken up at Bloemfontein.

ON the 1st January, 1900, the 17th left Ireland for Aldershot, to form, with the 7th Dragoon Guards and the 8th Hussars, the Fourth Cavalry Brigade.

A strong friendship has existed for many years between the 8th and the 17th, and a tradition is found among Mutiny men that the two regiments once formed a single corps—the "Old 25th Light Horse," but, unfortunately for this, like many traditions, there is no truth in it, the number 25 having been arrived at by the adding together of the two regimental numbers in a spirit of *cameraderie*.

At Aldershot the 17th were once more mounted on registered horses, and they were fortunate in securing a very respectable lot.

They were also joined by the reservists of the 21st Lancers, and for the next few weeks all ranks were busy preparing for active service.

Three months' hard fighting had passed before the 17th got "the route," and in the history of those three months are to be found some of the bravest and bloodiest pages of Britain's annals.

Talana Hill, Elandslaagte, Rietfontein, Lombard's Kop and Nicholson's Nek, Modder and Magersfontein, and the terrible Colenso battle, had thrilled the heart and dimmed the eye; and the memory of those slaughter lists will remain vividly with those of us who read them day after day, as long as we shall remember anything.

They had a peculiar interest for men under orders, and the regiment was impatient of every delay.

The band was turned into the ranks; lance-caps and tunics were sent into store, and they went into khaki, with the white metal badge on the left side of the helmet as the distinguishing mark of the regiment.

Bandoliers were issued, each holding fifty rounds for the Lee-Metford carbine, most of the officers carrying Mauser pistols; one suit of blue was taken—riding pants and serge frock—and the blue service-cap piped with white; the reservists having the white-topped service-cap, afterwards adopted by the regiment.

On the 15th January H.R.H. the Duke of Cambridge, their Colonel-in-Chief, inspected them on parade in a downpour of rain; the men, drawn up, dismounted, in review order; and the reservists, who paraded separately, were complimented for their smartness and the alacrity with which they had answered to the call to arms.

Still, there came delay after delay, until it seemed that the 4th Cavalry Brigade would never sail; but at last the eventful day arrived, and a furious blizzard swept over Aldershot.

It was the 14th February, and when the first party paraded at 3 a.m. snow had been falling heavily for some hours.

After a hasty mouthful they started for the Government siding in the teeth of a blinding storm, the first train leaving just before five, in charge of Major the Hon. Lionel Fortescue, the headquarter staff following at 7.30.

At Tilbury Docks, which they reached after a bitter journey, they found hot coffee and another breakfast, and the ss. *Victorian*—trooper No. 66—lying alongside the wharf. All morning relays of frozen lancers, buttoned up in their blue overcoats, kept arriving, and the horses were got aboard without accident. At half-past ten a draft of the Lancashire Fusiliers, 250 strong, came over by the ferry, and with them the band of the 4th Shropshires. Everything was grey and wintry; but, in spite of the miserable weather and the howling storm, all ranks were in high spirits. Early in the afternoon all were aboard, but the troopship had to wait for the morning's tide.

The exact strength of the 17th on the *Victorian* was 24 officers, 596 non-commissioned officers and men, and 505 horses.

There was little of interest to recount during the voyage of the *Victorian*. Several horses died, and they lost a man on the night of the 1st March. The service was read by the chaplain next morning, every one attending; the trumpeters sounded the "Last Post," and the three volleys were fired as the body was committed to the deep.

On 7th March each man was served out with 1 lb. of Lambert and Butler's Navy Cut, a Balaclava cap guernsey, large handkerchief, pipe, and pocket-case, containing twelve letter-cards and a pencil, from the regimental presents.

After a quick passage, they reached Cape Town on the 10th March, at noon, and, taking their turn for the quay, landed and disembarked stores on the 12th, finally moving off at 3 p.m., and leading their horses to Maitland Camp.

After picketing the horses, they pitched the tents they had brought with them, and in that camp they remained until 2nd April, practising the new cavalry tactics, the rest of the regiment joining on the 21st March. This latter portion — one troop of A squadron, two officers, 101 non-commissioned officers and men, and 39 horses—had an adventure which might have proved very serious.

They had embarked at Southampton on the *Pinemore*, and encountering severe weather off Land's End, had put into Queenstown with something wrong.

Divers discovered that one of the propeller blades had been lost during the gale, and, it being feared that the shaft might have sustained damage, it was decided to ship M Battery, R.H.A., with some other troops, and send the *Pinemore* to Liverpool to be overhauled, hence the delay.

While at Maitland Camp about 20 men were sent to do duty with the pompoms.

There was a rumour in Cape Town that Cecil Rhodes had offered a prize of £1,000 for the best trophy shield of regimental badges—I am not prepared to say whether there was any truth in it—but people were collecting wildly, and as thirty shillings were freely offered for the skull-and-crossbones of the 17th—the price at home is 4½d.—it is not surprising that some of the Death or Glory Boys went up country with the "Old Totts" marked in aniline pencil on the side of their helmets.

Orders to move to Bloemfontein were received on the 2nd April, to the intense delight of all ranks, and the regiment steamed out of Cape Town at 5 p.m., on the 3rd, amid great cheering and waving of Union Jacks by the spectators.

The strength on entraining was 23 officers, 475 N.C.O.'s and men, 65 chargers, and 433 troop horses.

On the 6th, at Norval's Point, where the bridge over the Orange River had been blown up, they left the train and crossed by a temporary bridge, and on resuming their journey they were ordered to keep fully dressed, with carbines and ammunition handy, being then in the enemy's country.

The line was guarded by patrols, and at Jacobsfontein Road Station magazines were charged, bandoliers put on, and no lights permitted on the train.

At Krugersdorp a good many old seventeenths who had been drafted into other regiments came by chance to look at the train from the large cavalry camp at that place; and there were no doubt many heartburnings among them at the sight of the old corps going up without them.

When they awoke at six o'clock on the morning of Sunday, the 8th, they found themselves at Bloemfontein, the capital of the Orange Free State, where they detrained, saddled up, breakfasted, and filed off through the town to the camp, four miles distant.

Bloemfontein had only been occupied by the British three days before the 17th landed in Cape Town, and rest was absolutely imperative for the Army.

Batteries required re-horsing, cavalry was in a sad state, the infantry battalions were over-marched and battle-thinned, and it was more than six weeks before the general advance began again.

At Bloemfontein, too, enteric first broke out seriously, and our losses from that cause amounted to more than 1,000 men in the town alone.

Nor were things quiet during the period of recuperation.

Karee, Sanna's Post, and Reddersburg, had to be entered on our battle-roll, as also the affair at Boshoff, where De Villebois Mareuil was killed.

At Bloemfontein the 17th went to the 3rd Cavalry Brigade, which was now to consist of the 9th, 16th, and 17th Lancers, under Brigadier-General J. R. P. Gordon, who had been gazetted from the 15th Hussars to the colonelcy of the 17th, and there they handed in swords and belts, carrying only lance and carbine.

Matches were not to be had for love or money, a cup of tea cost a shilling, as did also a shave; the whole town was given over to the troops, and all civilians had to be indoors by eight o'clock at night.

The following extract from a Regimental Order, by Major E. B. Herbert, commanding, dated Rustfontein, 18th April, 1900, is not without interest:—

Horses	No horse or pony is ever to be ridden without bit or briddoon in its mouth.
Cloaks	Cloaks will be carried on the front of the saddle, eyeletted blankets in rear.
Horses	The F. M. C.-in-C. again calls attention to the great necessity, when opportunity offers, of frequently dismounting men from their horses, and of watering, feeding, and grazing on every available opportunity.
Kits	The following will be carried on the buck waggons by each squadron:— Officers, 35 lbs. each; mess, 80 lbs. each squadron; squad sergt.-majors, squad quart.-mast.-sergt., 18 lbs., equal 36 lbs.; N.C.O.'s and men, 10 lbs. The following will be carried in the kit bag only:—1 kit bag, 1 shirt, 1 pair drawers,

	1 drill khaki jacket, 1 blanket, 1 towel and soap, 1 pair socks; knife, fork, and spoon will be carried in the haversack.
Food and Forage	One day's rations.

* * * * *

The men carried on the back of their saddles, in addition to the blanket, pegs, hay-nets, and built-up rope, and several times the entire regiment was turned out and paraded exactly as if they had received orders to march, one day the order coming in real earnest, during those operations known as the "clearing of the south-east."

De Wet was busy to eastward, and a forcible menace to our lines of communication.

Colonel Dalgetty, of the Cape Mounted Rifles, with 400 Cape Mounted Rifles, 1,000 of Brabant's horse, 400 Kaffrarian Horse, some scouts, and a hundred regulars, were surrounded by De Wet at Jammersberg, three miles from Wepener on the Basuto border, and it was in connection with the relief of that place that the 17th received their baptism of fire.

Dalgetty's defence reflected the highest honour upon himself and his entire command, and he maintained his position against a very superior force for seventeen days, until the enemy retired, thoroughly worsted.

The weather became very bad during the latter part of April; the country was in a sodden condition, the veldt very heavy going and beginning to lose its grass.

On Sunday, the 22nd, the countersign was "Curlew," and Divine service was ordered for 8.30, but, about 10 a.m., when they were at stables, the trumpets suddenly sounded "boots and saddles," and the Brigade had orders to be ready to march in three-quarters of an hour.

For a moment there was great bustle and confusion,

but the regiment paraded in double-quick time, and dismounted to draw rations of bully beef, some of them borrowing handkerchiefs to hold coffee.

When everything was ready—in the words of our corporal—"the topic of conversation was not fighting, but football."

Then they went off across the veldt on their way to smell powder!

The first trek was about 18 miles, the horses were linked, and the men used their saddles for pillows.

Réveille went at 4 a.m. next morning, and everyone expected to come in touch with the enemy that day.

The Brigade gained its first experience of Boer "slimness" during the march, as after passing a house covered with white flags, the rearguard of the Scarlet Lancers was fired on and a sergeant killed. A party returned, and, very properly, burned the place to the ground.

On the 24th a good deal of firing was heard among the hills, and the Brigade halted in front of Kleep's Drift; a squadron of the 17th was pushed forward as advance guard, and, seeing the Boers making for some kopjes, dismounted with their carbines and gained the height before them.

The Brigade arrived in support, and after a sharp fire of some half-hour's duration, the enemy retired.

Unfortunately the Maxim-gun detachment of the 17th suffered considerably, losing Sergeant Sutherton, killed, and having Lieut. Skeffington, Sergeant Cook, and Privates Collins and Hamer wounded.

They speak of this affair as the scrap at Grootfontein, and the next day General French took over command of all the cavalry.

On the 25th the 17th marched off at 6 a.m., leading

tne advance, reconnoitring kopjes and examining all the farms and buildings *en route*, in search of arms and ammunition.

In the afternoon a patrol got under fire and had to ride for it, but the enemy disappeared when they went back and opened fire with their carbines; and after fifteen hours in the saddle the troop returned to the Brigade Camp at Dewetsdorp, men and horses thoroughly done, to find the rest of the regiment out on escort duty. On the 26th they started on a six days' march, with half rations, to Thabanchu, the Boer force that menaced Wepener having suddenly disappeared; and the new trek was not without its incidents and hardships.

So far the regiment had procured good water, but most of their early campaigning was done on biscuit and a pull at the belt, with the hope of a good supper at the end of the day if all went well.

They were nearly falling into a trap before they had gone far, when reconnoitring during the afternoon.

They were riding over a level tract of land with hills on three sides, and horsemen were seen coming out in front and on both flanks. At first they were believed to be some of our own fellows, but while the officers were taking stock with their field glasses, the new-comers settled all doubts by galloping forward, and opening fire on all three sides at once.

Discretion was the better part of valour, and we retired on the spur, fortunately getting clear in time, although the horses were in bad condition, and had been without corn for two days.

To chronicle every little affair of this kind that happened to the regiment would fill a volume.

The history of the war is largely made up of them; sometimes we fell back, sometimes the enemy; many a bright young lad found an end to his soldiering in just such an incident which has not even a name in history, many a sturdy *dopper* fell from his saddle and was left on the veldt, or the hillside, to be buried by some future colonist who will find the whitening bones, and wonder who he was, and how he died.

On the 27th took place an abortive attempt to surround the enemy on Thabanchu Mountain, a tall, precipitous height enclosing a grassy basin in which the Boer laagers were reported to lie.

The mountain is crescent-shaped, with a long spur stretching out from its face in a north-westerly direction, and another roughly at right angles, and the position was strongly held by guns and riflemen.

There had been a sharp fight the evening before, when Kitchener's Horse, who had been holding a hill, were attacked as they retired into the town.

Major Fowle, now commanding the 21st Lancers, brought them off after beating back the enemy, and sustaining some loss, and early next morning we sallied out of the town to drive the Boers from their mountain and to capture their laagers if possible.

The 3rd Cavalry Brigade was sent to the right to pass the east of the mountain by a defile, and force a way into the plains behind; Ian Hamilton was to attack the Boer right and open the road for Dickson's Cavalry, while Rundle, who had come up from Dewetsdorp, was to hold the town and feint against the enemy's centre.

Smith-Dorrien's infantry and Ridley's Mounted Infantry began the action, the former re-occupying Kitchener's Horse Hill, Dickson's Cavalry passing through a gap to the rear of the Boer right.

The Boer strength was not definitely known, being variously given as "2,000," and, later on, as "small parties," but, as we were to discover, the enemy was in considerable force.

Dickson and Ridley turned their right, and the Horse Artillery and the pompoms were busy.

It was expected that the 3rd Cavalry Brigade would get them on the move and drive them into our arms, but the Lancers found it impossible to make headway.

C Squadron of the 17th and a squadron of the 9th went round the eastern end of the mountain and entered the plain behind it, and A troop, B squadron, of the 17th, passed through the defile, but that was the extent of our advance on that side.

A very hot fire was suddenly opened by the enemy, who were swarming on the kopjes and the side of a high hill, and word was sent to Sergeant Paul of the detached troop of the 17th to get back as the Boers advanced.

He went about and galloped through the defile again, not a moment too soon, as Lieutenant Theobald of the 9th and three men were captured, the other squadrons retiring on the Brigade.

Squadron Quartermaster-Sergeant Lewns of the 17th was taken through his horse falling, and there was nothing for it but to pound away with our guns.

The Boers were masters of the situation, and when, on the approach of evening, Dickson decided to return, he was hardly pressed, and not only did the "small parties" open on him at long range, but practically charged him, capturing the brigadier's mess cart and the regimental water-carts, until Ian Hamilton drove them back with heavy fire.

The main body of the enemy—whose numbers seem to have been about 6,000—had in the meantime trekked way to north-east and escaped from the trap.

On the 28th the regiment was reconnoitring, losing one man shot through the head, and three horses, and after a hard day's work on biscuit and water, they were posted to guard a pass.

Sunday, the 29th, was one of action, after a bitterly cold night, and they started off at dawn on empty stomachs until 10 a.m., when they halted, and unsaddled for the first time for two days.

After a meal—the patrols having reported all safe, and when they were washing in the river, and looking forward to a rest—firing was heard among the kopjes about Thabanchu, and they saddled up in haste.

A squadron went to the left, B to the front, and Captain Warner took a flag message from the 9th Lancers, "Boers advancing in hundreds"; B squadron was ordered to dismount. They were under shell fire all the remainder of the day, and eventually retired, getting back to camp at 6 o'clock, joining the Brigade at Izraal Port. Our corporal records that his wash was the first one for six days!

The nights were now very cold, but the sun shone brightly during the whole of these operations.

On the 1st May the enemy were surrounded on a big kopje called Thaba Mountain; the Artillery shelled them out, and the Lancers decimated them with carbine fire when they moved; the Brigade had no losses, but 300 Boers were reported killed, and many wounded.

On the 3rd the Brigade was ordered back to Bloemfontein to its great delight, and camped that night at Bushman's Kop, reached Bloemfontein on the 4th, and began preparations for another march.

The advance on Pretoria had already commenced, the centre column having started with hearts high, and bands playing on the 1st, thankful to leave the fever-stricken town that had filled the hospitals and thinned the ranks.

At Bloemfontein the regiment re-equipped: there were fatigues all day, inspections of clothing, arms, saddlery, and weeding out of horses that had become used up on the march.

The Regimental After Orders for the 5th contain particular instructions for the waggons; the mules were not to be trotted under any circumstances, and it was pointed out that harness had been seen to press upon fresh sores among some of the waggons of the Brigade, due to carelessness.

A private of the regiment, condemned to death for sleeping at his post, had his sentence commuted by the Lieut.-General commanding the Division, to two years' hard labour, and our corporal thus comments on the affair, "Everyone of us is sorry for him, as everyone is liable to do it. Sometimes a man doesn't get any sleep for three nights, and perhaps working hard all day, so that it cannot be wondered at, although it is such a serious crime."

On the 7th the Brigade marched, passed the ruins of Glen Bridge over the Modder, which had been blown up by the Boers, crossed the battle-ground at Karee Siding, where the newly made graves were visible on the kopje sides, and camped three miles off.

On the 8th they passed through Brandfort, and there our corporal obtained a glass of milk for sixpence.

They were escorting three miles of baggage, and had to keep their eyes open.

About 10 o'clock on the morning of the 9th of May they found the enemy, who opened from some kopjes with two Long Toms and a pompom, but our guns came up and cleared them out, and they galloped out of sight, leaving the way free for the Brigade to join Lord Roberts' force at Virginia Siding.

From this place French took the left of the advance with the 1st, 2nd, and 4th Brigades, and the 3rd Lancer Brigade, under Gordon, marched on the right.

Thursday, the 10th, there was no fighting for the 17th, but the following day they found the Boers strongly entrenched at Boschrand, about six miles in front of Kroonstadt.

The Boers opened a very hot Mauser fire, to which we replied, and when our artillery came up we dosed them with shrapnel, the fight continuing until dark, and the Brigade bivouacking where they stood.

Fortunately, there were some stray sheep, which were promptly annexed, and came in handy after two days on biscuit and water.

Réveille went at four in the morning, and the regiment moved off as advance guard, expecting a heavy fight, but the enemy had retired during the night, leaving a network of elaborate trenches and shelter pits, and an immense quantity of picks and shovels.

Capturing about a score of prisoners by the way, the advance guard reached Kroonstadt about 11 o'clock the Landrost and principal officials handing over possession of the town.

The regiment remained in camp until the 17th, when they were sent off, hot foot, to the south, to capture a force of 800 of the enemy, who were attempting the lines of communications; but at Boschrand, where they halted for the night, they heard that the foe had given in, and returned once more to camp.

At Kroonstadt Lord Roberts made an eight days' halt, until the railway had been repaired and supplies brought up, and before the end of that time food was running low in the town, a 2-lb. loaf costing two shillings, and other things in proportion.

But it was about time to trek once more, as witnessed by the Regimental Orders issued on the 20th, from which we take some extracts:—

(1.) "*Réveille* 4.30 a.m.; feed and breakfast, stand-to and ready to march off at 6.10 a.m. The task allotted to the Brigade is to reconnoitre and clear up the country between Honingspruit and Boschpoort.

(2.) "The 16th Lancers will find the Advance Guard, one squadron on the Heilbron Road, one squadron to move *viâ* Swellendam and Doornland. The headquarter squadron to move on the line bisecting the angle formed by the railway and the Heilbron Road.

(3.) "B Squadron, 17th Lancers, will furnish an officer's patrol (one section), to move through Welgevomden, Gelucks, Krall, Fonteinspruit, to a point on the Heilbron Road $1\frac{1}{2}$ miles beyond Boschpoort, then to regain the Brigade.

(4.) "The main body will move at first on the Heilbron Road, and then strike N.E. towards Klip Kraal and Kleindoornkop.

(5.) "Reports to be sent to the G.O.C., who will ride at the head of the column. Negative reports to be sent every hour."

On the 22nd the march was resumed, *réveille* went at 4 a.m., and the 17th moved off an hour later in the bitterly cold dawn.

One troop was missed, and believed to have been captured, but it turned up three days later, having fallen in with Lord Roberts' column, and acted as his bodyguard.

On the 24th, the Queen's Birthday, the 17th went out to hunt up an overdue convoy, found it at Rodewall in the afternoon, and escorted it; were hung up at a steep drift for five hours, marched until three in the morning, had a two hours' halt, and got into Vredefort the following afternoon, where the transport awaited them with beef and biscuit, finally reaching the Brigade at 8 p.m., thoroughly done up.

On the 26th they acted as rearguard to Roberts' advance, and arrived at the Vaal River on Sunday the 27th.

The 17th had continued on the right of the advance all the way from Bloemfontein, and, while the main body halted, patrols reconnoitred, were fired upon, and reported swarms of Boers in the kopjes ahead.

The 17th opened a hot fire on them, and used their pompom with considerable effect, the Boers picking up their wounded and retiring quickly over the hill.

The 3rd Brigade then moved about eight miles to the west, to Viljoen's Drift, and crossed the river into the Transvaal, their casualties being one wounded and two captured, and their bivouack at Vereeniging, a town of coal mines.

"It was awfully cold in the night," says our journal, "couldn't get warm nohow; in the morning we had to break the ice in the necks of our water-bottles."

The movements of the rest of the advancing force are matter of history: how Louis Botha fell back from Rhenoster, how French had crossed on the 24th at Parys, and Ian Hamilton had been brought from our right flank to the left, hoodwinking the enemy, who mistook him for the main body and concentrated to no purpose twenty miles east of Vereeniging.

The hard work and short rations were beginning to tell severely on men and horses, and on the 29th our corporal found his mount so done up that he had to follow on foot, falling in with several other men in the same case.

"We are all very near starved," he writes, "being on half rations, horses as well. After it got dark we lost our Brigade, and stopped where we were for the night. All we had to eat was some bread-crumbs one of the men found in an empty house. That was after going all day with nothing.—May 30th. Caught the Brigade up in the morning, and found some mealie flour, which we boiled and ate. It wasn't up to much, but goodness knows what you wouldn't eat when you're hungry. The Boers started attacking us with big guns, but retired after about three hours' firing on both sides. We were served out with a biscuit and a half this morning as a day's food, having had no meat for three days."

The Lancer Brigade continued to work on the right of the advance and moved on Boksberg.

They did not go into Johannesburg, but on the morning following Lord Roberts' entry, and which was to have been a much-needed day of rest, instead of "revallay" going at 7 o'clock as laid down in orders, the enemy sounded it at 6.15, with shell fire, and after a mutual exchange of courtesies and continuous "scrapping" until four, the Brigade moved off for the dynamite works at Modderfontein, B squadron of the 17th having to report all clear within ten miles of that place.

At eight o'clock on the night of the 30th, a composite force of 200 men from all three regiments, including about 70 of the 17th, started, under Major Hunter-Weston, with Burnham, the celebrated American scout, to blow up the Delagoa Railway, and so cut off the Boer retreat; but, after walking all night, they were unexpectedly attacked at dawn by a strong commando, and had to retire, with a loss of 5 killed and 14 wounded.

Of the 17th, Lance-Corporal Rose was severely wounded, a private was wounded, and another captured.

Sergeant Witts and Corporal Page made a very plucky attempt to rescue Rose, and remained with him until the Boers were within a few yards.

The Brigade moved on Pretoria on the 3rd June, and started shelling it, and the shelling was continued against the hills all the next day.

On the 4th, A squadron, under Major Lionel Fortescue, was surrounded on a kopje, but was reinforced from the Brigade, but had to retire as the Boers fired the long grass.

That night they bivouacked at Six Mile Spruit, and next day the Brigade halted just outside Pretoria.

The capture of the seat of the Boer Government is too well known to need more than a few words here.

The advance had been resumed on the 3rd June, French's cavalry forming the left, and Ian Hamilton the centre, the main column, under Lord Roberts in person, consisting of the 7th and 11th Divisions, the Lancer Brigade, and the Corps Troops.

Some resistance was experienced on the 4th from the range of hills to the south of the town, where two strong forts guarded the Nek, but the absence of heavy gun fire showed that the guns had been removed, and the affair resolved itself into a stand by the Boer rearguard to cover Botha's retreat.

While we pounded them in front, Broadwood's cavalry turned their right flank, and De Lisle's mounted infantry made a charge, and about four o'clock the Boers were in full retreat.

The town was entered on the 5th, the enemy, who had surrendered, getting a train of horse trucks away under our very noses, the Grenadier Guards preventing the escape of others by going forward at the double and seizing the station.

As at Johannesburg, the 17th did not enter Pretoria, but moved from camp to camp for the next few days.

A sergeant was sent into the town for much-needed remounts, and from the 75 Boer ponies set aside for the regiment's use he selected about 20.

In the Regimental Orders for the 8th June appears a lengthy congratulation from the Field-Marshal Commander-in-Chief, in which he "desires to place on record his high appreciation of the gallantry and endurance displayed by the troops, both those who have taken part in the advance across the Vaal River and those who have been employed in the less arduous duty of protecting the lines of communication through the Orange River Colony. . . . ."

In R.O.'s, 9th June, we find that "the 3rd Cavalry Brigade under Major-General Gordon will henceforth form part of General Hamilton's force," and on that date the 17th moved off towards the hills for Bronkerspruit.

The Boers, who seemed to be wavering for a moment whether or not to throw up the sponge, had withdrawn to a strong position at Pienaars Poort, fifteen miles east of Pretoria, where they had 25 guns and about 7,000 men, commanded by Botha and De la Rey.

The army, while it had accomplished its work in seizing the enemy's political capital, was not in a particularly enviable position after all said and done. It was thinned by disease, losses in action, and the necessity of detaching the 14th Brigade to hold Johannesburg; it had suffered severely in horses, and its lines of communication were insecure, Steyn's burghers being also in arms behind it.

On the 7th June De Wet had cut the railway and

the telegraph at Roodeval, north of Kroonstadt, thus isolating the Field Marshal, and no time must be lost if things were to be remedied.

It was this news that decided Botha not to meet Lord Roberts, which he had arranged to do.

The 18th Brigade was left to garrison Pretoria; Smith-Dorrien's was distributed along the line between Kroonstadt and the capital, where were also sent our released prisoners, three thousand strong, hastily armed with Boer weapons, and Lord Roberts marched with the remainder of the forces upon Botha and De la Rey.

The Delagoa Railway ran through Pienaars Poort, which was a cleft in a chain of steep hills running north and south for some fifteen miles, and about the same distance from Pretoria itself.

Far away behind the enemy, out of danger, Kruger waited developments in his saloon carriage.

Lord Roberts' plan was to turn both flanks of the enemy with our cavalry, and cut the line in his rear, while he pressed them in front; French was on the left, Pole-Carew advanced along the railway, Ian Hamilton moved parallel to him some six miles farther south, while south again rode Broadwood, with the rest of the cavalry to tackle the Boers' left flank.

The Lancer Brigade operated a little south of Broadwood, their line of direction curving outward towards the Tigerspoort Ridge, so that they formed the extreme right of the British force.

We advanced on the 11th, and at 10 a.m. the 17th Lancers were under heavy shell fire.

Lieutenant Morritt with 40 dismounted men had previously lined a pass in the hills to cover our advance.

The regiment, forming the right of the Brigade, lay among the kopjes for the next two days—in fact, until the afternoon of the 13th—and experienced a very hot time.

During the action Major Fortescue, Lieutenant Cavendish, and five men went on to a kopje, and of the seven, Sergeant Davis and Private Bird came off alive.

Major Fortescue was shot through the heart, Lieutenant Cavendish through the head, and the regiment lost two of their most popular officers.

In September, 1901, Sir Drury Lowe unveiled a cross which had been erected to Major Fortescue's memory, and to those of others from the parish who had fallen in the war, at Filleigh, North Devon.

Sir Drury Lowe said that "there were none present to whom the Major was more dear than to himself. He was a man with a high sense of duty, a loving and devoted son, a staunch friend and comrade, and a gallant soldier. It would be a solace in their sorrow at the loss of Major Fortescue and others whom the monument commemorated to feel that they lost their lives in a just and righteous war."

Fortescue would seem to have fallen about the same time that the gallant Earl of Airlie met his death.

As in so many other instances, Boer treachery cost us dear at Diamond Hill, and a body of them came through the long grass towards our guns, crying, "Don't fire!" and then, opening suddenly, shot five of the gunners, the 12th Lancers having to charge and clear them out.

With the main body, and the advance of the Sussex and the C.I.V.'s, the 17th had little to do. The 3rd Brigade had its own work against the enemy's left, which it was not strong enough to turn, but it held its ground until the Boers retreated along the railway line, and if the horses had been fit might have pressed the pursuit to some purpose.

Their rations on the night of the 12th, after two days' hard pounding, were a biscuit and a quarter per man!

The Field Marshal's object having been gained, the troops returned, the Brigade leaving Bronkerspruit on the 15th and reaching the capital at 3 p.m., where it lay for about a week.

On the 16th, 80 of "The Death or Glory Boys" entrained for Kroonstadt to bring up remounts, marching off at six o'clock in the morning in pouring rain to the station, where, after a dreary wait of two hours, they were packed into open trucks, wet through, and perished with cold.

In one truck there were 43 men, and the pressure was so great that they could not sleep: such are some of the joys of a khaki campaign!

The sun dried them next morning, but they had to leave the train at Koppe, where the bridge over the Rhenoster River had been blown up, and after a march of five miles they reached the spot where De Wet had burned a mail train.

There, among torn papers, and ripped-up clothing of all descriptions, they found three letters still intact addressed to the regiment.

It was not safe to proceed that night, but they reached Kroonstadt at noon on the 18th, where they received extra rations, of bread, jam, and potatoes.

On the 19th they took over the remounts, for the most part English, and in good condition.

Next day they moved to the other side of the town and were suddenly called out to pursue De Wet up the line. This celebrated guerilla leader had been very busy along our lines of communication, doing infinite damage with his Freestaters.

Three hundred of our released prisoners armed with Martinis, under Bullock of the Devons, held out against shell fire for seven hours at Honing Spruit Station, until the detachment of the 17th, some Yeomanry, and the guns of the C.I.V.'s came up and relieved them.

The mobile De Wet retired at dusk, and next day our fellows moved farther up the line.

On the 23rd they halted, bathed, and sewed buttons on, and next day went farm-burning.

"I saw some frightful scenes," writes our corporal, "women imploring our officers not to do it; all the nippers turned outside, crying, watching their homes being burned. It was very hard, but if you were out here you would know that it has to be done."

The law of reprisals is one of the stern necessities of war, and the attack on Honing Spruit alone had just cost us the lives of Major Hobbs and four men, and a grim total of seventeen wounded.

From the 25th to the 29th the Lancers patrolled the line. On the 30th they were at Wolverhoeck, and on the 1st July they trekked for Heilbron, reaching it on the 3rd.

A large convoy of 45 waggons was starting for Frankfort next day, intended for Bruce Hamilton, and the detachment of the 17th moved off as escort.

On the way they were fired at by snipers, some of whom when captured were found to have been released on pass by Lord Roberts, and as a natural sequence to their treachery their houses were promptly burned.

On the 6th the detachment joined the Brigade at Frankfort. After about a week's stay in Pretoria, they were moving down to get in touch with Buller, who was coming up from Natal.

The Brigade had come by way of Springs, Heidelburg, and Villiersdorp, and had had some "scrapping" on the road, but nothing of any importance.

At Nigel Mines they had released Privates Taylor and Holmes, and at Springs, Brigadier-General Gordon had left them to take over the command of the 1st Cavalry Brigade.

Major E. B. Herbert had been gazetted Lieutenant-Colonel in his place in May, but on the 16th July there appeared in Regimental After Orders the following farewell from one of the best brigadiers the 17th ever served under :—

"Brigadier-General Gordon, having been ordered to proceed to the Transvaal to take over command of the 1st Cavalry Brigade, desires to thank all ranks of the Lancer Brigade for the good work they have done for him since he has had the honour to take over the command on the 11th February. With regiments like the 9th, 16th, and 17th Lancers, and R Battery, R.H.A., Brigade work becomes simple, either in field or camp. On handing over the Brigade to his friend of long-standing, Colonel Little, General Gordon wishes both him and the Lancer Brigade the very best of good luck."

Ian Hamilton having broken his collar-bone, the column was now under Archibald Hunter, who joined it on the 9th, and the 2nd Cavalry Brigade was working with the 3rd, Hector Macdonald having also joined with the Highlanders at Frankfort.

On the 7th they marched south, with orders to commandeer all cattle, and burn any transport likely to be of use to the enemy.

They stayed the night of the 8th at Reitz, and reached Bethlehem at noon next day, the weather at nights being now fearfully cold, and the blankets frozen in the morning.

Orders had been given for the preparation of medal rolls, with the names of those men actually present at Thabanchu, Pretoria, and Diamond Hill, and our corporal says, "We have an idea we shall be coming home soon!"

They little thought that nearly two years were to elapse before they finished their South African trek.

On the 11th they doubled back again towards Heilbron, halting at Reitz on the 12th, and with them went 100 ox waggons to refill, 22 of them carrying 112 of our sick and wounded.

Forty prisoners also marched under an escort of M.I., and 120 sick horses from General Clement's column, the 17th Lancers forming the baggage guard.

They trekked all day on the 13th, and on the 14th were fired upon from a farm, which was shelled and burned to the ground.

Heilbron was reached in the afternoon of the 15th, and a detachment sent at once to Kroonstadt for fresh mounts.

A night in an open truck was to some degree compensated for by one under canvas—the first for four months—and they were served out with winter clothing, though the issue proved thinner than their summer kit!

The regiment was sadly in want of underclothing and boots; our corporal made himself up a pair from some cast-off ones, getting a number 8 and a number 10.

On the way back to rejoin, acting as escort to a convoy, they fell in with a patrol of the 17th, lost on the veldt, and learned that the enemy were about in force.

T

The Boers, 2,000 strong, hunting for the convoy, attacked the regimental baggage by mistake, and had a warm reception, one wounded man being brought in with half his face and shoulder blown away by a pompom.

At Paarde Kraal, on the 17th, it having been discovered that the enemy, with 1,800 men and 5 guns, had broken through the cordon, and was reported as making for Lindley, all our dismounteds and sick horses were packed off for Kroonstadt, and the Brigade put on three-quarter rations.

On the 20th they learned that the enemy was marching in a north-easterly direction, and the pompoms of the 17th were ordered to make a reconnaissance at 6.30.

On the 21st the enemy was discovered on a kopje a mile from camp, and opened fire, but the pompoms cleared them out, and we followed them up all day.

On the 22nd the Brigade halted twelve miles from Kroonstadt, rather weak by this time, and expecting to be sent into that town to refit, but the ubiquitous De Wet was breaking out in fresh places, and only the dismounted men went to Kroonstadt, while the rest trekked off in pursuit.

A few miles outside Lindley the Brigade got into a tight place, and was practically surrounded, the Regiment having Sir Francis Burdett and one man wounded; but the Boers drew off after dark and the pursuit was renewed to Kopjes, and thence to Ælian Kop, where they once more formed a cordon about De Wet.

The 17th Lancers, under Lieut.-Colonel Herbert, were detached at Essenbosch Farm in the centre, the 2nd Cavalry Brigade remaining at Ælian Kop, the 9th and 16th Lancers being posted on the right.

While in this position there occurred a happening of

no little interest—namely, the first V.C. won by the 17th since Evelyn Wood's exploit in the old Mutiny days.

On August 7th, on patrol in the neighbourhood of the farm, Sergeant Lawrence and Private Hayman were suddenly attacked by more than a dozen Boers at dawn.

Lawrence retired at speed through a gap in some barbed wire, but, looking round, saw that Hayman's horse had come a cropper, throwing his rider with a dislocated shoulder and a broken collar-bone, and the sergeant rode back to his assistance.

Finding Hayman's horse useless, and the Boers almost upon them, Lawrence hoisted him on to his own —a dun pony—set his head for the picket, gave the brute a kick in the belly to start him, and remained with his carbine and the private's to cover the latter's retreat.

Under heavy fire, the solitary sergeant retired on foot, keeping the Boers at bay for about two miles, until Lieutenant Morritt came out and brought him off, and for his gallantry he was gazetted to the Victoria Cross, 15th January, 1901.

In spite of every precaution, De Wet slipped through the cordon, and on the 10th August the Brigade crossed the Vaal River in pursuit, and once more entered the Transvaal, having parted company with the 2nd Cavalry Brigade and Smith-Dorrien at Ælian Kop.

On the 11th the 17th got in touch with his rear-guard, and pursued as far as Oliphant's Nek, where, in that time of hard tack, and little of it, the orange groves became a regimental recollection.

If you ask a man of the 17th what he remembers about Oliphant's Nek, it is a thousand to one that his first words will be, "That's where we got the oranges."

The transport of 250 waggons lagged behind the

Brigade, the mules so exhausted that several times it was necessary to harness in troop horses to get along.

On 16th August the Brigade had orders to push on to Elands River, where Colonel Hore, of the Rhodesian Horse, in charge of a convoy, had been rounded up by De la Rey, and was making a very gallant stand. He had formed his waggons in laager, thrown up earthworks and banks of stones, and was besieged for fourteen days before the Brigade relieved him.

He had 70 casualties, including 16 killed, and only 7 horses out of 170 survived.

The 17th was the advanced regiment, and B Squadron, under Lord Beauclerck, the advanced squadron.

At Elands River the Brigade rested, waiting for Lord Methuen, who was coming up, and who joined them on the night of the 18th, and next morning, early—*réveille* went at 3.15 a.m.—they marched off for Zeerust to westward, which they reached at noon on the 21st.

The Boers retired as we came in sight, and during the pursuit a corporal of the 17th was shot through the heart—his first day in the ranks as it chanced, he having been previously employed on transport service.

The Brigade remained in camp at Zeerust for a few days, and provisions were at war prices: butter 3s. 6d. lb., milk 1s. 6d. a tin, and matches 1s. 6d. a dozen.

The country around Zeerust was very bushy and difficult, and the enemy troublesome, the Scarlet Lancers losing some men while on observation.

Carrington's force came in on the 24th, *en route* for Mafeking with mails, and next day all dismounted men were attached to Methuen, with orders to march to Mafeking and entrain there.

The Brigade left for the lead mines, and, Brigadier-General Little getting hit, Colonel Herbert of the 17th took command of the Brigade, the regiment having Sergeant Mason killed and Private Langley wounded at the same time.

They took a circuitous route to the lead mines, and were scrapping all the way, and at Quaggasfontein there was a big fight.

De la Rey roused them from their bivouac in the grey of a foggy morning with his snipers, and they found him strongly posted across their path.

All day long they were at it, hammer and tongs, and at night Surgeon-Major Thompson, attached to the 16th Lancers, went out with the ambulance, which was promptly seized by the Boers.

Dalgetty, who was in command of the column, formed up the convoy next morning and prepared to cut his way through at all costs, and after heavy fighting until noon succeeded, the little British force eventually camping on the Jameson Raid ground.

After a two days' rest at Krugersdorp the Brigade marched to Johannesburg, where they stayed three days.

While there Colonel Porter took the Brigade, which marched to Elandsfontein, from whence, after a few days' halt, it entrained for Kroonstadt to refit.

Meanwhile, the dismounted men had been attached to the 3rd Yeomanry, and marched with Methuen, burning many houses *en route* which were found to contain arms, one having a maxim in the roof; and on the afternoon of the 28th August they reached Mafeking.

They camped outside the town with every sign of a terrific storm coming on.

Our corporal, who was with the party, constructed a shelter tent with the aid of his chum: a branch, a carbine, a pair of reins, two blankets, and odd bits of string providing the materials.

The wind howled, the thunder crashed like a thousand batteries in action, the rain burst as it only can in South Africa, and the lightning played about the lance points.

The tent blew down after a while; kit, caps, pots and pans went whistling away, and the horses stampeded, and when they got their shelter up again they sat all night in four inches of water, waiting for the dawn.

Journeying through Kimberley, Magersfontein, Modder, and Belmont, De Aar, and Norvals Point, they reached Bloemfontein on the 4th, the line ahead being blown up, but on the 6th they marched to the station again, wearing Boer slouch hats and carrying their kits anyhow, "whistling marches, imitating the native transport drivers, and kicking up a devil of a row altogether, just to let the inhabitants know we were leaving them," and, packed 60 in a truck, reached Kroonstadt at 7 p.m.

The Brigade straggled in in details; the 9th Lancers and R Battery, R.H.A., arriving, the remainder, delayed through the blowing up of the line between Kroonstadt and Krugersdorp, getting in on the 12th.

At Kroonstadt the Brigade re-equipped, and there they remained until the 23rd, when a composite regiment of squadrons was suddenly ordered off, leaving their packs behind them, and marched north at six in the morning, under Knox, on a strong reconnaissance.

At Heilbron they met Colonels De Lisle and Dalgetty, and went on to Vrede Ford Road, Ælian Kop, and back to Kroonstadt, which they reached on the 13th October.

In the meantime a draft had joined at Kroonstadt on the 5th, mostly recruits with twelve months' service, and two days later they left to pick up the Brigade.

About 8 o'clock on the evening of the 13th (twelve months and two days after the Boer ultimatum) the advance party of the Brigade came in quite unexpectedly and by the time the main body arrived there was a big fire and tea awaiting them.

They had been in camp near Rhenoster for five days when they were ordered back to Kroonstadt.

After a day's rest they were off again at 7.30 a.m. on the 15th, to make an irregular loop out westward, farm-burning about Boschrand and Tweefontein.

A man of the 17th fell from his horse ten miles out, and was killed, and one private, who was severely wounded, died the same night.

At Tweefontein, too, the Boers, dressed in khaki, got close up to us before they were identified, and wounded a man before they were driven off.

The murder of Private Greenwood happened at this time. He had been sent to an isolated spot by himself and was wounded in the thigh.

The Boers galloped up, took his horse, saddlery, and arms, and told him to get back to his camp, but, as the poor fellow was limping away, the scoundrels fired two shots at him, one piercing the muscle of his arm, and the other driving the hoofpick attached to his belt into his spine, from the effect of which he died soon after.

The Brigade returned to Kroonstadt, and later on went out to Bothaville and Commandoes Drift; returning to Bothaville, where they joined Le Gallais, and scouted while the town was burned.

They had rounded up all the women and children to the number of nearly four hundred, and brought them into Kroonstadt with all the cattle they could find.

On the 23rd five men of the pompom section rejoined, one of them bringing a good story with him.

While in action round Thabanchu a Boer got detached from his people, and a lancer pursued him at full gallop.

When he was overtaken, the Boer went down on his knees, crying, " Spare me, I am a field-cornet."

" I don't care a —— if you're a brass band!" was the reply, and through went the lance!

On the 27th, the Brigade left Kroonstadt at 8 a.m., making south, and bivouacking at Boschrand.

They left 106 men behind for want of mounts, and a terrific rainstorm deluged the camp two days later.

Men began to talk of home now; on the 30th the Foot Guards went through Kroonstadt, and on 1st November the Household Cavalry.

On the 3rd, the dismounted men received orders to entrain for Bloemfontein next day, and packed up the regimental stores. They reached Bloemfontein on the 6th November, and on the 10th the Brigade came in at 2 p.m., bivouacking a mile and a half out of the town.

It proved to be their last bivouac, for the Lancer Brigade was about to be broken up.

A squadron of the 16th had been left to garrison Winberg, and another Brandfort, and on the 13th two squadrons of the 9th left for Modder River.

CHAPTER XVI.

"DEATH OR GLORY" ON THE VELDT.

Lances Given In—Dewetsdorp Again—Hot Pursuit—"Smasher Hats"—Insubordination Refuted—Death of Queen Victoria—Cape Colony—An Awkward Mistake—A Water Party—A Sniper and his Fate—A Night March and a Hot Fight—Lieut.-Colonel Herbert Leaves Them—The Camp Fire of the Colonials—Bayonets—A Fight on a Kopje—Gallant Stand at Modderfontein—No Surrender—The Roll of Honour.

THE 17th was re-equipped, and, to its great regret, the lances and carbines were now ordered to be given in, and the Regiment to draw rifles!

The date of this drastic alteration was the 14th November, and for the remainder of the war "The Death or Glory Boys" were to play a Mounted Infantry *rôle*.

On the 15th the Regiment left at 4 p.m. for Springfontein, with a squadron of the 9th Lancers, and two guns of R Battery, R.H.A., filling four trains.

They stopped at Kaalspruit that night, and reached Edenburg about 11 a.m. next morning, where, their orders being cancelled, they detrained and bivouacked, as a small commando was prowling about the town, blowing up the rails, and sniping patrols.

The position of the enemy at this time was briefly as follows:—

The Boers had lost more than half their artillery, and ammunition was becoming scarce, but there were still five important commandoes in the field, to say nothing of isolated bands and snipers.

Hertzog was in the south-west of Orange River Colony; De Wet and Fourie in the east; while, in the Transvaal, De la Rey was in the neighbourhood of Magaliesberg, Beyers somewhere to the north of Pretoria, and, the largest commando of all, under Louis Botha, Schalk Burger, and other leaders, was farther away in the north-east.

The veldt was growing green again, which meant fodder for the Boer ponies, and consequently the enemy grew bolder; De Wet, foiled in an attempt to join hands with Botha, and badly licked by Barton, De Lisle, and poor Le Gallais, made a daring attempt to carry the war into Cape Colony, and by way of a start laid siege to Dewetsdorp, south of Thabanchu on the night of the 17th November.

Major Massy was in command, and the position was a fairly strong one, but there was scarcity of water.

De Wet was in force, and had also a Krupp gun, and fire was kept up on our position day and night.

On the 20th the Boers cut off the water supply, and for three days the sufferings of the little garrison were very great, so much so, that at 6 o'clock on the 23rd there was no alternative left but to hoist the white flag, De Wet and Steyn riding over to receive the surrender.

In the meantime, the regiment, which had remained at Edenburg, got sudden orders to march at 1.30 p.m. on the 22nd, forming part of a column under Lieut.-Colonel Herbert of the 17th, the rest consisting of the 9th Lancers, Irish Yeomanry, Mounted Infantry, Grenadier Guards, and Argyll and Sutherland Highlanders.

They halted at six that night, marched at five next morning, and when near Reddersberg saw about forty Boers gallop away for their lives.

The column bivouacked near a lake, and there heard that they were marching to the relief of Dewetsdorp.

On the 24th, after a skilful reconnaissance, the enemy was discovered entrenched on a kopje, and, opening upon them with rifle and pompom fire, they were driven back.

Lord Beauclerck's troop galloped a mile and occupied the kopje, and B Squadron went to support them.

Leaving the horses at the bottom of the hill, the men swarmed up and, taking cover, began to fire.

They had not been there long, when the Hon. Mr. Baring was hit in two places, and Sergeant Paul was wounded almost simultaneously.

A ball knocked the sergeant's backsight clean away, entered between his finger and thumb, ploughed up the wrist, made three holes in the upper part of the arm, and one in the chest; he is uncertain whether it was an explosive bullet, or whether he received a volley.

The firing was very hot, and all the mounted men came up, with three pompoms, four twelve- and four fifteen-pounders; the enemy using a Long Tom and two lighter guns, besides their Mausers.

The Dewetsdorp garrison had been sent off by their captors the night before, and the Boers occupied the British trenches which had been so gallantly defended, peppering us with our own cordite shrapnel.

About 9 o'clock the firing ceased, and the Lancers drew off to camp until next morning in rear of a kopje.

On the 25th *réveille* went at 3.30, both sides occupying the same positions, and desultory firing going on all day, one of the 17th being wounded by a shell.

One squadron had a narrow escape when ordered out to discover the position of one of the Boer guns.

They had advanced over three ridges, and were moving to the right, when the gun dropped a shell into the middle of them, singularly enough hurting none, and, as they galloped back, eight more shells were fired at them without effect.

On the 26th we sent four shells into the Boer position without eliciting any response, and after waiting until 11 o'clock a scout was sent out, who brought back the intelligence that the enemy had stolen away, south-east, about eight, carrying 400 prisoners with them.

From two men of the R.A.M.C. who came out of the town we learned that the Boers numbered about 3,500, and had been on the point of rushing our position, when, hearing that reinforcements were approaching, they had retired, De Wet leaving behind him a proclamation, saying that he was marching south, and would burn every farm and homestead in Cape Colony.

Reinforcements came up under General Charles Knox, who had been ordered to take the command, while Colonel Pilcher was to hasten from De Aar.

The loyalty of the Cape Dutch was strongly open to suspicion, and there was not a moment to be lost if the firebrand were to be stayed before he set the Colony aflame.

Knox sent a galloper back to Pilcher, directing him to leave Dewetsdorp alone and push with all speed to Vaal Bank, where Barker's and Herbert's columns would join him.

Marching light—though there was never a trek during the whole war when our columns marched light enough—Herbert's column started at 5 a.m. on the 27th, and engaged De Wet's rear about eleven.

The Boers only made stand sufficient to allow their main body to get away, nevertheless we took 46 prisoners, 3 waggons laden with bread, and found 6 dead burghers, and camped for the night at Helvetia, where the column was put on half rations.

On the 28th Pilcher, making for Vaal Bank, learned that a Boer laager lay in a basin three miles ahead, and almost at the same moment a mounted man dashed away from a farm close by.

Pilcher instantly acted upon his information and made for the basin, while the farmer, knowing that De Wet and Steyn were at a house some distance from their men, rode to warn the leaders, who escaped in a Cape cart.

The laager was surprised, there was a hot fight, U Battery fired shrapnel, and 300 Boer ponies stampeded, but, with their almost superhuman celerity, the enemy inspanned and got away, leaving two waggons behind them, and for the next four days we lost touch of them.

Herbert's column, meanwhile, had marched at 4.30 through a difficult country full of kopjes, which tried the horses severely, and after a long trek of thirty miles they reached Smithfield.

On the 29th, proceeding in a westerly direction, they passed a place where concealed ammunition had been recently dug up, and after an easy march halted 18 miles from Bethulie Bridge.

On the 1st December they reached Silverspruit, the weather excessively hot, on the same day Pilcher and Barker joined forces at Bethulie, where they picked up a column under Colonel Williams, consisting of Strathcona's Horse, the 1st M.I., and the 85th Field Battery.

On the morning of 2nd Herbert sent out a squadron of the 17th northwards to scout, and they had only been out about two hours when they saw the enemy coming towards them in full force.

Taking up a position on a kopje, the Lancers lay low

until the Boers were within range, and then letting drive, sent them back helter-skelter, and pursued for half an hour

Colonel Herbert, sending a man on the spur to Knox, who was issuing supplies at Bethulie, moved his column forward, and, the enemy taking up a good position, we did the same, and opened a hot fire.

The whole of that day the firing went on, the hills around Sterkspruit echoing to the flipflop of the Mausers and the crack of the Lee-Metfords.

"If we just showed our helmets, whizz would come a bullet, and we did the same with them."

Both sides made good shooting, the Boers going particularly for our convoy, putting a shell through a water-cart and wounding an officer.

One of the patrols brought in seven Italians, who had shot one of the 17th dead before they were captured; they were dressed like brigands, with ostrich feathers in their hats, Free State badges, and brown gaiters.

Williams hurried up from Bethulie, followed by the other columns, Knox continuing Herbert in the centre, posting Barker on the left, and sending Williams away on the right, rather far out, while the Suffolks occupied a ridge in the rear to protect Bethulie in case of need.

At dawn on the 3rd the fight began again; two of the 17th were killed, two more wounded, and a horse shot. An officer of the 9th Lancers, who had lost an arm at Magersfontein, was hit in the other one.

At 1 o'clock the men were served out with one biscuit and 4 oz. of bully beef, the first ration since the three biscuits of the 1st.

During the afternoon we shelled the enemy with lyddite, and they bolted like rabbits; one shell was seen to burst in the centre of a party of them, bits of horses, men, and rock flying in all directions.

Williams, in the meantime, had made a circuit, and Strathcona's "Toughs" headed De Wet off.

The slim Boer general, who had all the time been amusing us with a rearguard action, trekked away north-east, and Williams' scouts brought word at nightfall that he was making for Bushman's Kop.

The total of his dead left at Sterkspruit varies from 30 to 90 in various accounts.

It began to rain at five o'clock, and the night was one of sodden discomfort, and at 4 a.m., the columns marched north in a pitiless deluge, camping about 2 p.m., Knox's scouts having discovered that De Wet's retreat towards Bushman's Kop was only a feint, and that he had gone south, still carrying the Dewetsdorp prisoners with him, having successfully slipped past our right wing.

Knox now went on north with Williams and Barker to pick up the "spoor" at Carmel Farm, where the Boers had halted for the night, and he sent Pilcher and Herbert south, to cross the Orange River and lie in wait for the enemy when they should attempt to cross.

The storm was still raging when we started, and on the road the 17th passed a party burying a sergeant who had been killed by lightning.

They camped beside Slick Drift, finding it impossible to pass it in the dark, and on the 6th, after waiting two hours until the transport was got over, they went through Bethulie, crossed the Orange into British territory, and camped three miles farther on.

Knox was meanwhile "on the heels of De Wet," who crossed the Caledon, then rapidly rising; when we reached it, it was in spate, the passage by our men being a fine piece of work, and the greatest praise due to Colonel Williams, who got the thirty guns over in safety, crossing more than sixty times in person.

De Wet now released the Dewetsdorp prisoners, as they encumbered his march, but he still carried the officers with him, in waggons, and he made an attempt to get across the Orange River at Odendaal Drift, some fifteen miles west of Aliwal North, where Hector Macdonald commanded.

Finding Odendaal garrisoned, and time precious, De Wet turned up stream, to find all the drifts held by the British, and on the 6th December the wily one headed north again as far as Rouxville, where he divided his force into two parts, one of which tried to bluff a post of the Highland Light Infantry under Lieutenant Blair at Commassie Bridge.

The Boers were 300 strong, the Highland Lights 40, and the Scotsmen had the best of it.

De Wet now passed the Caledon, his guns submerged, and by dint of hard trekking, reached Helvetia Farm, near Dewetsdorp, on the 9th December.

Knox was hard after him, and fought his rearguard during the 9th and 10th, releasing four of the captured officers, and compelling De Wet to retreat to Geluk, and then towards Thabanchu.

How they eventually rounded him up; how White and Thorneycroft joined in, and how, when success seemed certain, the daring guerilla broke through the cordon and escaped again, does not belong to this place, and we must return to Herbert's column, which reached Aliwal North on the 8th December.

The column received a hearty welcome, and it was good to be among English people once more.

They crossed the bridge and camped in the

Free State, in full view of the town; but at 5 p.m. on the 10th they saddled up, off on the trek once more.

On the way to Rouxville next day, they captured a Dutchman and a Kaffir carrying flour into the Boer lines, and one of the 17th was shot, as were also five horses out of a patrol of seven men.

On the 13th they met Brabant's Horse; on the 14th the regiment was out all day reconnoitring; on the 15th the column reached Rouxville, and left in three hours, hearing that the enemy was out to westward.

On the 16th they arrived at Oliphant's Spruit, where the drift over the Orange River is about 300 yards across, and the rushing torrent was then 4 feet deep, with a rocky bottom full of clefts and holes.

A day's ration was issued to each man, in the event of the waggons being unable to cross, and teams of 30 horses were hitched to the transport.

They were over into Cape Colony about three in the afternoon, only to hear that the enemy had crossed earlier and were then nine miles ahead.

The mounted men of the column now set off, and galloped 12 miles, 2 Horse Artillery guns and a pompom keeping up with them, and they arrived in time to prevent the raiding of an English farm, which was defended by a small force of 25 Cape Police.

The guns unlimbered and shelled the enemy out, and a squadron of the 17th, making a side movement, took post on a ridge, for which the Boers also rode, to be received by an unexpected rifle fire, which sent them post-haste off into the hills.

The commando was about 700 strong, and soon disappeared, thanks to their superior mobility.

Remounts were now urgently needed, and rations

were also wired for from Knapdaar Station, the convoy having remained at Oliphant's Drift.

A party left by train for fresh horses, and were away some days, spending Christmas at Silhoombee, where some of them struck a good dinner, most unexpectedly, at the house of a friendly farmer.

After numerous adventures they rejoined on 3rd January, 1901, finding the regiment once more near Aliwal North, but on the opposite of the river.

On the 4th new clothing and boots were served out, and, there being no helmets to hand, "The Death or Glory Boys' had to be content with "smasher" hats —a note for future military painters!

The next morning, while the regiment was starting on a 35-mile march to Jamestown, there appeared in *The Army and Navy Gazette* at home a paragraph of no little regimental interest.

A lurid report had been published in the London papers on the 17th December, headed "Insubordinate Lancers—90 Men Placed under Arrest," and had reference to the Reserve Squadron of the 17th at Ballincollig, who were said to have mutinied on the eve of their embarcation, a corporal flinging his cap at his commanding officer by way of a start.

As the statement was widely circulated, and reflected discredit on the regiment in the minds of many people, we give *in extenso* the very emphatic disclaimer of Captain Nickalls from the above-mentioned journal:—

"I wish it to be clearly understood," wrote the commander of the Reserve Squadron, "that not a single man of the 17th (D.C.O.) Lancers was implicated in the disturbance. The 17th Lancers left Ballincollig for Cork and Limerick in September last, since which time no

17th Lancers have been quartered at Ballincollig, which is occupied by the Reserve Regiment of Lancers. I only wish to add that the men were transferred to me after the disturbance, to form part of a large draft for the 17th Lancers in South Africa, and were the best behaved lot of men I have ever had to do with. In a draft of over 200 men there was not a single case of drunkenness or crime (except for one absentee), for some days previous to and during embarcation."

To return to the front. The regiment was now operating in wild and difficult country; on the 7th January they made a reconnaissance towards Lady Grey, covering about 40 miles.

On the 8th they moved to Flat Cop Drift, where they received news of the enemy that took them back to Roode Vek, over a range of rugged hills, that presented great difficulties to the transport.

On the 9th the horses were out grazing all day—this recalls the old "grass guards" at the time of the 17th's formation—and when the men were about to have tea the whistle was blown, and they filed back through a pass in the hills.

A shot was fired after they had crossed the Ostrich River, and everyone expected to find that they were in a tight place, it being very dark, and the valley surrounded by towering kopjes.

Word was given for perfect silence, no matches were to be struck, but after a wait some time the march was resumed.

All night long they rode, half asleep in their saddles, and reached Flat Cop at 4 a.m., to find the enemy had trekked west six hours ahead of them: a feed for the horses, and then on again, but the Boers were not to be caught, and the squadrons halted at seven for the night, fortunately able to get some bread and milk from an adjacent farm, as they had left the convoy.

Next morning they reached Jamestown, and were joined by the remainder of the Brigade later in the day.

On the 15th they camped near Burghersdorp; "was going fishing with a string and a bent nail," says our journal, "but had to go on kopje on observation duty instead."

At Oldfontein a man was sentenced to two years' hard labour for being asleep on outpost. "Very sorry for him. We subscribed £1 in our troop for him to cheer himself with till he arrived at prison."

On the 18th they forded the Orange at Sand Drift, and halted at Drunkfontein; the sun very hot.

There they lay until the 23rd, when they changed camp. "Was greatly shocked and deeply sorry to hear of Her Most Gracious Majesty's death. It is most deeply regretted by all troops here. Every man is expressing sorrow."

They patrolled along the Orange River for 10 miles on the 24th without discovering a sign of the enemy, and the patrol was invited into an orchard to help themselves from the ripe fruit. "There were grapes, figs, peaches, plums, greengages, apricots, quinces, and pomegranates," to which they did ample justice after their diet of "trek ox" and ration biscuit.

They got in touch with the enemy again on the 27th, when a patrol of the 9th Lancers was fired at by snipers, and the day after they had sudden orders to saddle up.

Reaching the Caledon, with the fires just lighted for tea, they were blazed at by Boers from a kopje, and replied with a pompom and a 12-pounder, sending two troops in pursuit of the Boers, who bolted out of reach.

On the 30th they halted at Slick Drift, the reconnoitring squadrons reporting 3,500 Boers on the Smithfield Road.

At Bethulie Bridge they were served out with bread, and marched off at 4.30 next morning.

"Had to lead three commandeered horses all day," says the journal; "never had such a job with horses. Couldn't get them along anyhow. Got off my horse to fight the other three. By help of Kaffirs and whips, and tying them to a waggon, we eventually got them to camp, where I was thankful to hand them over, retaining a fine chestnut for myself, which is *the thirteenth mount out here.*"

Two squadrons were left to assist in holding Rhenoster Drift on 2nd February, and on the 4th these squadrons reported killing a number of Boers who tried to cross.

They saw them coming, and let them get into the centre of the river before opening fire.

The regiment was at this time acting under Hector Macdonald, who had just captured 700 of the enemy.

The regiment continued in camp at Rhenoster Rock until the 15th, three days' heavy rain swamping everything, and then entrained at Kapdaar for Rosmead.

After a stay of three days, they proceeded by rail through Middelburg to Roodehookte: "here the stationmaster's wife gave us each a cup of coffee."

"Ye gentlemen of England who sit at home at ease," may find it difficult to realise the state of privation that makes a cup of coffee worthy of entry in a soldier's journal; the poor woman was about to suffer severely for her generous hospitality.

They reached Bethesda on the 20th, and marched thence at 4.3 a.m. on the 22nd, "the road taking us through some very rugged places. The kopjes round this part are very high and rocky, and if you were not very careful you could soon fall into an ambush. Halted at 11 a.m. for two hours. We had no sooner taken our saddles off and fed the horses than, flipflop, flipflop—the Mauser in action again, mingled with the crack of our Lee-Metfords. We discovered the enemy were engaged with our observation posts round the camp; one post was driven in by the Boers, who had charged the kopje they were on. The shots came into camp very thick, one man and five horses being shot in a few seconds. Of course we saddled up immediately, and galloped off to the kopje the Boers were making for. We arrived first, and were soon giving them what they asked for. We had one man shot through the thigh, the Boers having three killed and sixteen wounded, after which they retired to another kopje, and we were sniping at each other till darkness set in."

"Colonel Gorringe with a force of Cape Defence Corps joined us at daybreak, and the pursuit was taken up again.

"A farm was discovered where the enemy had burned a Union Jack, and they were then three hours ahead, leaving many exhausted horses on the road.

"Pushing on, we reached Roodehookte, to find the station burned to the ground and the rails shifted.

"The armoured train had arrived as the Boers were leaving, and shelled them, killing seven and capturing thirteen.

"The rest of the enemy took shelter near a ridge, and our force camped near the station ruins."

Three squadrons and a couple of guns went out next day, returning at dusk with two casualties, the rest of the column meanwhile waiting the arrival of supplies.

On the 26th, when the enemy's position was reconnoitred, he had gone, and passing the gigantic

Fafleberg, which towers above the surrounding kopjes to an altitude of 4,500 feet, the regiment camped four miles from Middelburg.

Gorringe joined them again on the 27th, and the prisoners were tried by court-martial, when two were acquitted, and the rest handed over to the civil authorities.

"Most of them were shivering and snivelling like a lot of frightened babies, just like all the *brave* Boers," says our journal, the writer of which was escort to them at the trial.

Having obtained some more remounts, the regiment went off on the 28th to keep up the pursuit of Kritzinger, leaving all four-wheeled transport behind.

On the 1st March they halted at Roodehookte with Gorringe, shooting several done up horses, and next day they drew rein at the mouth of a pass in the Swazi Mountains.

They were on a hot trail, but it took them five days to get through the pass; the road very rugged, and the Cape carts encumbering them.

A good deal of the way was performed on foot, the men leading their horses.

At seven o'clock on the morning of the 8th, they rode into the town of Pierston, to find that it had been looted by the Boer commando the day before, and that 21 Dutchmen had gone off with the enemy.

The townguard of 70 men had surrendered at the first shot, and the Dutch had pointed out the English shops, which were the only ones looted.

As soon as this was discovered, we entered the town and looted all the Dutch stores, taking the owners prisoners, and by the law of reprisals our men obtained supplies for a week — tinned fish, condensed milk, groceries, and underclothing.

On the 9th a squadron of the 17th went out to pick up the spoor, and was away two days, finding that the commando had trekked south-east towards Somerset East, which is at the junction of the lines from King William's Town and Port Elizabeth.

The column came up, and the pursuit was continued; the march being through mountainous country covered with prickly pear, and inhabited by monkeys.

One river was crossed twelve times, so sinuous were its windings, but in spite of every effort, when the column arrived at Middleton at 9.30 on the 12th, the Boers had cut the wires and passed the line six hours before.

Colonel De Lisle's column had them in touch, and as a result of his shells four dead Boers were found at a farm near the town, but unfortunately our horses were so done up that Herbert's men had to abandon the pursuit pending the arrival of remounts, which came by train next day from Port Elizabeth.

After a night at the English village of Cookhouse, they reached Cradock on the 15th, a good-sized town with a garrison, and surrounded with barbed wire hung with old tin cans to guard against a night surprise.

The 17th had bread and butter issued to them, the first time they had had butter for thirteen months.

On the 16th they received new boots, blankets, equipment and horses—not before they wanted them—and on the 19th they were *en route* for Maraisburg, learning that 250 Boers passed along the road the day before.

They found Maraisburg looted, reaching Kroomhookte at 6.30 on the 20th in a downpour lasting until 11 o'clock.

A draft of 30 men joined the 17th on the 21st, as also the transport, and letters from home.

Next morning, at 5 a.m., they continued their way in

the direction of Venterstad until a despatch rider overtook them and changed their course.

At 4 p.m. they camped, and ten minutes later a squadron was ordered to ride for a drift before nightfall.

As they neared it about 300 horsemen galloped towards them, to all appearance Boers, the squadron opening fire, notwithstanding disparity of numbers.

The fire was returned, and the 300 rode for them on the spur, so that nothing remained but to go about and gallop their hardest, when, to make matters worse, it was discovered in some mysterious fashion that their pursuers were part of Gorringe's column.

There was no means of explaining the mistake, it was growing rapidly dark, and a pompom and a 15 pounder now opened on the squadron, while ahead lay a barbed wire fence into which the Lancers plunged as they tried to take cover.

An officer was shot through the hand, and some horses bolted in the confusion, but the incident had its humorous side, over which they laughed next day when they met their opponents at the camp.

The weather now became dull and cold; on the 24th they were marching from 9 until 5 in a torrent of rain, and arrived in camp to go on outposts, spending the night on a kopje in the pitiless downpour, and leaving next morning without breakfast.

They were now moving on Steynsburg, which they reached on the 27th.

On the 28th, when halting at midday on the way to Colesberg, they were joined by Major Murray's column with Lovat's Scouts, and at Colesberg they camped on the old battleground, which was still littered with fragments of shell, and the graves of Briton and Boer.

Brackfontein, Venterstad, and so to the Burghersdorp

road, where they had news of the enemy on the 3rd April that sent them at a gallop towards the river.

The Boers were surrounded at last by the other columns, and the river was in flood; and all night, though very worn and weary with the continued trek, they guarded against possibility of escape southward.

Alas! it was the old story when dawn came.

"The slim burghers, taking the wheels off some of their waggons, had crossed the swollen river, swimming their ponies beside them, and once more the prize was snatched from our grasp. The only satisfaction that remained to us was the knowledge that the bulk of the enemy were now back in the Free State."

Marching by way of Knapdaar Station, the regiment camped three miles north of Bethulie on the Springfontein road, from the 6th until the 9th, and while there two drafts joined them.

April 7th was Easter Sunday, and the commanding officer held a special church parade; the Grenadier detachment, which had escorted their convoy for some time, left them on the Monday, and on the 9th they shifted camp about four miles nearer to Bethulie.

A private named Hardman, returning to the old camp to look for a strayed horse, was surprised by a handful of Boers, and died of his wounds shortly after.

A troop went out on the 11th to destroy boats; on the 12th new clothing was served out; on the 15th camp was shifted into Cape Colony again, five miles south of the Orange River, until the 20th, when they went back to their former ground.

On that day they played Baden-Powell's Police at football, and the 17th won—five goals to nil.

Another striking contrast to the daily routine is

recorded in the journal before us, at Odeidale Stroom Drift, where the regiment was on the 23rd.

"Watered horses in Orange River, and saw a very peaceful scene there, which would have dispelled all thoughts of war if it wasn't for the realistic facts which we were fully acquainted with. The scene in question was a pleasure party having an enjoyable evening on the tranquil waters. It is a very picturesque spot, with the water-mill and green trees on the banks, and a waterfall over which the water pushes in ever-increasing energy."

On the 24th they went to Aliwal North again, and next day trekked into the Free State, hearing heavy firing in front of them from Murray's column, 134 strong, with two guns and a maxim—which the Kaffirs called the piccaninny pompom—and they were holding up a commando of 500 Boers.

Herbert's column of 400, with two 12-pounders and another maxim, was a very welcome reinforcement when they came up on the 26th, the 17th patrolling the surrounding country after the enemy retired.

They were on half rations again, and on the 27th they crossed the Caledon at Kumassie Bridge, and passed through Smithfield, which was deserted, the only inhabitants being a few chickens and some stray dogs.

The weather was now very cold and frosty, the African winter approaching; they saw Boers ahead, moving north on the 29th, but they passed out of sight, and the column halted near Wepener.

They were burning forage and destroying everything that was likely to be of use to the enemy; on the 2nd May alone the 17th killed more than 3,000 sheep!

On the 3rd they were in the neighbourhood of Rouxville, on the 4th they joined Colonel Williams once more at Kumassie Bridge, and, finding a bullock convoy there, were on full rations again.

On the 5th they sighted more Boers in the distance, but they galloped out of range at our advance.

On the 6th one of the troop officers volunteered to try and catch some Boers who were believed to be staying the night at the neighbouring farms, and his men were mustered at 2 a.m.

"It was bitterly cold, no talking or smoking was allowed, and our horses' feet were muffled with sacking.

"We went to four large farms, walking quietly up till within fifty yards, and then surrounding them at a gallop. A bang at the door and a shout of 'Out you come!' galloping to the outhouses and corrals to search them, women and children crying and dogs barking; it was just a little lively for the time being. However, we found out there had been Boers there the previous night, but knowing that the British were advancing they scooted as usual."

The party picked up the column at seven next morning and fell in with snipers—a 17th and an I.Y. being killed, the neighbourhood being infested with small parties of these fellows, who hung on our flanks and vanished like smoke as we approached them.

"We halted at noon near a farm," says the journal; "a prisoner was taken from it. The man swore he had never been fighting, but we got positive proof that he had been on the kopje only yesterday, sniping at our column. We found one of our regulation saddles at his farm, which was damp with recent sweat, so *he* won't snipe any more!"

On the 7th they marched into Springfontein, and next day received 200 remounts, which, proving insufficient to mount all the men, all those riding with the transport were given mules.

"My pony is a very good one," says the journal, "the last three days we were out he carried me eighty miles, and is still fit."

On the 10th they marched under Colonel Wyndham: *réveille* at 4 o'clock, started at 5.30, halted at 1 p.m.

When the men were settling down to sleep, orders were issued for a night march, and at eleven they moved off with the utmost silence to Philipopolis, which they entered at midnight, finding it empty, but raking out six Boers who were in hiding.

Pressing on, they covered another twenty miles, and halted at a large farm just before dawn, capturing four more Boers with Mausers after a bitterly cold trek of thirty miles in all.

"Most of the prisoners had been fighting since the start, and told us the remainder would never surrender."

They were now on the track of Commandant Hertzog —or "Hedgehog," as the troops nicknamed him—and picked up a number of ponies and cattle abandoned by him.

On the 13th they discovered fifteen Dutch women and children in a deep kloof, almost starving, who, however, declined to go on to the refugee camp, saying they would rather be shot than accompany the English, so there was no alternative but to leave them to their fate.

On the 15th 2,000 rounds of ball cartridge were discovered in a bed-tick, and the house burned down.

Every farm was thoroughly searched, and in one a man of the 17th found a diamond ring worth about £45, which he lost on the march next day.

After a long series of marches, everyone on the *qui vive* the whole time, they returned to Philipopolis on the 30th May, this particular trek having taken them in the direction of Hoptown, roughly parallel, out and in, with the course of the Orange River.

On the 31st they moved towards Norvals Point, from thence on the 2nd June to Springfontein, and there entrained for Burghersdorp, in the Colony.

On the 6th June they marched south to Steynsburg, and an incident occurred, very typical of the campaign, which I will give in the words of one of the actors in it.

"We off-saddled, cooked our food, and were just anchored down for the night, when an order came that we were in for a night march.

"Marched at 10.30 p.m. No smoking or noise allowed. Arrived at a farm twelve miles out, when we noticed a lot of ponies, which looked rather suspicious, so the officer in charge of the advance guard sent back this message to the colonel, 'A lot of ponies, am going to search the farm,' which he did, and found about fifty Boers there. It was so dark that matches had to be lit to find the arms before they woke up. Before this could be done, some of the Boers awoke, and then the firing commenced. Those that secured their rifles got behind the walls and other places to conceal themselves, and as soon as our men showed the least part of themselves, bang went the shooting-iron. A squadron of our men was in position near the farm, putting chance volleys into some men who were trying to get away. The Boers who were firing were using explosive bullets, which sounded very nasty as they burst over our heads. If they happen to hit one they make a hole in you as large as your fist. The scrimmage was all over at 4 a.m., after which we found we had one officer and two men wounded. We killed one Boer: he was shot dead by a sergeant as he was aiming at the colonel. Twelve were wounded and 28 captured, with their arms and a large quantity of ammunition, and 30 good ponies. The regiment then marched back to Steynsburg with the prisoners, who were mostly rebels. The doctor was left behind with the wounded, and when he arrived in camp on the 7th he told us that half an hour after we had left a Boer commando under Nolan came up and surrounded the farm, thinking to entrap us—but we weren't there: so ended that sketch!"

They now went to Kroomhaughte, during a movement against Kritzinger, pursued Commandant Smith without success, and spent the rest of the month between that place and Steynsdorp, making reconnaissances, and occasionally getting a shot at the springbok which were plentiful in that district.

On the 27th Lieut.-Colonel Herbert left them, to their great regret, and on the 30th Lieut.-Colonel Haig took over the regiment.

A race meeting was arranged on the 1st July at Steynsdorp, a band was improvised for the occasion, and the officers of the 17th brought several winners past the post, but the chief event was won by a private of the regiment on a horse he had commandeered on the veldt during one of their treks, and it was bought after the race by one of the officers for £20.

On the 3rd they marched to Springfontein, in the Zuirburg, 16 miles off, to turn a commando under Van Reenan, heading him into the arms of the column under Gorringe, of the R.E., who shelled him to some purpose, the Boer leader having to abandon most of his horses.

Captain D'Arcy Legard was severely wounded in the left shoulder on the 7th, near Steynsburg, and the month opened merrily for all concerned.

The enemy, although greatly reduced, were still active in Cape Colony, but General French had now taken the direction of affairs there, and organised several columns which gave them little rest.

Elsewhere, the blockhouse system was in full force, and we were slowly but surely bringing matters to a climax.

A squadron of Tasmanians was working with the 17th at this time, and they went up to Dornbeck on the 11th to hold a position.

The Colonials held a sing-song round the camp-fire one night, and some of the 17th went over to their lines. "Their singing was awful," says the journal, "no tune to be found anywhere, and their songs were all in the same strain, about Mother, and the Home Across the Sea, etc., which isn't calculated to cheer a man much in our circumstances. Our fellows livened them up with a few classics and comics." The column now went up into the Stormberg Mountains, and encountered bitter weather, with snow and sleet clouds.

Near Molteno they commandeered a quantity of provisions intended for the Boers at a farm, and took the farmer prisoner.

On the 20th some of the officers played tennis with the ladies at Glenrock, and on the 22nd a helio from Maraisburg hurried them towards Cradock, where Colonel Crabbe was in a tight place.

They did twenty-two miles that day before they off-saddled at Bushman's Kraal, and marched at dawn next morning, to find that Crabbe had been relieved by another column, after which followed more mountain climbing, the horses having to be led, and the Boers always fleeing before we could get to them.

At the end of the month the 17th were at Tarkastad,

where a box of presents was distributed among the squadron to which our corporal belonged.

The good folk at home could hardly have realised what those simple gifts of tobacco, and handkerchiefs, stationery, and the like, meant to those hard-bitten men out on the veldt, carrying their lives in their hands night and day, with few comforts and no luxuries.

On the 7th they visited a farm and store looted by Botha, and, as a big clearing move was now being planned by General French, there was a great concentration of columns.

Lieut.-Colonel Haig inspected the horses on Sunday, the 11th, and the next day bayonets were served out, "so that we are now fully converted into mounted infantrymen, which is not exactly calculated to please a crack lancer regiment."

On the 13th they marched northwards—hearing on the way of a successful fight which the column under Gorringe had had; and next day they passed through the Zuirburg, camping outside Venterstad.

After much marching and countermarching they returned to this camp again on the 24th, looking less like brigands than they had done for some time in new clothing and equipment, and there they waited for orders, in touch with Knox, Gorringe, and Crabbe.

Another move to Steynsburg, which they reached on the 6th, and then a march to Henning, in the Stormberg country.

"My troop left Henning at 6 a.m." (on the 8th September), says the journal, "to reconnoitre Glendoorn Hoek, a mountain pass leading to Maraisburg. Remainder of squadron marching on to Molteno, a small town eleven miles south of Stormberg, from which place Gatacre marched when he met with his reverse. Travelled about six miles up the pass, and discovered that some Boers had stayed at a farm near by the previous night.

"The intelligence officer, Captain Disten, took six of our men, and native scouts, to follow up a spoor, while the remainder of us went on.

"We had gone a mile when we heard firing on our left, so we at once made for it, and took up a position on a high kopje, where we found Captain Disten was engaged with a number of Boers on another mountain in front of us, about 12,000 yards' range.

"We immediately opened fire, to which they replied.

"We could see a lot of them, mounted, going along a ridge, and saw a few drop out!

"We were sniping each other for about three hours, when one man holding the horses at the foot of the kopje was shot in the leg by one of the enemy, who managed to work to the back of us.

"The horses were put under better protection, and we continued the 'sketch.'

"In another half-hour, a man who had been with Captain Disten came to us in a weak condition, shot in the side.

"The enemy's bullet had struck his bandolier, knocked a bullet from the cartridge case, and both bullets had gone five inches round the ribs, making a nasty jagged wound.

"We bound up both of them, and then continued the ball for half an hour, when the Boers ceased fire and retired.

"My troop officer took three men, and made for the part where Captain Disten had been, and found that all his party had been put out of action.

"Disten himself was wounded in the arm, one of our men was shot through the heart, and the Boers had taken his watch and boots: we buried him, using bayonets to dig the grave with.

"Three native scouts were shot dead after being captured, and three of our own men were captured, but released after being relieved of their arms.

"If the Boers had known our strength, they could have captured the lot of us, as we were only 30 strong, and they numbered 80 to 100.

"One of the natives seemed to know what to expect when he was captured, as he suddenly seized one of our men round the neck, thinking that by so doing the Boers wouldn't fire; but it was no good, as a Boer pointed his rifle at him and dropped him, nearly hitting our man. . . . .

"We carried the wounded men from the kopje to the road in a blanket off our saddles, and sent to the nearest farm for a conveyance, which arrived two hours after in the shape of a bullock-cart.

"The troop went on back to Henning, and I handed my pony and rifle to one of them to take care of, and then went to the farm with the wounded men, to look after them till the doctor arrived.

"The inmates, who were Dutch, made us all as comfortable as possible, and did all they could for us.

"Next morning (the 9th) Colonel Doran's column came along. The officers came to the farm, and, finding us there, wanted to know all about it.

"The column passed on, leaving two doctors, who dressed the wounded men. . . .

"Besides the man we had buried, one of the wounded native scouts told me he saw another white man dead on the mountains, and, as we had one man missing, I thought perhaps he would be the same, so I went up to the place, accompanied by the doctor, farmer, and a

Kaffir with a spade, but on reaching the spot we could not find any sign of the man.

"Two Kaffirs and two horses were lying in a pool of blood dead, and the feet of the man who was buried were sticking through the ground.

"We buried him properly, and I wrote his name on a boulder near by, leaving the farmer and Kaffir to bury the native scouts.

"The place where we had the fight was called 'Devil's Kop,' and a very rough mountainous part of the road near it was called 'Hell's Gate.'"

Our diarist eventually joined the squadron at Stormberg Junction, where he found them entraining for Tarkastad. A wretched night, the rain pouring in torrents, brought them to Tarkastad at 5 a.m. on the 15th, and, tying their horses up in the churchyard, the squadron took shelter in the Town Hall, where the ladies of the town sent them hot coffee.

Marching at 9.30 next morning, still in the pouring rain, they reached Modderfontein at 1 p.m., hanging their blankets to dry on the trees, the rain having ceased by that time.

The next day, the 17th September, was one destined to live for all time in the regimental annals.

C Squadron, under Captain Victor S. Sandeman, who had gone out with the regiment as adjutant, was on its way to hold a poort when it halted at Modderfontein.

It was part of a cordon intended to prevent the enemy, now growing desperate, from breaking through Elands River Poort and Evans Hock into the Craddock district.

The Lancers' camp was on the southern slope of a gentle rise, encircled on the west by a spruit.

They were at dinner, the officers at a farm close by,

when a man galloped in from an observation post to say that a large number of Boers were approaching, and, as he was reporting, shots were heard some distance away.

"The men saddled up and took up positions round the camp," says the journal; "a lot of Boers were on a ridge running halfway round the camp, firing at us, while others were seen advancing, and there were soon a number laid low on each side.

"Some of the enemy were in khaki, which at first led our men to suppose them to be Colonel Gorringe's column, which was expected—a dastardly *ruse* practised many times by the Boers during the war.

"The 7-pounder gun had to be abandoned as two men were shot dead, and the officer in charge and one man wounded, they having absolutely no cover.

"With the first shot, however, three Boers were knocked over.

"The firing was fast and furious, and presently some Boers were seen coming up a river bed which ran halfway round the camp.

"Our casualties soon ran up to an alarming number.

"The enemy were working right round us, and were soon right on top of us.

"It was almost a hand-to-hand fight.

"Three of our officers were shot dead, and the three remaining wounded.

"The sergeants immediately took their places, and they were all shot except one.

"Still the men fought on; no one ever thought of showing the white flag or surrendering till we were absolutely overpowered and overwhelmed by numbers.

"Men absolutely refused to surrender, and many were the deeds of bravery enacted.

"One officer (Lieutenant Russell) said to the man

next him, 'Fix bayonets, charge!' and no sooner did they rise than they were both shot dead. Another man of my troop was helping a wounded man to ambulance when he was shot dead through the temple. A sergeant had his arm shattered, but he managed to mount a horse and galloped to another camp for help. Some men were lying dead with their rifles in the death-grip; most of the bullets were explosives, some horrible wounds being made. One officer (this was Lieutenant Morritt), a well-made young chap of 6 ft. 4 in., had his scalp blown clean off and his brains were lying on the kopje. One man was shot dead at the ambulance; another, waiting to be dressed for a wound in the hand, got another in the shoulder. Some of the Boers got among the waggons, shooting anybody they saw. I don't know how any of us escaped—just pure luck. I could feel the wind made by the bullets going by, and dirt and bits of stone splashed in my face. The Boers soon looted the camp and set fire to the waggons; they were in a deplorable condition—no boots, trousers made of blankets and sheepskins, no hats, and starving. They soon got among the eatables, and then some went round robbing us of our money, watches, etc.; one took my telescope, a change of washing, and my hat. Some of the men were left standing in their drawers. All of the enemy were Transvaalers, and told us they had been trekking night and day from the Transvaal, and were starving. We couldn't tell the exact number of casualties the enemy had, but Commandant Smuts said he had paid dearly for it. While they were removing their dead and wounded they kept us out of the way so we shouldn't see, but six were seen to be put on a Cape cart, and a lot across horses, and the Boer doctor came to ours for lint and bandages. The Boers were 600 strong, as far as we could see, while we numbered 150! They told us we were reckless, and we told them it was DEATH OR GLORY!

"Of course, we were beaten, but I'm glad to say not disgraced; we lost 37 killed and 45 wounded, 82 casualties in all, so that just over every other man was put out of action—I happened to be one of the *other* ones!

"The captain in charge was hit in the chest"—this occurred just before the finish—"and was carried to a farm: lady in house said she was so sorry.

"The captain said, 'Don't be sorry at all—I wish I was numbered with the slain.'

"All the wounded bore their pains most heroically.

"My officer (Lord Vivian) was shot in the thigh; expect he will have his leg off. (Happily this proved unnecessary).

"My sergeant had his arm shattered, and I expect this will come off too.

"Just as the Boers were retiring (they went south towards Bedford), leaving one dead and one wounded as a blind, a column came up with another squadron of our regiment (Captain Nickalls).

"They said they saw the Boers in the camp, but couldn't fire for fear of hitting us.

"Doctors were sent for to Tarkastad, and later, after totalling all up, we found we had 82 killed and wounded —a frightful number for one squadron.

"We stopped at the farm all night and next day."

This account, from the pen of one who was there, needs no comment, and very little amplification.

The squadron held its own until its ranks were decimated, and then the enemy attacked from the rear.

Then Captain Sandeman attempted to make for

some neighbouring kraals, but was shot down with most of the men that were with him, and the Boers rushed the camp.

Not a single man surrendered, and "the action throughout was characteristic of the regiment, and reflected the greatest credit on all ranks."

Lord Kitchener telegraphed to the War Office, "Squadron fought most gallantly, inflicting heavy loss to the enemy, who, being dressed in khaki, were mistaken for our own troops."

A letter from the Rev. J. Catling, rector of Tarkastad, who afterwards buried the dead, is of interest.

"The 17th, true to their motto, 'Death or Glory,' preferred to die rather than surrender. They contested every inch of the ground—but what could 150 do against 400?—and many were killed at 20, 10, and even five yards. The Boers used explosive bullets. I found some, and have them, and I saw the awful wounds."

"September 18th"—to quote again from the journal —"we dug a grave 60 feet long near the rocks, where the greatest number fell. The minister came, and we buried them just as the sun was going down. We put three officers in first, then 30 N.C.O.'s and men, then two artillerymen of the 4th Mountain Battery, and then a Boer.

"The service was very impressive. Just imagine thirty-six men, side by side in one long grave, all wrapped in blankets! How many hearts will be sore later on! They all died heroes, and what is death *supposed* to be to a soldier! We afterwards filled the grave up, and marked it off with big stones, and erected three wooden crosses, by which time it was quite dark. We then marched back—all that was left of the squadron—to the next camp, about three miles back.

The first man I met was an old chum of mine. He gripped my hand, *and it did feel good!"*

Such is the simple story of Modderfontein as narrated by one of the survivors; one must fill in the setting for oneself: the flipflop of the Mausers, the answering crack of the Lee-Metfords, the rain-soaked veldt, and the empty cartridge cases littering the blood-stained kopje on which the lads of the 17th died.

A picture has been painted of the subject, and although the details are woefully inaccurate, the spirit of the thing is well rendered.

That death-fight will gain in interest when the halo of time has gathered round it: many a regimental medal has been struck for actions not one whit more heroic!

The official list of the casualties is a roll of honour that must find a place in these pages.

MODDERFONTEIN.—17*th September*, 1901.

KILLED.

Lieut. Richard Brinsley Sheridan.

Mr. Sheridan, who joined in 1896 from the 3rd Battalion Royal Scots, was a direct descendant of the famous dramatist, and his mother was a daughter of Motley, the historian of the "Rise and Fall of the Dutch Republic."

Lieut. Robert Alexander Morritt, of Rokeby Park.

Mr. Morritt came to the regiment from the 7th Dragoon Guards, and had been at the front a year.

2nd Lieut. Philip Leslie Russell.

This officer was a son of the late Hon. P. Russell, of Ballarat, New Zealand, and had only joined the previous March from Cambridge University.

Sergt. A. Applegate; Corpl. A. Kellard; Lance-Corpl. W. Nichols; Privates W. Davis, J. Todd, F. Thomas, H. Sherriff, T. Large, C. Richardson, J. Bailey, R. Rose, A. Stephens, H. W. Peers, J. Gilligan, C. Bushby, H. Harley, W. Thomas, A. Thompson, H. Dooley, T. Rice, J. Wheelhouse, A. Tallis, W. Roberts, W. Raison.

WOUNDED, SINCE DEAD.

Sergt. G. Wort; Privates G. Hall, J. Francis, J. Walker, A. Aird, C. Kennedy.

WOUNDED.

Capt. Sandeman, Lieut. Lord Vivian; Sergts. G. Marsh, T. Naylor, E. May, O. Sandwith; Corpls. J. Tucker, E. Barnes; Lance-Corpls. P. Gillon, Law, H. Belford; Shoeing-smiths, A. Neale, R. Brown; Privates J. Clutterbuck, J. Wallace, H. Fitch, G. Drumm, J. Ayres, J. Sheffield, C. Linder, T. Harvey, M. Owen, W. Martin, J. Poole, A. Saunders, T. Barnfather, J. Marsden, W. Steenton, G. Wildman, J. Moylan, J. Naughton, A. Birtwhistle, W. Anders, H. Hayes, R. Gilbert, J. Lyna.

CHAPTER XVII.

THE END OF THE WAR.

Captain Shaw-Stewart's Death—Stormberg and Molteno—Inspected at Dordrecht by French—The Siberia Mountains—The Drakensberg—Aliwal North—Campaigning in the Great Karoo—Talk of Peace—Peace Proclaimed—Cape Town—Home Again.

A VERY sad occurrence about this time was the death of Captain H. M. Shaw-Stewart, one of the most popular of the regiment's officers, who, being invalided home, had sailed in the *Candia;* and in August came the news of his tragic ending. An officer of the I.Y., named Stone, died on board, and was buried with all the solemn impressiveness of a funeral at sea; and Captain Shaw-Stewart, whose Kodak was never very far from his hand, springing on to the gunwale to take a snapshot as the body was launched into the deep, overbalanced, and disappeared. He rose once, waist high out of the water, but before help could be rendered sank altogether, and although every effort was made, they could find no trace of him.

After the fight at Modderfontein the squadron returned to Steynsburg by train from Tarkastad, and on the 8th November they reached Stormberg, where a considerable concentration of troops was in progress.

They found the 9th Lancers and the Cape Mounted Rifles there, and met many old friends in the ranks of the former regiment, as the 17th had sent several large drafts, including many of their best recruits, to the 9th before that regiment went out.

From Stormberg they went to Molteno, and then to Dordrecht, where General French inspected them on the 15th.

Colonel Munro's column was drawn up in a line nearly a mile long, with their waggons in the rear, and, followed by a large staff of aides-de-camp, gallopers, and orderlies, the general came on parade at a gallop.

After the inspection "he made reference to the gallant stand made by us at Modderfontein, and said it was a noble example to every other corps in the country. . . . He left us in the same way that he came, viz. at a gallop!"

And now began again—if, indeed, it can be said to have ever ceased—a toilsome and persistent trek, very difficult to follow.

The net was closing round the enemy, but they still showed fight, and turned and twisted in a marvellous manner.

The column toiled up the Siberia Mountains, meeting their convoy at Coetzy's Kraal, and for several days their route lay in the high latitudes, with bitter cold and heavy rains thrown in.

On 22nd November the main body attacked, killing two and wounding seven of the enemy without casualties on our side.

On the 24th they were in camp, and played the I.Y.'s at football—one goal each; the next day they beat them at cricket by 10 runs; on the 26th they were on the march again, reaching Barkly East at seven in the evening.

The following day the camp was visited by terrific dust storms, and half the column marched next morning to an English farm which the Myburgh commando had looted at midnight.

During the three hours' halt there they were soaked to the skin, and pelted by hailstones the size of sparrow's eggs, and at 7 p.m. they moved off along the Lady Grey road, fording the Kraal River up to their girths.

The other portion of the column had taken another route, and at half-past five in the morning their guns were heard about two miles off, the Boers having run into them unexpectedly, and finding themselves suddenly called upon to face the music of two 15-pounders, a pompom, and a maxim, which made them bolt over the fairly level country.

Men and horses were thoroughly done up, having been in the saddle thirteen consecutive hours, but after a day's rest they went on again, camping on the 7th on a slope so steep that they slept in an almost perpendicular position, the keen air of the mountains giving them tremendous appetites, which they had no means of satisfying.

On the 8th they flushed a commando, and captured all their pack-horses and blankets, rescuing one of the Cape Police who was about to be shot and who told them he had counted 203 Boers in bad condition, Fouché himself having robbed the man of his boots.

A hot chase was kept up, the column climbed a ridge of the Drakensberg, some 15,000 feet above the sea level, the men clinging to their horses tails, so steep was the going, and the wind so terrific that two horses of the I.Y. were blown over a precipice; but the enemy were found to have crossed the border into native territory, and our men, worn and thin, with mounts well-nigh at the last gasp, turned rein for Barkly once more by way of Mount Moubine, getting a handful of flour apiece, which the C.O. commandeered at a lonely farm.

On the 11th they were served out with rations, and our corporal notes in his diary that "the cast-iron biscuits tasted like wedding-cake!"

They reached Aliwal North on the 21st, heartily glad to leave the mountainous Barkly district, and next day the column pushed on again.

Another Christmas Day was to be spent on service, and the story of one day's work is almost a repetition of every other.

Headquarters moved to Matjesfontein at the end of December, and the regiment had experience of campaigning in the Great Karoo Desert, where the ironstone rocks gave out such heat that "it was torment to sit down."

One squadron of the 17th with one of the 9th, and Brabant's Horse, formed a column under Major Lund, of the 9th, and worked with Capper's column, doing some long and continuous treks, and often getting in touch with the enemy.

On the 5th February they hustled a strong commando which had attacked Colonel Crabbe's convoy near Roger's Valley, and the squadron of the 17th covered the columns at Molteno Pass the day after.

Capper parted company with them on the 9th, and on the 5th March their old friends the 9th Lancers left for India, heartily glad to turn their backs on the veldt.

All ranks were weary of the protracted struggle kept alive by certain irreconcilables who had to be worn down before the war could be considered over, and there still remained several months of hard work for the 17th.

They were now in the north-west part of Cape Colony, the column being under command of Major

Russell, R.A., and the same twisting and turning continued, almost as difficult to follow in detail as the enemy themselves.

Glen Parde Kloof, Garst Kolk, Reitaar, and Bokpoort mean nothing to English readers, but they will awaken regimental memories of marches by night and day, of no water when they did not chance upon a rock-well, of far too much when the rain came down in torrents.

On the 17th, two days after they had reconnoitred Vosberg, and drawn blank, they had a camp concert, which was quite an event.

On the 24th the column was inspected by General Stevenson, at Victoria Road Station, and on the 25th they made a night march to round up some of Malan's commando, who, however, were not to be found.

On Easter Monday Bethune's column marched along the Prieska Road, a squadron of the 17th and one of the Yeomanry taking a parallel track, and eight miles out the latter column was fired on from a farm.

They saw the enemy bolting, and a troop of the 17th charged after them up a kopje, afterwards returning to the farm, where they found a Cape cart and a Mauser.

Our corporal, passing through the garden with his hat full of tomatoes, came upon a Boer hiding in the bushes, and promptly collared him, the man yielding some useful information to the C.O.

On-saddling and marching off again, the column was attacked by the enemy, who had returned in force, but they were beaten off.

They made a desperate attempt on the convoy next day as the waggons were passing a nek, the troops being on ahead, and carried away thirteen, laden with corn, and a few men of the Yeomanry with them.

The column's veterinary surgeon fell into their hands, and was despitefully used, coming into camp in nothing but his collar and tie, to the huge amusement of everyone, the provost-marshal taking a snapshot of him.

"You want to go over there and take some!" said the denuded vet., pointing in the direction of the enemy, amid a roar of laughter.

On the 10th April the lighter side of campaigning showed itself again, and the 17th Lancers beat the 16th at cricket by 58 runs.

This was followed by a football match, and after a splendid game the I.Y.'s won by 2 goals.

Next day, *réveille* at 5 a.m., horses exercised, a march towards De Aar, and flanking patrols.

Peace began to form the chief topic of conversation; the column reached Deelfontein on the 16th, and Richmond Road Station on the 18th, the Boers trying to cross the line the night before.

The blockhouses were ordered to be strengthened on the 21st, as the enemy were expected to make a dash for it, but nothing happened, and on the 22nd the advance guard of Imperial Yeomanry surprised a Boer outpost at a farm.

Three were captured, the rest getting away barebacked, leaving their blankets and forty saddles behind them, hotly pressed by the column, but escaping in the darkness.

The enemy, very desperate by this time, opened hot fire on the column on the 23rd, but the 12th Lancers wheeled to the right and charged a kopje; the 17th went to the left, and cleared the snipers out of some small kopjes in that direction; while the pompom put the main body to the right about, killing five and wounding twenty-eight, as was reported.

They found 2,000 spent cartridges on one kopje alone, showing how hot was the fire that had been opened on the Yeomanry.

The column was now in a district where all the water was salt.

The column still kept on the move, through terrific dust storms blown up by piercing wind, and on the 1st June, when camped at an outspan station called Gorras, near Klipfontein, they received a sudden order to parade at 8.30 p.m.

They turned out with rifles and bandoliers, expecting to be attacked, but a more pleasurable surprise awaited them, and Major Hoare called for a light, which our corporal provided in the shape of a candle, shielded from the wind in an empty biscuit tin.

Peace was proclaimed in the Transvaal and the Free State, and there was every prospect of the rebels surrendering shortly.

The hard-bitten, veldt-wearied men went mad with delight; shouted until they were hoarse, and sang "God Save the King!"

The candle was flung high in the air, and an indescribable scene of joy ensued, followed by a double allowance of rum.

The next day they went round the camp with a Union Jack and a blanket, and paid off some old scores among the staff men and the military police, holding a concert at night with the aid of a borrowed piano.

On the 3rd our corporal, to his great surprise, found himself chosen for one of the ten men from his squadron who were to go home at once to represent the regiment at the Coronation.

It wanted only twenty-three days to that historic event, and the little party were off and away in two hours at a gallop, amid the hearty cheers of their less fortunate comrades.

Before they went the Column Commander took their photographs, the officers shook hands with them all round, and the officer who was to take them was chaired out of camp.

They did sixty miles before dark, halting at Pom Pere Poort, going on next day with fresh horses.

At Cape Town, which they reached at something after six on the morning of the 7th June, they were met with the alarming information that the boat sailed in half an hour, so, springing out of the train, leaving kits and blankets behind them, they ran helter-skelter for a mile and a half, to find the steamer had already left at midnight.

Fortunately a tug had just returned from the transport, and the lieutenant rose to the occasion, offering the captain £50 if he would put them aboard.

Even then their troubles were not over; it was discovered that they had three men too many, and there was a hasty ballot, the unlucky trio going back with the tug, bitterly disappointed; the others reaching Southampton on the 25th June, where they were welcomed by Lord Roberts.

The regiment remained in South Africa for several months longer, but at last the day came when they started from Victoria West Station and embarked on the Union Castle liner *German*.

At the very moment that the "Old Comrades" were dining together in London, the *German* was steaming up the Solent, bringing home 14 officers and 527 men, under Colonel Haig's command.

They landed on the 19th October, and were met by their old chief, Sir Drury Lowe, who made a brave little speech in the embarcation shed, in which he regretted that he was now too old to don the regimental jacket.

Colonel Haig called for three cheers for the General, and later on they entrained for Edinburgh and Glasgow, where they still lie.

Their casualties during the campaign, of which I here give an official list, form a roll of which any regiment might be proud; it is a record of good work done, and of good lives unhesitatingly surrendered in the doing.

Killed or died of wounds:—Officers, 5; men, 58. Died of disease in hospital:—Officers, nil; men, 32. Died at sea:—Officers, 1; men, 3. Wounded and recovered:—Officers, 9; men, 67. Invalided:—men, 438.

About 2,000 horses were received by the regiment during the war, and their marches totalling roughly 2,000 miles, each mile cost them a horse!

Several events of interest remain to be set down here since the Regiment's return.

On the 4th March, 1903, the lance was abolished, except for escorts, and certain ceremonial parades.

In the opinion of many distinguished officers, and certainly of every lancer, the step is unwise, and unnecessary, and it is to be hoped that the order will be rescinded ere long.

We have all read the evidence of Colonel Haig before the late Commission, and the protests of other cavalry officers would fill a volume.

Of the new service-dress, and the Russo-German cap that has replaced the smart pill-box, it is not our intention to speak; both are as ugly as sin, and universally disliked by the great majority of the service.

When the King visited Scotland in May, the 17th were on duty in Edinburgh, and on the 13th they rode out to Dalkeith to receive their medals from his Majesty's hand.

The 1st Battalion Black Watch followed them, and about a dozen of the Royal Artillery, the Gordons, and the Army Service Corps.

"I am well aware," said his Majesty, "of the admirable manner in which both regiments have behaved. They have shown their old spirit, and I hope they will always continue to show it, and that that spirit will increase and go on in the British Army. I hope you will maintain the high position you have attained in the army, and always do your duty to your sovereign, and to your country."

They afterwards marched past to the band of the Black Watch.

A happening of the keenest regimental interest was the winning of the Inter-Regimental Polo Competition at Hurlingham on the 11th July, before her Majesty the Queen, the Prince and Princess of Wales, and a distinguished company.

Fifteen teams had competed, and the final issue lay between the Blues and the 17th.

The 17th had an old Indian reputation for polo, when Captains Renton, Miller, and Portal, and Mr. Rawlinson played in the team, but neither regiment had ever won the cup, and the competition was remarkably keen.

The respective teams were :—Mr. H. G. Brassey, Capt. the Hon. R. Ward, the Duke of Roxburghe, the Hon. D. Marjoribanks (back) for the Blues ; and Capt. Carden, Major Tilney, Mr. A. Fletcher, and Col. Haig (back) for the 17th, and the Lancers scored five goals to one.

Colonel Haig, C.B., A.D.C., who had previously played in three winning teams for the 7th Hussars, and is one of the first authorities on the game, has been appointed Inspector-General of Cavalry for India.

In August Lord Roberts visited the regiment at "Jock's Lodge," and expressed himself as highly pleased with its condition.

To conclude what, after all, is but a brief outline of its doings, the regiment gained during the war 1 V.C., 1 C.B., 3 D.S.O.'s, 3 D.C. medals, and 50 individual mentions in despatches.

CHAPTER XVIII.

THE "OLD COMRADES" DINNER.

"My Old Regiment"—*Esprit de Corps*—Rise and Progress of the "Old Comrades" Dinner—Sergeant O'Gorman's Medals—A Pathetic Story—An American Gentleman and His Letter—Liberal Support by Officers, Past and Present—*L'Envoi*.

To the soldier who has done honourable service, either in peace or war, and passed from the army into civilian existence again, there is nothing under heaven so thrilling as the words "my old regiment."

In days of yore they meant more to him than perhaps they do now, but it is only a question of degree, and, "long service" or "short," if he has been a good soldier it does not matter whether fate has turned his sword into a ploughshare or exchanged it for an office quill, or even a crossing sweeper's broom, those words retain the same magnetic influence for him until the day of his death.

He is prepared to proclaim it "the smartest corps in the service"; if it is not now, it was in *his* time, and there is no gainsaying him—he gives you chapter and verse, and sometimes, when his enthusiasm gets the better of his judgment, he enlarges on its achievements in a manner very confusing to the seeker after hard facts.

But his intentions are honourable, and if some of his stories are "old soldiers' stories," they are prompted by *esprit de corps*, which is a sentiment to be assiduously cultivated.

To *esprit de corps*, well fostered, our little British army owes a great deal, and though recent reforms have done much to destroy it, there are signs at the present time of a reaction in its favour, which will bear great fruit in the future.

In the 17th Lancers regimental tradition has been kept very much alive; and, to their honour be it said, the sentiment is not allowed to cease when they leave the colours.

I have received letters during the compilation of these records from men whose connection with the regiment has been severed thirty years and more, yet they still proudly sketch the skull and crossbones after their signatures, and can show you the old sword and lance exercise without a mistake.

Nine years ago a few old members of the corps met together to dine, and out of that little gathering has grown an annual function now known as the "Old Comrades' Dinner," which may be strongly recommended to the notice of the army at large.

Officers' dinners have existed for generations, but anything like a gathering of retired non-commissioned officers and men has been a rarity hitherto, and in the present instance much of the success is due to the efforts of the secretary, Sergeant-Major Paul, a veteran of Ulundi, who served for thirty-two years in the regiment, and was their first musketry instructor when they received the carbine.

The second dinner showed a marked increase in numbers, about 60 old comrades assembling at the Horseshoe to effect a "reconnaissance in force" through a menu every item of which was named after some officer or regimental tradition, from the soup, which was "Death or Glory," to the sirloin, christened "Duke of Cambridge's Own."

The officers of the 17th, then stationed at York, sent a deputation of non-coms. to represent the corps, assisted the committee with the sinews of war, and despatched a welcome telegram during the evening, which was received with great enthusiasm.

At the third meeting the squadron of "Death or Glory Boys" mustered 80 strong, 4 Balaclava heroes among them; and the fourth dinner, to which 97 sat down, was marked by an incident which had a ring of genuine pathos in it.

An American gentleman—Mr. R. H. Wyeth—was present as a guest, and he told them a story which carries the mind back to a glorious period in the regiment's history, and touches on the seamy side of soldiering.

Years before, when a journalist in Philadelphia, he saw two British medals in the window of a pawnbroker, and, going in, inquired their origin.

On the yellow and blue ribbon of one of them were the Alma, Balaclava, and Sebastopol clasps, telling of the "death ride" and the horrible Crimean winter; dangling to the red and white of the other hung the silver guerdon of Mutiny days, and both had belonged to Sergeant James O'Gorman, of the 17th Lancers.

The pawnbroker informed him how O'Gorman, falling on evil times, had been reduced to the dread necessity of pawning his hardly-won medals, and how for *seven years* in succession he had paid the interest, unable to redeem them, yet hoping against hope.

And then there came a day when the gallant old fellow presented himself no more!

Whether to the pinch of poverty there was added the pang of knowing that the medals had passed beyond his reach, or whether he had died in the meantime, is not known; only that he *did* die, somewhere in Philadelphia, where the 17th had lain under Howe in the old, old days of battle!

Mr. Wyeth bought the medals, and for years they remained in his possession, until, hearing by chance, when staying at Leamington in Warwickshire, of the "Old Comrades'" meeting, he wrote a letter to the secretary, offering the trophies to them.

I have his correspondence before me, and its tenour does him honour.

It would have astonished the scarlet-coated Light Dragoons of American war time, and have made Dennis O'Lavery open his eyes!

At the fourth annual dinner, in 1898, this worthy American citizen presented the medals to O'Gorman's comrades amid tremendous applause, and received as a memento the silver motto worn for many years on the lance cap of Sergeant-Major Paul.

I am tempted to reproduce here some words he subsequently wrote to the sergeant-major on the eve of his departure.

"The simple dedication," he says, "will be placed under glass at the back of the frame, which will be of *English* oak, and you may rest assured that should anything happen to me your wishes as to the motto will be respected. I go to the United States able to tell my countrymen, when and where I can, that a crazy king and a corrupt ministry could not sever utterly the hearts of a people the same in thoughts, language, and religion."

At the fifth annual meeting, held at the Temple

Bar Restaurant, on October 21st, 1899, 81 old members of the 17th met to fight their battles over again under the shadow of the crossed lances and John Hale's famous emblem.

Each succeeding year greater interest is displayed in the gathering; the Duke of Cambridge, Lord Tredegar, General Sir Robert White, Sir William Gordon, and a host of former officers, contribute guineas, game, and champagne to the cause of regimental *cameraderie*, and the present officers never allow them to pass unremembered.

"Balaclava Pudding' and "Death or Glory Sauce" still figure on the menu and in the intervals between the loyal toasts, they revive ancient memories of " my old regiment "—that regiment whose varied fortunes we have traced in this volume through the four quarters of the globe; in storm and sunshine, in scarlet and blue; sometimes under circumstances of great trial, but always with honour to itself, true to its old traditions and to its stirring name—

"THE DEATH OR GLORY BOYS!"

APPENDICES.

APPENDIX A.

THE SUCCESSION OF COLONELS.

1763 (27th April) John Hale.
1770 (2nd Nov.) George Preston.
1782 (18th April) Hon. Thomas Gage.
1785 (4th Feb.) Thomas Fiennes Pelham Clinton, 10th Earl of Lincoln.
1795 (20th May) Oliver de Lancey.
1822 (9th Sept.) Lord R. E. H. Somerset, K.C.B.
1829 (23rd Nov.) Sir John Elley, K.C.B., K.C.H.
1839 (28th June) Sir Joseph Straton, K.C.H.
1839 (24th Aug.) Sir A. B. Clifton, K.C.B., K.C.H.
1842 (25th April) H.R.H. Prince George of Cambridge.
1852 (23rd Sept.) Thomas William Taylor, C.B.
1854 (28th Jan.) Sir James Maxwell Wallace, K.H.
1867 (4th Feb.) Charles William Morley Balders, C.B.
1875 (22nd Sept.) John Charles Hope Gibsone.
1876 (21st June) H.R.H. Duke of Cambridge (colonel-in-chief).
1884 (19th July) Henry Roxby Benson, C.B.
1892 (24th Jan.) Sir Drury Curzon Drury Lowe, G.C.B.

It is worthy of remark that all the sixteen colonels of the regiment, with the exception of the Earl of Lincoln, have seen war service, and that no less than *six* were Waterloo men.

1. JOHN HALE. Appointed 27th April, 1763.

Raised the regiment by warrant dated 7th November, 1759. For life and services, *see* Chapters I., II.

2. GEORGE PRESTON. Appointed 2nd November, 1770.

General Preston was a picturesque figure in the military history of the 18th century. He is said to have entered the service as a common soldier, and to have been kettle-drummer at the coronation of Queen Anne.

After serving under Marlborough in Flanders, he was present with his regiment at Dettingen, Fontenoy, Roucoux, and Val, where he was wounded, at that time holding the rank of captain.

The lieut.-colonelcy was given to him in 1757, and he commanded the Greys during the war in Germany, from 1758 to 1762, establishing a reputation for skill, valour, and personal eccentricity, always going into action in an old buff coat of an earlier fashion.

He was at Minden, Warbourg, Kirch Denkern, and Grobenstein, besides innumerable skirmishes and minor actions, and on the retirement of John Hale was made colonel of the 17th.

Major-general in 1772, lieut.-general in 1777, he returned to his old corps in 1782, the colonelcy of which he held until his demise at Bath three years later.

3. THE HON. THOMAS GAGE. Appointed 18th April, 1782.

The Honourable Thomas Gage was second son of Thomas, 1st Viscount Gage, in the peerage of Ireland, and was born in 1721.

On the 30th January, 1741, he was made lieutenant in the Hon. James Cholmondeley's regiment of foot, afterwards the 48th—now 1st Northamptons,—and in 1745 was a captain in Batterean's, the old 62nd.

In 1748 he was major in the 55th which became

the 44th when the old marine corps were disbanded in that year.

He wore their scarlet and yellow for some years, becoming lieut.-colonel 2nd March, 1751, and commanding them in the North American troubles under Braddock, Gage himself being badly wounded with the advanced column on the 9th July, 1755.

He raised a provincial regiment, under warrant, 5th May, 1758, called the "80th Light Armed Foot," an early attempt in the direction of riflemen, save that they had smooth bores with the barrels shortened.

He married Miss Kemble in December, the daughter of the President of the Council in New Jersey; saw more service in Canada the following year; commanded the rearguard under Amherst, and was made Governor of Montreal.

He became major-general 1761, and Commander-in-Chief in North America, with headquarters at New York, from 1763 to 1772, holding during that period the colonelcy of the 60th Royal Americans for two months, until Jeffery Amherst's reinstation, and then that of the 22nd Foot.

He became lieut.-general in 1770, and in 1774 was appointed Governor and Captain-General of the Province of Massachusetts Bay, which brought him into some connection with the first stage of the War of Independence.

He was well received on his arrival at Boston in May, and was personally popular with the colonists, but a series of proclamations, and several attempts to seize their war stores, irritated them against him, and, though an undoubtedly brave man, he soon proved himself an indifferent general.

He embarked at Boston, 10th October, 1775, barely

four months after the battle of Bunker's Hill, leaving everything to Howe; was made colonel of the 17th Light Dragoons, 18th April, 1782, became full general the following November, and was removed to the colonelcy of the 11th Dragoons in 1785, dying on the 2nd April, 1787.

Of the general's eleven children, his youngest son, Sir William Hall Gage, Admiral of the Fleet, died as recently as 1864, with a good record of naval service.

4. THOMAS FIENNES PELHAM CLINTON, 10th Earl of Lincoln. Appointed 4th February, 1785.

Lord Thomas was born in July, 1752, and was third son of the 9th Earl, who afterwards became Duke of Newcastle.

He was appointed captain and lieut.-colonel in the 1st Foot Guards, 5th April, 1775, becoming Earl of Lincoln three years later on the death of his brother Henry.

Colonel in 1780, he obtained the colonelcy of the old 75th in 1782, going on half-pay when the regiment was disbanded the following year, and succeeding General Gage in the command of the 17th in 1785.

Major-general in 1787, he became Duke of Newcastle in 1794, but did not enjoy the dignity long, for, catching the hooping cough from his children, he burst a blood vessel after taking an emetic, and died on the 18th May, 1795, at Sunninghill, Berkshire.

5. OLIVER DE LANCEY, M.P. Appointed 20th May, 1795.

Oliver de Lancey was an American by birth, his family having settled there and accumulated considerable wealth. He published a pamphlet on taxation in the British colonies, and was gazetted cornet in the 14th Dragoons in 1766, getting his troop in the 17th in May, 1773.

He was sent out on the outbreak of hostilities in advance of his regiment, with despatches to Howe, and a commission to buy horses for the 17th—a mission that proved futile owing to the wide spread of the revolt; and, joining his regiment on their arrival in Boston, he served with them during the earlier stages of the war.

He commanded a squadron on Long Island in 1776, at the driving in of the enemy's pickets and the affair at Brooklyn, and again in the Jerseys during the following spring he was repeatedly under fire with his men.

In the spring of 1778, he was constantly to the front, and had some hard service with the rearguard during Howe's march to New York.

On the 3rd June, 1778 he became major, and commanded the regiment on Long Island and in the lines in front of New York, afterwards proceeding to South Carolina with Cornwallis, as deputy-quartermaster-general.

In 1781 he was promoted lieut.-colonel (though he retained his regimental majority for some years to come), and succeeded Major André as adjutant-general to the forces in America. When the war was over he had the arrangement of all military claims, and sat as president of the commission for settling the accounts of the army; was appointed deputy-adjutant-general with the rank of colonel in the army in 1790, and, four years after, succeeded Samuel Birch, the last of John Hale's original officers, as lieut.-colonel of the 17th.

That same year he received the barrack-master generalship, and was promoted major-general on the 3rd October.

On the 20th May, 1795, two days after the death of the Duke of Newcastle, Oliver de Lancey became colonel of his regiment, a proud and well-deserved position which he continued to hold for the next twenty-seven years.

In 1801 he was made lieut.-general; general in 1812; and when he died, in September, 1822, he closed a military career that had extended to the unusual period of fifty-six years.

6. LORD ROBERT EDWARD HENRY SOMERSET, K.C.B.
Appointed 9th September, 1822.

This officer, generally known as Lord Edward Somerset, was born in 1776, third son of the 5th Duke of Beaufort, and he joined the 10th Light Dragoons, as cornet, 4th February, 1793, at the age of seventeen

He was lieutenant in December; captain, 28th August, 1794, and in 1799 served in Holland as aide-de-camp to the Duke of York.

A majority in the 12th Light Dragoons was given to him in November, transferred twelve months later to the 28th Lights; and on Christmas Day, 1800, he became lieut.-colonel of the 5th Foot, from which he exchanged in 1801 into the 4th Dragoon Guards, with which regiment he was destined to see a good deal of hard fighting.

From 1799 to 1802 he was M.P. for the Monmouth Boroughs, and was returned for Gloucester in 1803, continuing to represent that place until 1823, but his attendance in the House must have been strangely intermittent, as from 1809 until the close of the Peninsular War he was almost always in the field.

In April, 1809, he went to Portugal with the 4th, and commanded them at Talavera and Busaco.

At Usagre, 25th May, 1811, he was engaged in a brilliant encounter, where our 3rd and 4th Dragoons cut up and captured about 200 men belonging to a couple of French cavalry regiments.

In the charge of General Marchant's heavy brigade at Salamanca, Lord Edward Somerset led one squadron with a gallantry that earned for him mention in the despatches and a place in Napier's history of the war.

He had already been made colonel, and aide-de-camp to the king in July, 1810, and after the campaign of 1812, Wellington himself recommended him for a brigade.

He became major-general in June, 1813, and was presented by his brother officers with a sword of honour on his leaving the regiment to command the Hussar brigade of the 7th, 10th and 15th.

He continued at the head of those dashing light horsemen, at Vittoria, through the Pyrenees, Orthes, where he charged, and Toulouse, receiving the thanks of Parliament, 26th June, 1814, and the gold cross with one clasp for the Peninsular.

In January, 1815, he was made a K.C.B., and his name will ever be associated with Somerset's heavy brigade at Waterloo.

He was in the thick of that charge, when the Lifeguards, Blues, and 1st Dragoon Guards, tore down the slope, round and about La Haye Sainte; and, losing his cocked hat, Lord Edward wore a Lifeguard's helmet for the rest of the day, it being also rumoured that his own sword had not been idle!

After Napoleon's overthrow, he held command of the 1st Cavalry Brigade of the army of occupation in France, from 30th November till the end of 1818, again receiving the thanks of Parliament, and the orders of Maria Theresa, St. Vladimir, and the Tower and Sword.

In January, 1818, he received the colonelcy of the 21st Light Dragoons; in September, 1822, that of the 17th Lancers; the Royal Dragoons, November, 1829; and finally his old regiment, the 4th Dragoon Guards, in March, 1836.

He was subsequently inspector-general of cavalry; lieut.-general, 27th May, 1825; lieut.-general of ordnance, 1829—1830; G.C.B., 1834; surveyor-general, 1835; general, 23rd November, 1841, and died 1st September, 1842.

He was the first of the "Waterloo" colonels of the 17th Lancers.

7. Sir John Elley, K.C.B., K.C.H. Appointed 23rd November, 1829.

This officer began life in romantic fashion, of which there are two accounts extant.

The one, quoted by Cannon, makes him a native of Leeds, articled to a London solicitor, but, preferring the army, enlisting in the Blues at Leeds as a private trooper. The other, and I believe the more correct, is given in "Biographia Leodiensis," on the authority of the Rev. John Smithson, incumbent of Headingley, who died in 1835.

John Elley was born in London, about 1770, and was the son of an eating-house proprietor in Furnival's Inn Cellars, Holborn.

In his fourteenth year he was apprenticed to a Mr. John Gelderd, of Meanwood Tannery, near Leeds, and lost no time in falling desperately in love with his master's buxom daughter, Anne, who was a year or two older than young Elley.

The girl being rather hot-tempered, and inclined to be a little flighty, the course of true love did not run as smoothly as her swain desired, and, after a serious quarrel, he came to London and enlisted on the 5th November, 1789, in the Royal Horse Guards Blue.

Unhappily, the lady took it so much to heart that she fell into a rapid decline, died, and was buried in Armley Chapel, the trooper getting leave to attend the funeral "in great grief."

It was a bad start, and he begged his father to buy him out, without success; but, later on, he found the money for the then warrant rank of a troop-quartermastership, in 1790.

He went to Flanders with the four troops of the regiment in 1793, as acting adjutant, and attracted notice for his bravery at Cateau, April, 1794, afterwards purchasing a cornetcy in June.

Lieutenant, by purchase, 26th January, 1796; captain-lieutenant, 24th October, 1799; he purchased a troop, 26th February, 1801, and served as aide-de-camp to Major-General Staveley during the invasion scare.

Major, 29th November, 1804; lieut.-colonel, 6th March, 1808, he was appointed assistant adjutant-general to Sir John Moore's cavalry, and served during the Corunna campaign, being present at Sahagun, Majorca, Benevente, Lugo, and Corunna; continuing to hold the appointment until 1814.

He was thanked by Wellington for his gallantry and skill at Fuentes d'Onoro and Llerecna; had two horses killed under him at Salamanca, and was severely bayoneted in the side with Le Marchant's heavy cavalry brigade.

He was often wounded, and saw an immense amount of active service during the war, being promoted colonel, 7th March, 1813; and assistant adjutant-general of the cavalry when Napoleon escaped from Elba, and we were preparing to oppose him once more.

At Waterloo he played the double rôle of staff officer and combatant, and, possessed of great physical strength, he was reported to have slain several cuirassiers with his own sword.

Loaded with medals, crosses, clasps, and orders, the runaway apprentice was made K.C.B.; major-general, 12th August, 1819; Governor of Galway, 1821; colonel of the 17th Lancers, 1829; and lieutenant-general, 1837.

He had been returned for the borough of Windsor in 1835, but the sands of life were running out, and on the 23rd April, 1839, he died at his seat, Cholderton Lodge, Wiltshire, and was buried in St. George's Chapel, where a bust and slab commemorate the virtues of a fine soldier.

His personalty was something under £25,000, and, after a number of charitable bequests, he left two sums of £300 to be spent on mess plate by his regiment.

8. Sir Joseph Straton, K.C.H. Appointed 28th June, 1839.

Joseph Muter entered the 2nd Dragoon Guards as cornet in December, 1794, and did all his service under his proper name, changing it in 1816 on coming into the estates of his aunt, Miss Straton, of Kirkside, near Montrose.

Lieutenant in December, 1795, he was promoted to a troop in the 13th Light Dragoons on the 2nd March, 1797, got his majority in 1801, and after studying at the Royal Military College, High Wycombe, during 1804 and 1805, he passed out well, and was appointed to the Duke of Gloucester's staff.

A lieut.-colonel in 1808, he sailed for the Peninsula with the 13th in the early part of 1810, and served through three campaigns with a regiment that was always hard at it.

He was mentioned in despatches for the gallantry with which he led them at Arroyo de Molinos, and on the 4th June, 1813, he was transferred to the Inniskilling Dragoons.

Colonel, June, 1814, he commanded the Inniskillings at Waterloo, where they formed part of the famous Union Brigade, and later in the day, after the death of Ponsonby, Colonel Muter took charge of the brigade until, wounded towards the end, he was succeeded by Clifton, of the Royals, who, oddly enough, followed him in the colonelcy of the 17th Lancers.

Medal and C.B.; 4th class of St. Vladimir of Russia, and K.C.H., Sir Joseph—now Straton—became major-general, 1825; lieut.-general, 1838; colonel of the 17th, June, 1839; and was transferred to the 8th Hussars in August, following Keir Grant, under whom the 17th had served in the Pindari wars, and who had followed Banastre Tarleton in the colonelcy of the King's Royal Irish.

Leaving the 8th, Sir Joseph Straton died in October, 1840, six months after his removal to his old regiment, the Inniskilling Dragoons.

9. Sir Arthur Benjamin Clifton, K.C.B., K.C.H. Appointed 24th August, 1830.

General Clifton entered the army as cornet, 6th June, 1794; was lieutenant, 7th August the same year; captain, 27th February, 1799; major, 17th December, 1803; lieut.-colonel, 25th July, 1810; colonel, 12th August, 1819; major-general, 22nd July, 1830; lieut.-general, 23rd November, 1841; and general, 20th June, 1854.

His campaigning lasted from 1809 to the crowning glory of Waterloo, and he smelt powder for seven consecutive years.

He commanded a squadron in support of Spanish guns at Talavera; served at Busaco, and in the pursuit of Massena from Santarem. Fuentes d'Onoro, Nave d'Aver, El Bodon, Fuentes Guinaldo, Aldea de Ponte, and several affairs during the retreat from Salamanca, killing or taking nearly a hundred of the enemy with his red Dragoons.

The Royals were in the rear at Vittoria, but there was service to be seen at Pampeluna, in the Pyrenees, and at Toulouse, all of which has gone to the general's credit, and he commanded the regiment at Waterloo, where it was on the right of the Union Brigade.

He received the gold medal and one clasp for Fuentes d'Onoro and Vittoria; the silver war medal and three clasps for Talavera, Busaco, and Toulouse; was made a Knight of the 2nd Class of St. Anne of Russia and the 4th Class of Wilhelm of Holland, and getting the colonelcy of the 17th Lancers in August, 1839, held it until he obtained that of his old corps, the 1st Royal Dragoons, 30th August, 1842.

10. H.R.H. Prince George of Cambridge. Appointed 25th April, 1842. [See 14, p. 287.]

APPENDIX. 361

11. Thomas William Taylor, C.B. Appointed 23rd September, 1852.

Cornet, 14th July, 1804; lieutenant, 12th June, 1805; captain, 22nd January, 1807; major, 7th July, 1814; lieut.-colonel, 18th June, 1815; colonel, 10th January, 1837; major-general, 9th November, 1846.

General Taylor, when a lieutenant, served as assistant adjutant-general under Sir James Craig in the Mediterranean, 1805 and 1806; and in 1811, when captain, he was employed on the staff at the attack and capture of Java, including the attack of the outpost near Wettevreden, and the storming of the lines of Cornelia.

In the campaign of 1815 he served with the 10th Hussars, and was present at Waterloo.

War medal and clasp for Java.

12. Sir James Maxwell Wallace, K.H. Appointed 28th January, 1854.

Cornet, 14th August, 1805; lieutenant, 6th June, 1806; captain, 22nd October, 1807; major, 1st January, 1817; lieut.-colonel, 25th September, 1823; colonel, 28th June, 1838; major-general, 11th November, 1851; lieut.-general, 6th February, 1855.

When a captain in the 21st Light Dragoons at the Cape of Good Hope, he commanded a squadron of the regiment in 1812 with the expedition under Brigadier-General Graham, and had a very arduous seven months before the Kaffirs were driven across the Great Fish River.

In the Waterloo campaign he was appointed orderly officer on the 16th June, to assist Dornberg's brigade-major, Captain Robais, but during the retreat on to our position on the 17th from Quatre Bras, Dornberg's aide, Krachenburg, was taken by the French, Robais made aide in his place, and Wallace acted as brigade-major, until—Robais being killed at Waterloo—the Baron recommended Wallace to the Duke of Wellington, who confirmed him in the appointment.

13. CHARLES WILLIAM MORLEY BALDERS, C.B. Appointed 4th February, 1867.

Major-General Balders entered the service as cornet, by purchase, 10th November, 1825; lieutenant, 25th November, 1828; captain, 15th July, 1836; major, 16th May, 1845; brevet lieut.-colonel, 3rd April, 1846; colonel, 20th June, 1854; lieut.-colonel, 8th January, 1858; major-general, 31st August, 1860.

He commanded the 3rd Light Dragoons in the Sutlej (1845-6), and led them at Moodkee and Ferozeshah, at which latter place he was wounded in the groin while charging the guns in the evening. Medal with one clasp, brevet lieut.-colonel, C.B.

14. JOHN CHARLES HOPE GIBSONE. Appointed 22nd September, 1875.

General Gibsone entered the service as cornet, 8th October, 1830; lieutenant, 16th August, 1833; captain, 24th July, 1835; major, 25th February, 1845; lieut.-colonel, 3rd September, 1847; colonel, 28th November, 1854; major-general, 28th June, 1862; lieut.-general, 25th October, 1871; general, 1st October, 1877.

General Gibsone saw considerable service in the Kaffir war of 1846-7; leading the cavalry charge on the Gwanga, 8th June, 1846, when 400 of the enemy were killed. He was complimented in the despatches, and particularly mentioned in general orders.

(*Colonel-in-Chief*) H.R.H. GEORGE WILLIAM FREDERICK CHARLES, DUKE OF CAMBRIDGE, COMMANDER-IN-CHIEF (now K.G., K.T., K.P., G.C.B., G.C.S.I., G.C.M.G., G.C.I.E., G.C.V.D., A.D.C., Honorary Colonel-in-Chief to the Forces). Appointed 21st June, 1876.

The Duke of Cambridge commanded the 1st Division throughout the campaign of 1854, and was present at the battles of Alma, Balaclava, and Inkerman, where his horse was shot. His services also include the Siege of Sebastopol. Medal with four clasps and Turkish medal.

15. HENRY ROXBY BENSON, C.B. Appointed 19th July, 1884.

General Benson entered the service as cornet, 31st January, 1840; lieutenant, 15th April, 1842; captain, 27th June, 1845; major, 23rd October, 1854; lieut.-colonel, 20th September, 1856; colonel, 23rd September, 1859; major-general, 6th March, 1868; lieut.-general, 1st October, 1877; general, 1st July, 1881.

General Benson commanded the 17th Lancers in the Crimea from the 14th January, 1855, including the battle of the Tchernaya; siege and fall of Sebastopol; commanded the squadron of the Light Brigade in the night attack on the Russian outposts, 19th February, 1855. Medal with clasp, 5th Class of the Medjidie, and Turkish medal. He also served with the regiment in the Mutiny.

16. SIR DRURY CURZON DRURY LOWE, G.C.B. Appointed 24th January, 1892.

Cornet, 28th July, 1854; lieutenant, 7th November, 1854; captain, 9th November, 1856; major, 10th June,

1862; lieut.-colonel, 15th June, 1866; colonel, 15th June, 1871; major-general, 9th December, 1881; lieut.-general, 1st April, 1890.

Their present colonel joined the regiment on the 18th June, 1855, in the Crimea; was present at the battle of the Tchernaya, and at Sebastopol, for which he received the medal, clasp, and the Turkish medal. He took his share of the Tantia Topee pursuit, capturing 4 elephants at Zirápúr, and receiving the medal and clasp of Central India.

Called unexpectedly to the command, on the disabling of Colonel Gonne, he took the 17th out to Africa, and was slightly wounded at Ulundi.

In the Boer war of 1881 he served in command of a cavalry brigade under Sir Evelyn Wood, and in Egypt, 1882, the 17th's popular colonel greatly distinguished himself in command of the cavalry division. He was present at El Magfar, Mahsama, the two affairs at Kassassin, and the battle of Tel-el-Kebir, and immediately after the last-named made his celebrated forced march on Cairo, capturing the citadel and Arabi.

He was mentioned six times in despatches, was thanked by both Houses of Parliament; made a K.C.B., and received the medal and clasp, the Osmanieh, and the Khedive's star.

APPENDIX B.

THE WAR SERVICES OF THE SEVENTEENTH.

1761. A draft to Germany to serve under Granby and Prince Ferdinand: no details obtainable.
1763—1775. Several times called to assist the Civil Power in Ireland.
1775. Bunker's Hill: dismounted volunteers.
1776. Long Island: several skirmishes.
  ,, Brooklyn.
  ,, Pelham Manor: skirmish.
  ,, White Plains.
  ,, Fort Washington.
  ,, Rhode Island.
1777. Danbury.
  ,, Forts Montgomery and Clinton.
1778. White Marsh.
  ,, Crooked Billet.
  ,, Barren Hill.
  ,, March from Philadelphia.
  ,, Freehold, or Monmouth Court House.
1779. Various little affairs before New York: the whole war affords innumerable instances of individual actions on the part of isolated detachments of the 17th, the records of which were lost with the regimental papers in 1797.
1780. War in Carolina.
  ,, Charleston.
  ,, Monk's Corner.
  ,, Lenew's Ferry.
  ,, Wacsaw

1780. Camden.
1781. Cowpens.
  „   Guildford Court House.
  „   Various affairs before Gloucester.
1794. Aiding the Civil Power in Ireland.
1795. Jamaica and St. Domingo.
1796. Jamaica, Grenada, and St. Domingo.
1798. Detachment to Ostend.
1800. Aiding the Civil Power.
1806. Capture of Monte Video.
1807. Buenos Ayres.
1810. Engaged against fanatics in the Bombay Presidency.
  „   A detachment on escort to Persia.
1813—1815. Detachments on active service.
1815. Capture of Anjar.
1816. Capture of Dwarka.
1817—1819. Pindaree War.
1820. 2nd Expedition into Cutch.
1854—1856. Crimea—Bulganak—Mackenzie's Farm—Balaclava—Inkerman—Sebastopol.
  „   Aiding the Civil Power at Nenagh.
1858—1859. Indian Mutiny; Pursuit of Tantia Topee.
1878. Aiding the Civil Power.
1879. Zulu War, — July, transport duty on the Candahar route.
1893. Aiding the Civil Power.
1900—1901. The War in South Africa.

APPENDIX C.

THE TITLES OF THE REGIMENT; ITS FIRST UNIFORM, AND A RÉSUMÉ OF THE CHANGES IN ITS DRESS AND EQUIPMENT.

1759. Hale's, or The 18th Regiment of Light Dragoons.
1763. Hale's 17th Light Dragoons.
1766. Hale's 3rd Light Dragoons.
1769. Hale's 17th Light Dragoons.
1770. Preston's „   „   „
1782. Gage's   „   „   „
1785 (Feb.). The „   „   „
1822. The 17th Lancers.
1876 (June). The 17th, Duke of Cambridge's Own, Lancers.

Regimental Nicknames.

"The Death or Glory Boys"—from its formation.
"Bingham's Dandies"—about the early "Thirties."
"The Pipeclay Boys" }
"The Gentlemen Dragoons" } period uncertain.
"The Pride of England—the Terror of India—and the Glory of the World"—after the Mutiny.

The Original Uniform. Circa 1764.

The dress of officers and men was almost identical, differing only in the addition of silver lace for the former, and of course in the quality of the material used.

Scarlet long-skirted coats, lined white and faced with white half-lapels to the waist, the lapels 3 inches in breadth. The cuffs and turned-down collars (called capes at that period) were white, the skirts turned back with the same, and the collars capable of being raised in bad weather.

The sleeves were not to be slit, and the buttons, which bore the device 17 L.D., were set on lengthways up the arm, four on each sleeve, by twos.

Lace or embroidery was left to the option of the colonel, and in Hale's case it was silver, with worked buttonholes.

The officers sported two white cloth epaulettes with silver fringe, and scarlet velvet stocks, the men having white worsted epaulettes, black stocks on ordinary occasions, and white ones on Sundays.

Waistcoats and breeches were white, the latter either of leather or duck, the waistcoats made with cross pockets, no flaps, and no embroidery.

Boots, reaching to the knee, with black tops, were to be "round-toed and of a light sort," and a high polish was not affected in those days.

For dismounted duty a black cloth half-gaiter was used.

When the regiment was raised the officers' crimson silk sashes were worn over the left shoulder, the knot hanging to the top of the coatpocket hole, but in 1764 they were ordered to be worn round the waist under the coat, the knot on the right side.

The sword blade for mounted work was straight, 36 inches long, and carried in a white belt over the right shoulder under the coat; for dismounted duty the blade was 28 inches and worn in a waistbelt.

Both officers and men carried a pair of holster pistols with 9-inch barrels, the men in addition having the carbine, the barrel 2 feet 5 inches long, which was carried in two ways—either with the nozzle in a bucket below the right holster, the whole thing kept in position by a strap, together with the picket-post, or else sprung to the swivel on the shoulder belt, for service or exercise.

The helmets were of black leather, surrounded by a silk turban, possibly white at first, but scarlet before the regiment was many years old, topped by a silver crest from which whisked a pendant plume of red horsehair; two little tassels at the back, and on the front plate the Death's head in silver.

The horse furniture was of white cloth, housings and holster caps all in a piece, with a leather seat, that was held in place by the surcingle, and the men used theirs as an extra blanket on cold nights.

The officers had black bearskin tops to their holsters, the men goatskin, and housing and holster cap was edged with the mourning-lace.

From the corner of the housing, and from the centre of the holster cap, dangled a silver tassel, the holster being embroidered with the King's Crown and Cypher above the letters XVII. L.D.; the housing bearing the letters simply, on a red ground within a wreath of roses and thistles.

Quartermasters wore practically the same uniforms as the men, but with silver buttons, and a sash of crimson spun silk; their housings were like the officers', minus the tassels, and with a narrower lace, the furniture of all other ranks being ornamented with mohair instead of silver.

The distinguishing marks of a sergeant of Light Dragoons at that period were: a silver-worked button-hole, a narrow silver lace round the collar, and a silver fringe to the epaulettes; his waist being girded by a crimson spun silk sash with a white stripe in it.

A corporal differed from a private man, by having a narrow silver lace round the turn-up of the sleeve, and a white silk tape edging to his silk-fringed epaulettes.

All buttons were set on in twos; cloaks were red, with white collars and linings; the red watering cap had the regimental number on the little white flap in front, and in some regiments the officers affected a round topped stirrup in contradistinction to the square ones of the men, but whether that custom obtained in the 17th it is not possible to say.

As full details of trumpeters, farriers, and the regulation saddlery, have been given in Chapter I., it is not necessary to recapitulate them here.

1784.

Uniforms changed to a blue cutaway jacket; cuffed, collared, lined, and laced with white, the lacing of a square pattern. New helmet with bearskin crest and red and white side plume. Towards the close of the century the jacket was shortened to the waist, and the lacing placed in parallel lines.

1802.

Sleeve chevrons for non-coms. introduced in cavalry.

1812.

New uniform for Light Dragoons; date of adoption by the regiment uncertain, the 17th being then in India.

Blue coatee (cavalry grey for East Indies) with white revers. Flat-topped shako with white lace and lines. Wellington trouser of grey cloth with two white stripes down each seam. White worsted epaulettes, and girdle, blue and white for men, red and gold for officers.

1822.

Lancer uniform adopted by the 17th on returning to England in 1823. Blue jacket, white facings, blue-grey trouser. White-topped lance-cap with red and white plume. Moustaches. Gold aiguilette on left shoulder (done away with about 1824). Carbines given up.

1829.

White lapels abolished. Black plume. Dark grey "Oxford Mixture" trousers.

1831.

Scarlet jackets. Gold lace. Blue trousers with red stripes—gold for officers' full dress. Clean shaving.

1842.

Blue jackets. Grey trousers strapped with cloth.

1855.

Tunics with white lapel, to button back in fine weather.

OTHER CHANGES.

1857 (?).—White plumes.
1860.—Forage cap peaks abolished. Khaki.
1861.—White helmets.
1868.—Bamboo lances.
1869.—Black plumes.
1872.—Jack-boots.
1876.—White plastrons and plumes.
1878.—Martini carbines. The regiment has since been armed with the Lee-Metford and the Lee-Enfield carbine, and while in South Africa with the magazine rifle and bayonet. Two patterns of service cap have been worn, and the new forage cap; and the present service dress is piped with yellow.
1903.—Abolition of lance!

APPENDIX D.

LIGHT DRAGOON KIT AND ACCOUTREMENTS, 1759.

The following list may not be uninteresting to the student of military antiquities, and is taken from Hinde's "Discipline of the Light Horse, 1778"—a curious and somewhat rare book, in which the whole drill, dress, and duty of the British Light Dragoon is set forth with great minuteness:—

	£	s.	d.
A saddle	1	1	0
A pair of holsters	0	5	8
A pair of stirrup-leathers	0	1	3
A pair of tinned stirrups	0	3	6
A girt and surcingle	0	2	6
A crupper	0	0	11
A breastplate	0	1	2
A furniture compleat with a leathered seat and embroidered	1	7	6
A large crupper-pad	0	1	3
A pair of point straps and loops	0	1	0
A bucket	0	1	8
A bucket-strap	0	0	9
A carbine-strap	0	0	3½
A pair of long baggage-straps with double buckles	0	1	6
A pair of single baggage-straps	0	1	4
A middle baggage-strap	0	0	6½
A pair of cloak-straps	0	0	8
A middle cloak-strap	0	0	3
A bridle and bradoon	0	4	6
A tinned bitt	0	3	0
A linking brown leather collar	0	2	6
A linking white leather collar	0	1	6

	£	s.	d.
A pair of canvass bags, leathered, for the curry comb and brushes, etc.	0	3	2
A curry comb and brush	0	2	3
A mane comb and spunge	0	0	8
A horse cloth	0	4	9
A snaffle watering bridle	0	2	0
A carbine	2	0	0
A pair of pistols	1	10	0
A sword	0	12	0
A sword-belt	0	5	0
A shoulder belt	0	5	0
A cartridge-box and belt	0	2	8

NECESSARIES FOR A LIGHT DRAGOON, 1764.

A coat, waistcoat, breeches, and cloak, found by the colonel by contract.

	£	s.	d.
An helmet	0	16	0
Boots and spurs	1	3	0
A watering cap	0	2	6
Four shirts at 6s. 10d. each	1	7	4
Four pair of stockings at 2s. 10d. each	0	11	4
One pair of boot-stockings	0	2	0
Two pair of shoes at 6s. a pair	0	12	0
A black stock	0	0	8
A stock buckle	0	0	6
A pair of leather breeches	1	5	0
A pair of knee-buckles	0	0	8
Two pair of short black gaiters	0	7	4
A white jacket	0	8	6
A stable frock	0	4	8
A horse picker and turnscrew	0	0	2
A pick wire and pan brush	0	0	2
A worm and oil bottle	0	0	$3\frac{1}{2}$
Necessary bags	0	7	3
A corn bag	0	2	6
Goatskin topps	0	1	6
Blackball	0	1	0
Three shoe brushes	0	1	3

	£	s.	d.
A hair comb	0	0	6
A burnisher	0	0	6
A white portmanteau	0	8	0
A pair of gloves	0	1	6
A farrier's cap	0	14	0
A farrier's apron	0	1	8
A farrier's budgets	0	14	0
A farrier's ax (*sic*) and case	0	5	0
A farrier's saw and case	0	8	6
A brass trumpet	2	2	0
Sling and tossels (*sic*)	0	10	0
Trumpeter's hat and feather	1	0	0

APPENDIX E.

SOME OLD EXERCISES OF HALE'S LIGHT DRAGOONS ABOUT 1763.

THE manual of that period comprised thirty-one words of command, viz. :—

1. Poise your carbines.
2. Cock your carbines.
3. Present.
4. Fire.
5. Half-cock your carbines.
6. Handle your cartridge.
7. Prime.
8. Shut your pans.
9. Charge with cartridge.
10. Draw your rammers.
11. Ram down your cartridge.
12. Return your rammers.
13. Shoulder your carbines.
14. Rest your carbines.
15. Order your carbines.
16. Ground your carbines.
17. Take up your carbines
18. Rest your carbines.
19. Shoulder your carbines.
20. Secure your carbines.
21. Shoulder your carbines
22. Present your arms.
23. To the right face.
24. ,, ,, ,,
25. To the right about, face.
26. To the left face.
27. ,, ,, ,,
28. To the left about, face.
29. Shoulder your carbines.
30. Advance your carbines.
31. Shoulder your carbines.

TO PRIME, LOAD, AND FIRE.

Priming and loading were performed in fifteen motions, viz. :—

  Prime and load. 3 motions—recover, priming position, open pans.
  Handle cartridge.

Prime.
Shut pans.
Cast about.
Load. 2 motions.
Draw rammers. 2 motions.
Ram down cartridge.
Return rammers.
Shoulder. 2 motions.

The words of command for the firing were:—

As front rank, make ready!
Present!
Fire!
As rear rank, make ready!
Present!
Fire!

The front rank man turned a half-face to the right, the rear rank stepped out with his right foot so as to touch the front rank's left heel with his toe.

THE CAVALRY FUNERAL.

The military funeral of that day was pretty much as it is at present, all ranks from colonel downwards having the three sad volleys fired across the grave.

The trumpeters sounded their dead march. The "music" played the Dead March in Saul, the horse was led with the reversed boots, and if an officer's the empty saddle was covered with black cloth.

Insignia of the dead man's rank was laid on the coffin; sash, drawn sword, and pistols in case of an officer; for a chaplain, a Bible and cassock; the surgeon, an amputation knife and saw, in addition to his arms; a trumpet for the trumpeter; a whip for the riding-master; and on the farrier's coffin "with a drawn sword, to be laid a pair of pincers, a hammer, and horseshoe."

It was the practice for the entire regiment to attend as a mark of respect, the youngest officer leading, the oldest bringing up the rear; but on the return the commanding officer was in front, the trumpets sounding a march, generally a merry one.

"Why, soldiers, why, should we be melancholy boys?" would have been a peculiarly appropriate air for Hale's regiment on such occasions—perhaps they did use it—as, according to a tradition which I hope may never be dispelled, Wolfe sang that fine old song at mess the night before the storming of Quebec.

APPENDIX F.

THE TRUMPET DUTY OF THE LIGHT DRAGOONS.

The following calls were in use before the regulation of 1799, and were sounded by the trumpet, the bugle-horn, or the French horn, but the actual musical notation has been unfortunately lost.

For Stables,	Trumpet.
To Boot and Saddle,	"
Horse and Away,	{ Sometimes by the Bugle-horn.
The March,	Trumpet.
For Water,	"
For Stables,	"
Watch Setting or Tattoo at Night—For Stables in the Morning,	"
The Call.—For Parade or the Assembly,	"
Sounding to Horse.—For Stables in the Evening,	"
To Repair to the Alarm Post,	Bugle-horn.
The Standards Call,	Trumpet.
At Fetching and Lodging the Standards,	"
At Drawing and Returning Swords,	"
The Slow March on Foot,	By the Band.
The Quick March on Foot,	By the Fife.
Preparative for Firing,	Trumpet.
To Cease Firing,	"
To Form Squadrons,	Bugle-horn.
To Advance,	Trumpet.

To Charge—Or Attack,	Trumpet.
To Retreat,	French-horns.
To Trot,	Trumpet.
To Gallop.—To Front—To Form,	,,
To Form Squadrons, and the Line,	Bugle-horn.
To Rally,	,,
The Non-commissioned Officers' Call,	Trumpet.

INDEX.

Abdallah, The Thoroughbred, 78, 79
Abercromby's Army Delayed, 130
Aberdour's Corps, 25
Adam Wallace, Gallantry of, 88
"Admiral Christian's Storm," 131
Africa, The War in South, of 1899-1901, 265-341
Agent, First Regimental, 16
Ahua, The 17th at, 204
Alphonse de Neuville, 259
America at the Outbreak of War, 50
American Army, Pay of, 64
—— —— Uniform of, 73, 74
Amiens, Reduction at Peace of, 150
André, Major : his Fate, 96, 97
Anjar, Young de Lancey Wounded at, 175
Anniversary of Balaclava, The First, 222
—— —— Sad Coincidence, 225
—— of King's Birthday, 170
Arrears of Pay, 21

Badge, 17th's First, 10
Balaclava, Charge of, 204-223 ; Bugle, 221, 222
Balcarres, Earl of, in West Indies, 119 et seq.
Barbarous Cropping of Horses, 34
Barham Downs, Review on, 144 et seq
Baroda, 243
Barren Hill, Action at, 70, 71
Bass Drums Suppressed, 18
Bayonet for Light Horse, 7
—— Suppressed in Heavies, 5
Bearskin Caps for Farriers, 19
Belfast, 17th at, 111
Belts, Width of, 20
Benson at Zirápur, 242
——, Mrs., Carries Stretcher, 257
Berryman, 205, 214, 215, 252, 253
Bethel, Incident in Village of, 67
Bhooj, Capture of, 175
Bingham, Lord, Joins 17th, 195
—— —— Serves with Russian Army, 195
Black, Captain, Death of, 137
Blaquière, Lieut.-Col. : his duel, 40, 41 ; his death, 40, 41
"Blood" Smith, 221
Blue Uniform, 17th Put into, 109
Bombay, 17th Land at, 171
Boston, 53 ; Arrival of 17th at, 56 ; Letter from, 59 ; Evacuation of, 61
Boulderson, Major, 253
Bounty to American Army, 64
—— to 17th, 233
British Cheers, 261
Brooklyn, Action at, 63
Brown, Sergt., Gets Commission, 144
—— Trumpeter, Gets Commission, 252

Bronx River, 17th at, 65
Brutality during American War, 81
Buenos Ayres, Storming of, 164
Buff Coat, Last, in Service, 43
Buford, Colonel, at Wacsaw, 86-87
Bullion Epaulettes, 197
Bunker's Hill, Battle of, 56-57
Butcher Jack, 203
Butchery at Culloden, 6

Calcutta, 17th Land at, 170
Caledonia, Foundering of the, with Regimental Papers, 141
Camden, Battle of, 91
Camp Equipage, 67
Cannon, Richard, Errors in his Records, 115
Canterbury, First Visit of 17th to, 141 ; Second Visit, 192 ; Regimental Races at, 193 ; Chaplain at, 247 ; Expedition from, to Ostend, 142 ; Field Days, 145
Cape, Ordered to the, 265
Carbines, Early, 20 ; changed for Spanish Muskets, 155 ; given up, 183 ; resumed by the Lancers, 256
Cardigan, Lord, at Balaclava, 211, 212, 213, 216
Carolina, Campaign in, 75 et seq.
Cattermole, Sergt.-Major, 234
Cavalry, Light, Origin of, 5
—— Dismounted, for West Indies, 132
——, Defeat of American, at Biggin's Bridge, 80
——, Defeat of American, at Lenew's Ferry, 83
——, French, in America, 100-101
——, Gallant Charge of American, at Cowpens, 99
—— Horses, Method of Purchase in Last Century, 22
——, Lancers Added to British, 186
——, Reduced State of, in Crimea, 224
——, 17th serve as Dismounted, 123, 143, 155 et seq.
Chaloner, John Hale marries Mary, 36
Chatham, 17th at, 183
Cheetoo, Pursuit of, 180 et seq.
Chichester, 17th, The, Thanked by Corporation of, 169
Cholera, 17th Lose Three Men, 189 ; March, 248
Cleveland, Death of Cornet, 223
Coates, Introduction of, 176
Colonel, Status of Old-time, 2 ; Colonel-in-Chief appointed, 256
Comrades, Dinner of Old, Chap. XV.
Concord, 55

"THE DEATH OR GLORY BOYS."

Cork, 17th Leave, 49
Cornet, Rank of, Abolished, 255
Cornwallis at Camden, 91
Cossack Battery, 212
—— Trouser adopted, 191
Cowpens, Battle of, 98
Craufurd, at Buenos Ayres, 164
Crimea, 17th Embark for, 201-203
Cudjoe, a Maroon Leader, 118
Cumberland's Light Dragoons, 6
Cutch, Expedition to, 174-5

Dalrymple, Colonel, on Horse Purchase, 22; on Riding School, 33
Danbury, 17th at, 67
"Death or Glory," 11; "Sauce,' 269
Death of Wolfe, 1
—— — Adam Wallace, 88
—— — Balaclava Butcher, 249
—— — Baron de Kalb, 92
—— — Captain Black, 137
—— — —— Hale, 97
—— — —— Nolan, 212
—— — —— Shaw-Stewart, 331
—— — —— Wyatt Edgell, 261
—— — Co'onel Fitch, 122
—— — Cornet Cleveland, 223
—— — —— Paterson, 99
—— — Corporal Dennis O'Lavery, 102
—— — Lieutenant Marriott, 182
—— — Major Cotton, 171
—— — —— Fortescue, 265
—— — John Hale, 42
—— — the Prince Imperial, 259
—— of Tantia Topee, 246
De Lancey, Oliver, Appendix A
"Derby" and Saratoga, 68
Desecration of Church by 17th, 59
Deserters, Advertisements for, 14
—— Shoot Colonel of 28th Light Dragoons, 147
Douglas, of 10th Hussars, his Book, 222
Dragoons, Accoutrements of Light, 20, 21, 22
——, Ammunition for Light, 84
——, Band of Light, 18
——, Class of Recruit wanted for, 12
——, Cumberland's Light, 6
——, Extraordinary Conduct of Officers of Light, 26
—— for West Indies, 115
——, Kit and Pay for Light, 21; Appendix D
——, Light, Origin of, 5; put into Blue Uniforms, 109; another Change, 175
——, Punishments in the Light, 29
——, Renumbering of the Light, 39
——, Review of Light, 47
——, The Light Troops of, 7; "Broke," 87
——, Uniform of 17th Light, 17 et seq.; Appendix C
Drum Horse, 17th's, 263
Drummers, Light Dragoon, 8
Drums, Abolishment of, 18
Drunkards, Punishment of, 81
Drury Lowe, 242, 257, 258, 261, 262, 273, 287

Duffield, 17th Suppress Riots at, 148
Duke of Cambridge, 256, 273, 287

Elephants, Capture of, 242
Elliot, Colonel, Raises 15th Light Dragoons, 8
Embarkation, for America, 48; for Crimea, 201; for India, 170; for Mutiny, 228; for Zululand, 258
Emsdorf, 15th Light Dragoons at, 35
Emsworth, 17th Billetted at, 201
England, Part of 17th on the, 258
Erzunzayan Hill, Adjutant Shot at, 259
Esaughur, Tantia Topee Storms, 232
Evan Lloyd, last of American War Officers, 174
Eveline, the Headquarter Ship, 202
Eyre Coote, 142-3-4

Farce, an Interrupted, 60
Farriers, Uniform of, 18
Fearful Mortality in the West Indies, 139, 141
Fedioukine Hills, Charge of Chasseurs-à-cheval on, 217
Fédon, The Mulatto, 133
Flag, Strange Manufacture of American, 107
Flogging Drill in 17th Lancers, 234
France, Part of 17th Embark on the, 258
French Horn, Use of, 18
—— Lancers of Old Guard at Waterloo, 187
—— Lancers and Hussars in America, 100
—— Model, American Uniforms made on the, 74
—— Troops, Arrival of, 75
Friendship between 17th and Royal Marines, 131; between Wolfe and John Hale, 2-3
Froude, Quotation from, 111
Furious Storm, Clinton's Fleet Scattered by, 75
Furniture, Light Dragoon Horse-, 20, 21

Gage, Bad Generalship of, 57; his Services, 274
Garstin, of the 17th, Taken Prisoner, 116
George Grote, A Letter from, 42
Gift, Bravery of Marylanders under, 92; Escape of General, 92
Gloucester, Combat before, 101
Gonne, Colonel, Accident to, 257
Good Conduct of 17th at Chichester, 169
Gorse Creek, Messenger Captured at, 80
Gowan's Cove, American Fugitives Drowned in, 68
Granby, Detachment of 17th Serves under, 35
Grass Guard, Singular Custom of, 22
Grenada, Rising in, 133
Grays, 17th Receive Colonel from the, 45
Gubbins, Letter of Lieut., 115
Guidons 17th's first, 19
Guildford Court House, 17th probably at, 100

INDEX.

Gujerat, 17th Stationed in, 173

Hampstead, U.S.A., 17th in Winter Quarters at, 71
Hanger, George, 93
Hermione, 17th Serve as Marines on, 131
Horry, Anecdote of Colonel Peter, 96
Howard, John Eager, at Cowpens, 98; his Marriage, 100
Howe, His Staff all Hit at Bunker's Hill, 58
——— and the old Madeira, 64
———, Cruel Treatment of Officer by, 97
——— Takes the Field, 62
Hudson River, 17th Engaged on, 68
Huger, Flight of General, 82
Hull, 17th under Colonel, 127
Hussars, 11th and 8th at Balaclava, Chap. XII.
———, French Engage 17th, before Gloucester, 101
——— only to Retain Moustache, 198
———, 17th, Reviewed with 8th, 192
——— ———, Sail for Mutiny with 8th, 228

Ignorance of Recruits in the "Fifties," 235
India, First Visit of 17th to, 169; Second Tour in, 228; Third, 262
Ireland, 17th Land in, 38; Leave, for America, 50
———, — Leave, for Mutiny, 228
Irish, Corporal, Superb Gallantry of, 101
——— Deserter Shoots a Colonel, 147
Isle of Wight, Draft Run into off the, 235

Jackboots, Adoption, 295
Jack Penn, 213
Jamaica, 117 *et seq.*
Joy, Trumpet-Major, His Bugle, 221

Ker, Peter, Assault on, 26-7
Kerr, Kolapore, Makes a Dashing Charge, 240
Kilkenny, 17th Reviewed at, 44
Kingston's Light Horse, 6
Kinloch, Captain, Saves American Standard-bearer, 88

Lance, of Civil War, 185; Mercer's, 188; The, of 1816, 189
———, Crimean, and Mutiny, 229; Bamboo, 254
Lance, The, abolished, 339
Lancer, Revival of, 185
——— of Napoleon's Army, 185
——— — Russian Guard, 186
——— Uniform, *see* Uniform
Lancers, 17th, Take the London Duty, 192
———, —, at Balaclava, Chap. XII.
———, —, Made, 182
———, Lanzun's, 100
Lawrence, Sergeant, gets the V.C., 291

McMullins, Gallantry of Private, 103
Manchester, Strongest Muster of 17th held at, 149
———, Unpopularity of, as Military Station, 149

Man Singh Betrays Tantia Topee, 246
Maroons, Origin of, 118; Rising of, 119
Massachusetts, Armed Strength of, 54
Michel, Field Marshal, 230
Modderfontein, The Battle of, 322-330
Morris, Captain, Takes Command of 17th, 208; Expostulates with Nolan, 211; Unlucky Thrust of, 213; Surrenders, 216; Makes a Bolt for it, 219; Strange Coincidence, 220; His Rescue, 220; Death of, 220
Mungrowlee, Battle of, 232

Necessaries, for Light Dragoons, Appendix D
Nelson's Ferry, 85
Netley, Cavalry Camp at, 180
Nettles, Lieut., of 17th, Wounded, 99
Newcastle, Duke of, 276
New Corps, 189
——— Drill Book, 144
——— Town, Disaster at, 120
——— Uniform, 109. *See* Uniform.
Nibbs, Sergeant, 283
Nolan, Captain, Altercation with Lucan, 211; His Death, 212

O'Hara, Sergeant, 215, 221
O'Lavery, Dennis, Gallantry of, 101
"Old Dog Tray," at Church Parades, 247
Old Exercises, 299
——— Time Recruiting, 13
Order against Smoking, 254
Order of Review, 45
Original Officers of John Hale's, 16
Orphans, 17th give a Day's Pay to, 39
Ostend, Expedition to, 142
Oswald Werge, of 17th, 125, 128, 137, 143

Paget, Lord G., Mounts the Light Brigade, 207
Patterson, Cornet, killed, 99
Patrolling in Carolina, 82
Pawnshop, Medals in a, 267
Pay of Light Dragoons, 21
——— — American Troops, 64
Penn, Jack, 213
Perdita (Mary Robinson), 7
Philadelphia, 17th at, 70
Pindari, 176 *et seq*
Pipeclay Boys, 291
Plastron, White, 255
Platoff, Hetman, 186
Popham, Home, his plan, 142; another one, 151
Portsmouth, 17th embark at, for India, 168; Draft towed into, 235
Presentation Sword refused by Walpole, 129
Pride of the Ocean, Troopship, 201-2
Prince George of Cambridge, Colonel of 17th, 199
Prize Money, John Hale's, 35
Prussian Collar, 197
Pudding, Balaclava, 269

Quaker-brown, Adopted by Pennsylvania Regiments, 74
Raimond, Defence of Post at, 138
Rations, 31
Rawdon, Lord, 93, 102
Recruiting, Ancient, 13
Regent's Park Barracks, 17th at, 192
Regiment of Berwick, 139
Regulations for Standards, 19
Reports, Favourable, of 17th, 44
Retiro, Auchmuty takes the, 165
Review, Order of, 45
Revolver Practice, Accident at, 257
Riding, Dalrymple on, 33
Rogue's March, 29
Royal Waggon Train, Sergeant of 17th Receives Commission in, 144
Ruggeley's Mills, 90
Ruttapore, 17th at, 181

Saddles, Light Dragoon, 20; panel, 230
Sandford, Colonel, Death of, 121
Shadwell, Colonel, Murder of, 147
Shaving-dry, American Punishment, 95
Shubrick, Captain, Carries off Valuable Horses, 78
Sir William Gordon, 208, 218, 229 et seq.
Sleeve Chevrons, 294; regulation concerning, 235
Slinging Horses, 49
Soldiery and Populace, 53
Somerset, Lord E., Colonel of 17th, 184
Southampton, Part of 17th at, Under Orders for Egypt, 146
South Carolina, 75
Spanish Bloodhounds from Cuba, 126-7
Standards, Description of 17th's, 19, 22
"Star of the Evening," 247
"Star-Spangled Banner," 100
Stephenson, Sergeant, 127
Stevens, Gallantry of Brigadier-General, 92
"Storm, Admiral Christian's," 131
Subsistence, Light Dragoon's, 21
Surat, 17th at, 171
Sutherland's Camel Corps, 239

Tantia Topee, 230 et seq.; his Death, 246; his Hair, 247
Tarleton, Banastre, Birth of, 76; his Portrait, 77; wins Action at Wacsaw, 86; Terrible Brutality of his Men, 88; Pursuit by, after Camden, 92
Temple, Sergeant, of 17th, Deputy Provost-Sergeant, 225
Terrible Brutality after Wacsaw, 88-9
Thacher, Dr., his Journal, 59-60
Transport Duty, Party of 17th on, 268
Transports, Great Fleet of, 130
Transvaal War of 1899-1901, The, 265-341
Tremendous Losses of 17th by Sickness, 141
Trelawney, Maroons take up Position in District of, 111
Trumpeter's Dress, 18

Trumpeter Connor's Narrow Shave, 261
Trumpet-Major Joy, 221
Tryon, Detachment of 17th under, 67
Tucker, Sergeant, Gallantry of, 72; Promotion to Cornet, 72
Turks, Lord Bingham serves against the, 195

Ulundi, 17th Charge at, 261
Uniform, Alterations in, 196
——, American, 73-4
—— of Drogheda's Light Horse, 37
——, Farriers', 18
——, first, of John Hale's, 10, 17, Appendix C.
——, in India, during Mutiny, 229; during Pindari War, 175
——, Kingston's Light Horse, 5
——, Khaki for 17th, 248
——, Lancer, of 1816, 189
——, Lancer, French, 185
——, Lancer, in the Thirties, 197 et seq.
——, Lanzun's Legion, 100
——, Light Brigade, 209
——, Light Troops of Dragoons, 7-8
——, Neglect of old, 110
——, New, of 1784, 100
——, Pride of 17th in their old, 73
——, Price of Officer's 1829, 196
——, Russian Lancer, 186
——, Scarlet Cloth, 83-4
——, 17th as Lancers, 192
——, —— at Balaclava, 205
——, ——, one of the smartest, 255
——, 2nd Carolina Regiment, 95
——, Tight Lancer Uniform, 191
——, Wolfe's new, at Quebec, 4
Union Brigade at Waterloo, 17th receives Colonels from, Appendix A

Veigh, The Balaclava Butcher, 208; his Death, 249
Veterinary Surgeons appointed to Cavalry; 17th's first Vet., 140
Victoria Cross, no Bar granted, 253
Victoria Cross, for 17th Men, see Berryman; Farrell, 215, Evelyn Wood, and Wooden

Wacsaw, Action at, 86
Warrant, Arming, for Hale's, 10
Washington, George, Character of, 59
West, Benjamin, his Death of Wolfe a Speculation, 4
Winter, Captain, 202, 203, 208, 214
Webb, Captain, wounded, 214, 215
Wood, Sir Evelyn, 237, 238, 250-1, 259
Wooden, Sergt.-Major, wins V.C., 220; Anecdote of, 220
Wyatt Edgell, Death of, at Ulundi, 261

Xerxes' House, Private Cloyne's Name on Wall of, 173

Zululand, 17th in, 259

REGIMENTAL & DIVISIONAL HISTORIES

Read the real story of the worlds great conflicts in the histories of the regiments and divisions that were involved in them.

HISTORICAL RECORD OF THE EIGHTY-NINTH PRINCESS VICTORIA'S REGIMENT

A full unit history of an Irish regiment that saw service in the 1798 rebellion; the 1812 War with the U.S.; the Crimea and Indian Mutiny and the Suakim War in the Sudan. Fine colour illustrations and roll of officers.

9781845741020

HISTORY OF THE MANCHESTER REGIMENT (63RD and 96TH Regiments): VOLUMES I (1758-1883) AND II (1883-1922)

A massive two-volume history of the Manchester Regiment down to the end of the Great War: 'None more devoted, and none more valiant'. In effect a history of three regiments: 63rd and 96th Foot in volume I, and in volume II the Manchester Regiment.

9781845741433

HISTORY OF THE ROYAL IRISH RIFLES

The history of the regiment from its origins in 1793 as 83rd and 86th Regiments of Foot and ending in 1912

9781843424826

HISTORY OF THE 1ST BATTALION 6TH RAJPUTANA RIFLES (WELLESLEY'S)

History of an ancient Indian infantry battalion first formed in the 1770s, fighting under Wellesley (Wellington) in Mysore; before beign caught up in the tragic surrender at Kut in Iraq and entering Turkish captivity in the Great War.

9781847347565

HISTORY OF THE 12TH (THE SUFFOLK REGIMENT 1685-1913)

A very detailed regimental history recording almost 230 years of service at home and across the world – Flanders, Germany, Gibraltar, India, New Zealand and West India.

9781843421160

HISTORICAL RECORDS OF THE 14TH REGIMENT NOW THE PRINCE OF WALES OWN (WEST YORKSHIRE REGIMENT) FROM ITS FORMATION IN 1689 to 1892

Two hundred years in the history of a two-battalion county regiment with plenty of detail on its part in wars and expeditions and frequent lists of officers present for duty at various times.

9781843420965

HISTORY OF THE SERVICES OF THE 19TH REGIMENT NOW ALEXANDRA PRINCESS OF WALES OWN (YORKSHIRE REGIMENT)

Splendid history. Wars in Europe, American War of Independence, Kandyan Wars, Crimea, Egypt & Sudan, Boer War & NWF .Various casualty rolls.

9781843421887

ROYAL MUNSTER FUSILIERS (101 AND 104):

The History of the Bengal European Regiment, Now the Royal Munster Fusiliers and How it Helped to Win India The story of the Regiment's service with the British East India Company from 1652 till its transfer to the Crown in 1858.

9781843422730

NINTH (QUEEN'S ROYAL) LANCERS 1715-1903

A history set out in chronological form with a great deal of Regimental detail in a series of appendices – succession of Colonels, COs, Adjutants, QMs, Annual Army Lists and list of officers who served 1715-1903. 13 VCs won during the Indian Mutiny. Very good history.

9781843422365

HISTORY OF THE THIRTIETH REGIMENT, NOW THE FIRST BATTALION EAST LANCASHIRE REGIMENT 1689-1881

Greatly expanded 1923 edition of an 1887 history of one of the British army's oldest regiments, detailing its service, mainly as Marines, from the Glorious Revolution down to the Crimea.

9781843422419

HISTORICAL RECORDS OF THE 32ND (CORNWALL) LIGHT INFANTRY:

Now the 1st Battalion Duke of Cornwall's Light infantry, from the Formation of the Regiment in 1702 down to 1892. Beautifully illustrated history of a regiment, originally raised as Marines, which fought throughout the 18th and 19th centuries.

9781843425953

HISTORY OF THE RIFLE BRIGADE (THE PRINCE CONSORT'S OWN), FORMERLY THE 95TH

Standard, definitive history of the RB from raising in 1800-1874 inc. extensive services Peninsula & Waterloo, Kaffir Wars, Crimea, Indian Mutiny, Ashanti 1873-74. Awards roll.

9781843424024

EIGHTY-FIFTH KING'S LIGHT INFANTRY (NOW 2ND BATTN. THE KING'S SHROPSHIRE LIGHT INFANTRY)

An exceptionally full and detailed regimental history. Superply illustrated.

9781843425861

naval-military-press.com

www.ingramcontent.com/pod-product-compliance
Lightning Source LLC
Chambersburg PA
CBHW021133230426
43667CB00005B/98